The Attack on Literature and Other Essays

Other Books by René Wellek

Immanuel Kant in England

The Rise of English Literary History

Theory of Literature (with Austin Warren)

A History of Modern Criticism: 1750–1950, 4 volumes

Concepts of Criticism

Essays on Czech Literature

Confrontations

Discriminations

Four Critics: Croce, Valéry, Lukács, Ingarden

René Wellek

The Attack on

Literature

and Other Essays

The University of North Carolina Press Chapel Hill

© 1982 The University of North Carolina Press

All rights reserved

Manufactured in the United States of America

Library of Congress Cataloging in Publication Data

Wellek, René.
   The attack on literature and other essays.

   Bibliography: p.
   Includes indexes.
      1. Criticism—Addresses, essays,
lectures. 2. Literature—Addresses, essays,
lectures. I. Title.
PN85.W37   801'.95   81-21889
ISBN 0-8078-1512-8   AACR2
ISBN 0-8078-4090-4 (pbk.)

Contents

Prefatory Note

THIS collection of papers, all written in the seventies, is conceived as a continuation of two previous volumes of mine: *Concepts of Criticism* (1963) and *Discriminations* (1970). The papers cannot pretend to present a continuous argument but they do circle around related topics and present, let us hope, a coherent point of view. The title essay, "The Attack on Literature," tries to refute the wholesale attacks on the very idea of literature by the historical argument: the history of the term "literature." The nature of literature is then the concern of the second paper, on "Literature, Fiction, and Literariness," while the next papers, "Poetics, Interpretation, and Criticism" and "Criticism as Evaluation," defend the different stages of the process of literary study that begins with the interpretation of single texts, aims at a general theory of poetics, and inevitably leads up to a ranking or judging of literary works. "The Fall of Literary History" casts a skeptical glance at attempts to construe an evolutionary history of literature. The next item, "Science, Pseudoscience, and Intuition in Recent Criticism," raises doubts about quantifying and divinatory methods that have become fashionable, and the three following papers: "The New Criticism: Pro and Contra," "American Criticism of the Sixties," and "Russian Formalism," attempt to expound and to judge the main trends of twentieth-century criticism. In all these papers I hope my concern for clarity, coherence, and definiteness in my thinking about literature is apparent. I believe in literary scholarship and criticism as a rational enterprise that aims at a right interpretation of texts, at a systematic theory of literature, and at the recognition of quality and thus of rank among writers. The last two papers are apologies. "Reflections on my *History of Modern Criticism*" defends the method of the book, raising the whole question of how the writing of a history of ideas can be managed, and "Prospect and Retrospect" is a little intellectual autobiography that pays tribute to my teachers and reasserts my creed. The Bibliography that supplements those in *Concepts of Criticism* and *Discriminations* might be welcome. It lists the many pieces on individual critics that will eventually be incorporated in the last volumes of my *History of Modern Criticism* and the scattered articles and reviews devoted to Russian and Czech topics which I hope to collect in a separate volume.

Acknowledgments

"The Attack on Literature," *The American Scholar* 42 (December 1972): 27–42, is reprinted with permission of the United Chapters of Phi Beta Kappa.

"Literature, Fiction, and Literariness," in *Proceedings of the IXth Congress of the International Comparative Literature Association, Innsbruck, 1979*, ed. Zoran Konstantinović (Innsbruck: AMOE, 1981), 1:19–25, has been expanded and revised to appear in *Erkennen und Deuten: Essays zur Literatur und Literaturtheorie, Edgar Lohner in Memoriam*, eds. F. W. Lohnes and Martha Woodmansee (Berlin: Erich Schmidt Verlag). Permission to use the original paper has been granted by the publisher and the editors.

"Poetics, Interpretation, and Criticism," *Modern Language Review* 69 (October 1974): xxi–xxxi, was the presidential address at the Modern Humanities Research Association in 1974. Permission to reprint was granted by the general editor, H. B. Nisbet.

"Criticism as Evaluation," in *Herkommen und Erneuerung: Essays für Oskar Seidlin*, ed. Gerald Gillespie and Edgar Lohner (Tübingen: Max Niemeyer, 1976). Permission to reprint was granted by the publisher.

"The Fall of Literary History," in *Geschichte: Ereignis und Erzählung*, eds. Reinhart Kosseleck and Wolf-Dieter Stempel (Munich: Wilhelm Fink Verlag, 1973), pp. 427–40, is reprinted by permission of the publisher.

"Science, Pseudoscience, and Intuition in Recent Criticism," *Actes du VIIe Congrès de l'Association Internationale de Littérature Comparée [Montreal-Ottawa, 1973]* (Stuttgart: Kunst und Wissen, Erich Bieber, 1979), 2:465–69, was a paper prepared for the Congress of the International Comparative Literature Association. Permission was given by the joint holders of the copyright, the Association Internationale de Littérature Comparée and the Association Canadienne de Littérature Comparée.

"The New Criticism: Pro and Contra," *Critical Inquiry* 4 (1978): 611–24, is reprinted here by permission of the University of Chicago Press.

"American Criticism of the Sixties," previously called "Of the Last Ten Years," was published in *Amerikanische Literatur im 20. Jahrhundert*, eds. Alfred Weber and Dietmar Haack (Göttingen: Vandenhoeck & Ruprecht, 1972), pp. 13–28. Permission to reprint was granted by the publisher.

"Russian Formalism," *Arcadia* 6 (1971): 175–86. Walter de Gruyter in Berlin has given permission to reprint.

"Reflections on my *History of Modern Criticism*," *PTL: A Journal of Descriptive Poetics and Theory of Literature* (Amsterdam) 2, no. 3 (October 1977): 417–27. The North Holland Publishing Company of Amsterdam has granted permission to reprint.

"Prospect and Retrospect," *The Yale Review* 69 (1979): 301–12, is reprinted by permission of the editor and the Yale University Press.

The Attack on Literature

IN recent years we have heard much about the "death of literature," the "end of art," the "death of culture" and have become familiar with such terms as "anti-art" and "post-culture." We have been told that "literature, a dumping ground of fine feelings, a museum of *belles-lettres*, has had its day."[1] Norman Mailer believes that "we have passed the point in civilization where we can ever look at anything as an art work."[2]

I should like to examine the arguments for these views, to disentangle their motives and to set them in an historical perspective by tracing the term and the concept of "literature" through their history.

We can distinguish among several directions from which the attack on literature has come in recent decades.

One is politically motivated. It is the view that literature (and presumably all art) is conservative or at least a conserving power which serves only the interests of the ruling class. To quote some examples: Roland Barthes, in France, has said that "literature is constitutionally reactionary";[3] in Germany, Oswald Wiener has complained that "the alphabet was imposed by higher-ups";[4] and in the United States, Louis Kampf, who was President of the Modern Language Association in 1971, has charged that "the very category of art has become one more instrument of making class distinctions."[5] The concept of culture "is rooted in social elitism." It can be "little else but an instrument of class oppression."[6] "Initiating the underprivileged to the cultural treasures of the West could be a form of oppression—a weapon in the hands of those who rule" as "high culture tends to reinforce the given alignments of power within the society."[7] The logical deduction from Kampf's argument would be that people should be denied access to great literature and art in the name of their political advancement. Louis Kampf describes himself standing on the Piazza Navona in Rome, admiring the baroque fountains and architecture but thinking rather of "the crimes, the human suffering, which made both the scene and my being there possible." "My being there" alludes presumably to the grant he received from a foundation or university to travel to Rome, which he considers tainted as based in economic exploitation. He hates "the economic system which has invested finely chiseled stone with a price. Our esthetics are rooted in surplus value,"[8] he concludes, appealing to Marxist terminology but not of course rejecting the grant. In a different mood he recommends the destruction of what he considers a conspicuous symbol of High culture. "The movement should have harassed the Lincoln Center from the beginning. Not a performance should go by without disruption. The fountains should be dried with calcium chloride, the statuary pissed on, the walls smeared with shit."[9] These incitements to vandalism by the past President of the Modern Language Association of America are printed on fine paper in a volume entitled *The New Left*.

No doubt, many splendid works of architecture were built with slave labor, beginning with the Egyptian pyramids, and the money which paid for the fountains on the Piazza Navona came, presumably, from the Papal Treasury, which collected taxes in ways we might consider unjust and oppressive. But the generalized rage against all art and literature seems, to say the least, most unjust to large trends of literature in many lands. Even the briefest reflection will recall the eminently subversive, or at least liberalizing role of literature in many historical situations. The French revolution was prepared by the *philosophes*; the Russian revolution drew sustenance from a long line of writers critical of the Tsarist regime; the idea of a unified Italy was kept alive for centuries by her poets. The rebirth, in the nineteenth century, of the Greeks and the Hungarians, the Czechs and the Poles was triggered by poets and men of letters, and today few would refuse admiration for his heroic resistance against new oppression to Alexander Solzhenitzyn or deny the prominent role of writers in the Prague spring of 1968.

Thus the political attack on literature amounts simply to an attack on conservative ideology which has been necessarily expressed in print, just as revolutionary ideology has found expression in print, struggling, no doubt, with the obstacles of censorship and government monopoly of print long before the advent of modern totalitarianism, right or left. As long ago as 1816 William Hazlitt complained, on the occasion of Shakespeare's *Coriolanus*, that "imagination is an aristocratic faculty," that "it is right royal, putting the one above the infinite many, might before right," that "the language of poetry naturally falls in with the language of power" and that "the principle of poetry is a very anti-levelling principle."[10] Still, even in his time, Blake and Shelley showed that this is not necessarily true and that, as common sense tells us, literature and poetry as such cannot be guilty; men and writers say what they want to say: conservative and revolutionary thoughts, good and evil thoughts. The political attack on literature is a foolish generalization.

Much more serious and interesting is the attack on literature which is basically motivated by a distrust of language. Since the dawn of history many have felt that language fails to express their deepest emotions and insights, that the mystery of the universe or even of a flower eludes expression in language. Mystics have said so, in many variations, about their experience of the transcendent. Shakespeare has Othello say on meeting Desdemona again after landing on Cyprus: "I cannot speak enough of this content: it stops me here: it is too much of joy" (2. 1. 196). Cordelia in answering Lear's fatal question can say only "nothing, I cannot heave my heart into my mouth" (1. 1. 91–92). Goethe constantly complains of the inadequacy of language and the German language in particular. Philosophers, at least since Locke, have formulated their suspicion of words, and Bishop Berkeley has exhorted us "to draw the curtain of words to behold the fairest tree of knowledge."[11] Fritz Mauthner's three volume *Critique of Language*[12] accumulates massive evidence for this indictment; and the British analytical philosophers have made us more aware of the precariousness and shiftiness of our abstract and emotional vocabulary. The frightening inflation of the word in journalism and propaganda has brought home to a great many that the old certainties about terms such as "democracy," "justice," and "liberty" are gone forever. Linguists such as Benjamin Whorf have tried to show how closely grammatical and syntactical categories shape the view of the world of different people in different cultures; the Hopi Indians, he argued, see a very different order of the world from ours.[13] Philosophers such as Ernst Cassirer have, in extension of Kantian insights, demonstrated that language builds the very structure of our knowledge. We all speak of the indescribable, the unspeakable, we say that words fail us, that words cannot express this horror or that beauty.

This old feeling has in the last century led to a definite rejection of normal language by poets struggling with elusive inner states of mind. Mallarmé was one of the first to despair of expressing the mystery of the universe which he felt not only to be immensely dark but also hollow, empty, and silent. Hugo von Hofmannsthal in a fictitious letter of Lord Chandos to Bacon (1902) expressed his discontent with language, his (or rather his letter-writer's) justification for falling silent, because he wished only to "think with the heart."[14] Today this motif has become insistent and almost commonplace. J. Hillis Miller tells us that "all literature is necessarily a sham. It captures in its subtle pages not the reality of darkness but its verbal image." "Words, the medium of fiction, are a fabrication of man's intellect. They are part of the human lie."[15] In France, Roland Barthes complains that "literature is a system of deceptive signification": it is "emphatically signifying, but never finally signified."[16] The Saussurian terminology hides a simple thought: a word can never become a thing. Michel Foucault in *Les Mots et les Choses* has construed a whole history of the human mind in three stages of its attitude toward language. Before the advent of rationalism men assumed that words are things; they believed in the magic of words. In the Enlightenment people wanted to discover the order of things by words or, in Foucault's technical jargon, they wanted to find "a nomenclature which would be also a taxonomy." Our own period has concluded that "the thing being represented falls outside of the representation itself,"[17] and that man is thus unhappily trapped in a language game of which he knows nothing. There is no relation between language and reality. Language and literature have no cognitive value.

One result of this criticism of language has been the current cult of silence. Taken literally it lends itself to ridicule. In the nineteenth century one could laugh at Carlyle's gospel of silence in thirty volumes, and one might feel that there is nothing easier than to be silent. Still, George Steiner, Susan Sontag, Ihab Hassan, and other advocates of silence continue writing. But silence, as Susan Sontag recognizes, has become a metaphor for "a perceptual and cultural clean slate," the end of art, the ultimate horror.[18] Samuel Beckett in *Endgame* has been "looking for the voice of his silence."[19] Theodor Adorno's famous saying "no poetry after Auschwitz" is not a practical solution. The artist's dissatisfaction with language can only be expressed by language. Pause may be a device to express the inexpressible but the pause cannot be prolonged indefinitely, cannot be simply silence as such. It needs a contrast, it needs a beginning and an end. Even John Cage in his notorious piece of music in which a pianist or rather performer appeared and did nothing, had to time it four minutes and thirty-three seconds; he could not have kept it up for even four hours. Actually he replaced music by an act of pantomime that aroused expectations he disappointed. He manipulated his audience and their time sense, put on a show, made a joke but made no music of silence as there is no silent poetry or literature.

In France, Maurice Blanchot has prophesied the "disappearance of literature" and has envisaged "the death of the last writer." He recalls that there have been ages and countries without writers, and he dreams of ages without them in the future. He prophesies that "a great disgust against books will seize us." The age without words will announce itself by the "irruption of a new noise." "Nothing heavy, nothing noisy; at most a murmur which will not add anything to the great tumult of the cities which we think we suffer under today. Its only character will be: it never stops. It is speaking, it is as if the emptiness spoke, without mystery. The silence speaks." There will be no refuge for a minority in libraries and museums. They will be burned as Marinetti exhorted the Italians in 1909 to do, in his desire to rid them of their burdensome past. In Blanchot's vision, the dictator— from *dictare*, to say—will take the place of the writer, the artist, and the thinker.[20] A deep despair about the future of mankind and of civilization speaks loudly through him and many others. "The human voice conspires to desecrate everything on earth,"[21] says J. D. Salinger. Still, if we reflect upon this indictment of literature and language, we should recognize that it is man's actions, man's tools and inventions, his whole society which are here condemned. Admittedly, civilization would be impossible or, at the least, very different if man had not developed speech and writing, which have speeded communication and prolonged human memory. But to deplore this, as our apocalyptic prophets of doom and silence do so eloquently, means deploring that man is man and not a dumb animal—a mood, a gesture of despair but hardly a possible way of life and behavior. Men will continue speaking, and even writing.

Less apocalyptically, literature and writing have been seen as a transitory form of human communication to be replaced by the media of the electronic age. We all know of Marshall McLuhan's prophecy of the end of the Gutenberg era, his hope that our visual literature will be replaced by the double medium, television, which he argues is both aural and tactile. I won't enter into the difficulties of his theories: they have been aired by critics who believe that television is just as visual as the film, despite his argument that in television "the plastic contours appear by light *through*, and not light *on*, and the image so formed has the quality of sculpture or icon rather than picture."[22] McLuhan deliberately confuses visibility and legibility. He cannot prove that literacy has impoverished the spoken language. There is, however, little doubt that the new media have made inroads into the reading habits particularly of youngsters, but for the present at least, there are no indications of any extinction of literacy, reading, or the production of books. Any examination of statistics shows that book production and book sales have risen by leaps and bounds in all countries. In 1966, 460,000 new books were published. Even the usual assumption that the proportion of nonfiction compared to fiction has altered radically is not borne out by statistics. In Germany, as a recent article by Dieter Zimmer[23] showed, fiction accounted for 16.4 percent of all book production in 1913 and for 19.5 percent in 1969. Nor is it true that book production is mainly reprinting of older literature. Of the 36,000 books published in West Germany alone in 1971, 85 percent were new books. Similar studies made for the United States, England, and France yield similar results. The enormous expansion of the reading public in Eastern Europe and in the so-called Third World is an undeniable fact which makes the end of the Gutenberg era an event of the very far distant future.

All these attacks on literature, the politically motivated, the despair about the language, the retreat from the word, the cult of silence, and McLuhan's doubts about the future of literacy, assume a concept of literature that includes all acts of writing, from the most trivial to the most sublime. They make no distinction of quality, no aesthetic judgment.

The aesthetic concept of literature, the very concept of literature as art, has been under attack most insistently in recent decades. The collapse of aesthetics is the presupposition of the success of these attacks. The largely German theory of empathy which reduces aesthetic feeling to the physical action of inner mimicry; the aesthetics of Benedetto Croce in which "intuition" is identified with any act of perception of individual quality— even of *this* glass of water; John Dewey's *Art as Experience* (1934), which denies all distinction between aesthetic and other experiences in favor of a unified, heightened vitality; I. A. Richards's writings on literary criticism which abolish all distinction between aesthetic and other emotions, are just a few examples of this trend. More recently the analytical philosophers have tried to demonstrate "the dreariness of aesthetics," the "nonsense" of all traditional terms of aesthetics: beauty, form, and so on. Some of these criticisms are directed against aestheticism, the art for art's sake movement at the end of the last century which set up art in an ivory tower or, contradictorily, claimed to make all life "beautiful." Chiding "aestheticism" as it deserved, the reaction against it involved its presumed ancestors: the founders of aesthetics, Kant, Schiller, Schelling, and Hegel, none of whom would have ever dreamt of denying the enormous social and civilizing role of art. They were even extravagantly confident of its power. The aesthetic education propounded by Schiller was a scheme for freeing man from the necessities of nature and the evils of specialization.

The revolt against aesthetics was also a revolt against classical art with its demands for beauty, order, form, harmony, and clarity of meaning. But such a desire to make things new was not a denial of the ideal of art or literature; rather it was an attempt at a redefinition of art or an extension of its meaning to allow for the innovations of the twentieth century. A German volume of conference papers and debates called *Die nicht mehr schönen*

Künste[24] wittily formulates what has happened in recent decades: the inclusion in art of the ugly, the formless, the disorderly,
the outrageous and obscene, which culminated in Dada's thumb-
ing its nose at art and echoes today in such movements as Pop
art. Attempts have been made not only to widen the realm of art
but to abolish the boundary between art and nonart. In music,
noises of machines or the streets are used; in painting, collage
uses stuck-on newspapers, buttons, medals and so on, or "found
objects"—soup cans, bicycle wheels, electric bulbs, any piece of
junk—are exhibited. The newest fad is "earthworks," holes or
trenches in the ground, tracks through a cornfield, square sheets
of lead in the snow. A "sculptor," Christo, wrapped a million
square feet of Australian coastline in plastic. At the 1972 Bien-
nale in Venice, a painter, Gino de Dominicis, exhibited a mongo-
loid picked up from the streets as a work of art. In poetry, poems
have been concocted by the Dadaists by drawing newspaper clip-
pings from a bag at random; more recently poems have been
produced by computer, and a shuffle novel (by Marc Saporta)
has appeared, in which every page can be replaced by another
in any order. In these new techniques the old criteria of both
making and intentionality are denied: it is the extreme consequence of the rejection of the old conception of the poet as
prophet, as *poeta-vates*, the laureate, the "unacknowledged legis-
lator" with which the Western tradition has been familiar since
Dante, Petrarch, Tasso, Milton, and Shelley. The concept of inspiration is rejected: the new technological anti-art divorces the
poet from the poem, the artist from the object.

Yet, another attack on literature leads to different consequences. It urges the same objection to defining literature by the
quality of the art product. Northrop Frye's immensely influential and highly ingenious *Anatomy of Criticism* (1957) wants to
abolish all critical judgment in favor of a concept of literature that makes it an organ of myth-making, a part of man's
dream of self-definition. The result is that he can discuss any
fairy tale, legend or detective story as if it were on an equal
footing with the greatest works of Dante, Shakespeare, or Tolstoy. This breaking down of old barriers in favor of fictionality,
myth-making, or "fabulation" must be distinguished from other
attempts to disrupt the old concept. I am thinking of critics such

as Leslie Fiedler and Richard Poirier, who want to extend the concept of literature to include what used to be called subliterature: pornography, science fiction, and the popular song. Fiedler propagates a new, or possibly old, taste: in an essay "The Children's Hour" the song full of "lovely commonplaces, long-honored phrases, sentimental clichés" is exalted; the tritest poems of Longfellow appear alongside poems of the Beatles, Bob Dylan and black anti-verse, as Fiedler feels liberated, "sincere" for the first time. He can now repudiate Modernist poetry, "feel free at last to evoke in public the kind of poems which I have never ceased to love" but "which I've long felt obligated to recite in the catacombs, as it were."[25] This assertion of a different taste, a return to the folksy, the sentimental, the direct expression of simple feelings is the opposite of what is accomplished by computer poetry or by the graphic devices of so-called "concrete" poetry or even the automatic writings of surrealists. The dissolution of the concept of literature proceeds thus in two opposite directions: toward impersonal technology or toward subliterature, toward kitsch.

Still, both these extensions of the concept of literature are within the realm of art. One can argue (as Louis Mink has ingeniously) that even the most impersonal "found object" can be salvaged for art,[26] if we assume that the fact of its being singled out gives it some allegorical or iconographic meaning. Even the hospital urinal submitted by Marcel Duchamp or the grocery boxes of Andy Warhol are, somehow, works of art. They do express some rudimentary feeling. But the latest developments amount to a complete denial of art. Harold Rosenberg, in his aptly named book *The De-definition of Art* (1972), quotes an artist as saying, "I choose not to make objects. Instead, I have set out to create a quality of experience which locates itself in the world." The artist has become too big for art: he regards anything he makes or does as art. "No one can say with assurance what a work of art is—or, more important, what is not a work of art." We can't distinguish between a masterpiece and junk. Nothing is left of art but the fiction of the artist.

There is more to be said for the extension of the concept of literature to oral literature, to mere yarn-spinning, or to the popular song which returns literature to its oral origins. French and English literature is largely bookish but many literatures are still in close contact with their origins in oral folklore: in Eastern Europe, in Asia, and in Africa. A meaningful concept of literature as a world-wide phenomenon reaching into the dim past of humanity will include what in English has been called, awkwardly enough, "oral literature." Father Ong complains that the term implies that "oral poetry should have been written down but somehow was not."[27] Verbal art, *Wortkunst*, may be a better term: it would include Homer, whom Milman Parry has shown to belong to an oral tradition. But even much later, in the Middle Ages, the history of literature is incomprehensible without the constant interchange between the oral and the written word. Without sharing the taste for the sentimental banalities and comic obscenities admired by Leslie Fiedler, we should grant the fructification of modern literature by what the Russian formalists describe as the periodic need of "rebarbarization." We seem to be in such a period and can only hope that it will achieve the results that at the end of the eighteenth century flowed from the rediscovery of Scottish ballads and Elizabethan songs in Percy's *Reliques of Ancient English Poetry*.

This incorporation of the popular arts, of oral literature in a total concept of literature cannot, however, ignore the aesthetic question: there is good and bad popular art, as there is good and bad upper-class art. Paul Elmer More, a lover of detective stories, graded his collection into categories A, B, and C, and presumably the same could be done with science fiction or even pornography. The question of quality, the distinction between art and nonart, is unavoidable.

All these objections to the concept of literature have one trait in common: they do not recognize quality as a criterion of literature; quality that may be either aesthetic or intellectual, but which in either case sets off a specific realm of verbal expression from daily transactions in language. This denial of quality runs counter to the whole long history of the term "literature" and the concept. It may be useful to glance at this history in order to see the debate in some perspective and to refute the strange notion of some recent commentators such as Maurice Blanchot and Roland Barthes, who consider the term and concept creations of the nineteenth century.²⁸ What I can give is only a brief sketch for a topic that deserves a book-length study.

The term *litteratura*, which obviously comes from *littera*, "letter" in Latin, was called by Quintilian a "translation of the Greek *grammatikē*": it thus meant simply a knowledge of reading and writing.²⁹ Cicero, however, speaks of Julius Caesar as having *litteratura* in a list of his qualities, which includes "good sense, memory, reflexion and diligence."³⁰ It must mean here something like "literary culture." We have to go to Tertullian and Cassian in the second century after Christ to find the term used for a body of writing. They contrast secular *litteratura* with *scriptura*, pagan with Christian literature.³¹

Much more prevalent, however, was the term *litterae* in Rome. Cicero speaks of *Graecae litterae* and of *studium humanitatis ac litterarum*. Aulus Gellius expressly identifies *humanitas* with the Greek *paideia*;³² *litterae* in antiquity is simply the study of the arts and letters of the Greeks as far as they represent the Greek idea of man. In practice the study of letters was the study of the Greek writers, of Homer and the writers of the Periclean age. I need not enter into the remote history of the rise of this conception in opposition to the oral tradition crystallized in the Homeric poems. Eric Havelock's *Preface to Plato* (1963) traced this evolution persuasively.

In the Middle Ages the terms were used rarely. *Literatus* or *literator* meant anybody acquainted with the art of reading and writing. With the establishment of the seven liberal arts, including the trivium, literature as a term seems to have disappeared, though poetry was recognized as an art assigned to grammar and rhetoric.

With the Renaissance a clear consciousness of a new secular literature emerges and with it the terms *litterae humanae*, *lettres humains*, *bonnes lettres*, or as late as in Dryden, "good letters" (1692). These terms were used widely by Rabelais, Du Bellay, Montaigne, and other French writers of the sixteenth century. In the seventeenth century the term *belles-lettres* emerged. In 1666 Charles Perrault proposed to Colbert, the minister of finance of Louis XIV, an Academy with a section of *belles-lettres*, which was to include grammar, eloquence, and poetry. The term, as dictionaries show, was felt to be identical with *lettres humains* and had nothing of the faintly derisive implication with which we today speak of the "belletristic." The French term spread quickly to England: Thomas Rymer used it in 1692. Hugh Blair became Professor of Rhetoric and Belles Lettres at the University of Edinburgh in 1762.

By that time the term "literature" had re-emerged in the sense of a knowledge of literature, of literary culture. La Bruyère speaks, in 1688, of "men of agreeable literature." Voltaire calls Chapelain a man of "immense literature" and in a dictionary article, defines literature as "a knowledge of the works of taste, a smattering of history, poetry, eloquence and criticism."[33] Marmontel, Voltaire's follower, terms literature a "knowledge of *belles-lettres*" and contrasts it expressly with erudition. "With wit, talent, and taste," he promises, "one can produce ingenious works, without any erudition, and with little literature."[34]

In English, the same meaning became established. Thus the antiquary John Selden was, in 1691, called "a person of infinite literature" and Boswell refers to Giuseppe Baretti as an "Italian of considerable literature."[35] The use of the term survived in the nineteenth century when John Petherham wrote a *Sketch of the Progress and Present State of Anglo-Saxon Literature in England* (1840), where literature must mean the study of literature. (Incidentally, in the term "comparative literature," this older usage survives. It obviously means the comparative study of literatures and is not, as Lane Cooper complained, a "bogus term which makes neither sense nor syntax.")[36]

Apparently, very early in the eighteenth century, the term was used for a body of writing, though it is sometimes difficult to draw a sharp distinction between the concurrent use of "literary culture, erudition." Here is the title of a book by le Père Cl. F. Menestrier: *Bibliothèque curieuse et instructive des divers auteurs anciens et modernes de littérature et des arts* (1704).[37] It clearly refers to a body of writing in François Granet's little-known *Réflections sur les ouvrages de littérature* in 1737. Voltaire in *Le Siècle de Louis XIV* speaks in 1750 of "les genres de littérature" cultivated in Italy.[38] The Abbé Sabatier de Castres published *Les Siècles de littérature française* in 1772, the very year in which Girolamo Tiraboschi began his monumental, many-volumed *Storia della letteratura italiana.* In Germany the new use was completely established even earlier. Lessing's *Briefe die neueste Litteratur betreffend* (1759ff.) applies clearly to a body of writing, and so does Herder's *Über die neuere deutsche Litteratur* (1767).

In English the same process took place. The *Oxford Dictionary* is mistaken by at least sixty years when it quotes the first example for "body of writing" from 1822. In 1761 George Colman the elder thought that "Shakespeare and Milton seem to stand alone, like first-rate authors, amid the general wreck of old English literature."[39] In 1767 Adam Ferguson included a chapter "Of the History of Literature" in his *Essay on the History of Civil Society.* In 1774 Dr. Johnson, in a letter, wished that "what is undeservedly forgotten of our antiquated literature might be revived,"[40] and John Berkenhout in 1777 subtitled his *Biographia Literaria, A Biographical History of Literature*, in which he proposed to give a "concise view of the rise and progress of literature." Examples from the late eighteenth century could be easily multiplied. Still, the first book in English called *A History of English Language and Literature* by Robert Chambers dates from as late as 1836.

In all of these cases literature is used very inclusively. It refers to all kinds of writing, including those of erudite nature, history, theology, philosophy, and even natural science. Only very slowly was the term narrowed down to what we today call "imaginative literature": the poem, the tale, the play in particular. This is a process intimately connected with the rise of aesthetics, of the whole system of arts that in older times was not clearly set off from the sciences on the one side and crafts on the other. The traditional linkage of the arts and sciences was, I believe, first clearly dissolved in Charles Perrault's *Parallèle des Anciens et des Modernes* (1688–97) where the *beaux arts* are contrasted with the *sciences*, though the *Dictionnaire de Trévoux* in 1721 has still the term "Lettres" defined as "se dit aussi des Sciences." In the polemics between the conservatives and the *philosophes*, the term "littérature" emerges in the new narrow meaning of fictional literature, to set the humanities off against the new geometrical spirit, the new rationalism. Jean-Georges Le Franc de Pompignan, in *L'Essai sur l'état présent de la république des lettres* in 1743, uses "littérature" as a synonym of *belles lettres* and narrows it expressly to the "epic poem, the tragedy, the comedy, the ode,

the fable, history and eloquence."[41] Another early conscious dec-
laration of this new use I found in the Preface to Carlo Denina's
Discorso sopra le vicende della letteratura (1760), a widely read book
that was soon translated into French and English. Denina pro-
fesses "not to speak of the progress of the sciences and arts,
which are not properly a part of literature." He will speak of
works of learning only when they belong to "good taste, to eloquence, that is to say, to literature."[42] That literature was used
in this new aesthetic sense at that time may be illustrated by
Aurelio de Giorgi-Bertòla's *Idea della bella letteratura alemanna*
(1784), which is an expansion of an older *Idea della poesia alemanna* (1779). The change of title was made necessary by the
inclusion of a new chapter about the German novel, in particular
the *Sorrows of Young Werther*.

To speak sweepingly, one can say that in older times, in antiquity and in the Renaissance, literature or letters was understood
to include all writing of quality with any pretense to permanence.
Poetry was set apart mainly because of the clear distinction made
by verse. The view that there is an art of literature, a verbal art
that includes poetry and prose as far as it is imaginative fiction
and thus excludes information and even rhetorical persuasion
or didactic argumentation emerged slowly with the whole system
of the modern arts. It took about a century to prepare for Kant's
Critique of Judgment (1790), which gave a clear formulation for
distinguishing the good, the true, and the useful from the beautiful. The slow rise in the prestige of the novel, long frowned
upon as frivolous, collaborated in establishing a concept of literature parallel to the plastic arts and to music.

The meaning of a word is that given to it by its users. We
cannot prevent anybody from speaking about campaign literature or about the literature relating to a pharmaceutical product.
"Literature" has been and can be used to refer to anything in
print. On the other hand it has more often meant, as I have
shown, literary culture, the whole tradition of humane letters
descending from antiquity. It meant for centuries works valued
for their intellectual or imaginative eminence. In the eighteenth
century the term was often narrowed down to cover all imaginative literature: the novel, the epic, the lyric poem, the play. In
English the word "poetry" is limited more narrowly to works in

verse. We cannot speak, as the Germans do, of Dostoevsky or Kafka as a *Dichter*. I have used the term "literature" in this sense in *Theory of Literature*. Often, of course, literature has been rather contrasted with poetry. Thus Benedetto Croce made a distinction between *letteratura* and *poesia*. *Letteratura* has a great civilizing function, but *poesia* stands apart, outside of history, limited to the great peaks of what we would call imaginative literature. Sartre in *What is Literature?* draws the same distinction but values it differently. Literature is writing committed to changing man's consciousness, while poetry is assigned only a little nook and corner safely hidden from the stresses of history and historical change. Literature has also been used as a pejorative term for empty rhetoric, as in Verlaine's well-known poem *Art Poétique*. He wanted to "wring the neck of eloquence"; he exalted music in poetry and concluded "Et tout le reste est littérature."

In understanding these lexical distinctions,[43] we shall be able to reject the wholesale attack on literature: the political attack, which makes literature a reactionary force though it obviously can be and has been the opposite; the linguistic attack, which despairs of the very possibility of speech; and the anti-aesthetic attack, which revolts against quality and form in favor of subliterature or the impersonal permutations of the computer. Finally the replacement of literature by the new media will seem a very unlikely event of the distant future. None of these theories touches the capacity of man to create works of literature also in the future. The forms of literature will no doubt change radically, but as long as there is man in any conceivable shape, he will create, that is, speak, express, and communicate in writing and in print his observations, his feelings, his desires, his ideas, and his probings into himself and the nature of the world around him. Doubts about the exact limits of literature cannot obviate the difference between art and nonart, great and bad art, trash, kitsch, a Shakespeare play and a newspaper poem, a story by Tolstoy and a story in *True Confessions*. Doubts about language and its reach can only sharpen the poet's struggle to achieve what is difficult to formulate in language and to make him and us suspicious of the debasement of the word in propaganda, advertising, and bad journalism. Predictions of the end of literacy, of the triumph of television, should make us more aware of the need of a literary culture. The new barbarism, the know-nothingism, the mindless repudiation of the past in favor of so-called "relevance"—one trusts that these are only a passing mood dominating in the United States at this moment. We may reflect that this crisis of the concept of literature is confined to small, largely academic circles in France and the United States. It also flourishes among a group of neo-Marxists in Western Germany. It has not, I think, affected England, though in the writings of Raymond Williams and Richard Hoggart the uses of culture and literacy have been subjected to a stringent examination. Doubts about literature and its uses are, I think, completely absent in the Communist world because they have made literature a tool for the education and indoctrination of the masses.

We cannot predict the shape of things to come: in 1872 no-body could have forecast, in any detail, the literary situation as it is today. But there remain basic certainties: there will be, I am sure, no silence, and no incessant murmur, as forecast by Blanchot. There will still be the voice of men of letters and poets, in verse or prose, who will speak (as they have done since hoary antiquity) for their society and for mankind. Mankind will always need a voice and a record of that voice in writing and print, in literature.

Literature, Fiction, and Literariness

IN recent years, rather suddenly, an enormous debate has
sprung up about the nature of literature, its definition and
delimitation, and the meaning of such fairly new concepts
as "fictionality" and "literariness" (the last, an invention of
the Russian formalists, I believe). I can only allude to a tome of
594 pages by Bennison Gray, *The Phenomenon of Literature* (1975),
to a volume containing 19 papers, *What Is Literature?* (1978),
edited by Paul Hernadi, and to a special number of the periodical *New Literary History* devoted to the same question in 1973. In
German the debate is no less lively: Horst Rüdiger edited *Literatur und Dichtung: Versuch einer Begriffsbestimmung* (1973), Helmut
Kreuzer collected essays on the theme *Veränderung des Literatur-
begriffs* (1975), and recently András Horn, in *Das Literarische*
(1978), surveyed all the suggested answers. The debate goes
back to Sartre's *Qu'est-ce que la littérature?* (1947). Many discussions refer to my chapter on "The Nature of Literature" in
Austin Warren's and my *Theory of Literature* (1948), rarely to the
only other books expressly devoted to the question: Thomas
Clark Pollock's *The Nature of Literature* (1942) and Charles Du
Bos's English lectures *What Is Literature?* (1939). Needless to say
the question has been raised in the most diverse contexts before:
the term would have to be studied in a semantic field alongside
"poetry" and "fiction" with due regard to the different uses in
different languages.

All attempts to define literature in ways contrary to established
usage seem to me condemned to oblivion. Thus Bennison Gray
will never convince us that literature should be confined to fiction defined as a "moment-by-moment presentation of an un-
verifiable event,"[1] with the result that Eliot's *The Waste Land*,
Coleridge's *Kubla Khan*, Pope's *Essay on Man*, and Mallarmé's
Coup de dés are excluded from literature. Nor will definitions
that simply abandon the problem by declaring literature to be
anything in print or considering literature "any utterance which
known societies have regarded as of sufficient importance to

preserve permanently," as Archibald A. Hill argued in "A Program for the Definition of Literature."[2] Any law code, any legal
document, charter, liturgical text, verbal ceremony, or simply
remembered pronouncement such as the famous saying of General Cambronne at the battle of Waterloo would be literature,
contrary to all usage.

The question to my mind should be approached through a
study of the history of the word "literature" and its cognates.
I have attempted this in a contribution to Scribner's *Dictionary of
the History of Ideas* (1973) and in Hernadi's symposium *What Is
Literature?*[3] I must refer to the preceding essay for a summary.

Ignoring the unproblematic use of literature as "everything in
print" or such uses as "campaign literature" or the "literature"
about a pharmaceutical product, we are confronted with problems raised by two historically established meanings. Are they
purely descriptive or do they imply a value judgment? Can we
draw clear distinctions between imaginative literature and literature in general? Our first meaning, "literature including erudition, historiography, philosophy, etc." has always assumed some
distinction, not only artistic success but intellectual eminence,
moral authority, and national significance of some kind. If we
think, for instance, of the English eighteenth century, it would
be difficult to exclude the two philosophers, Berkeley and Hume,
the moralist and biographer Dr. Johnson, and the orator Edmund Burke from the concept of literature. Inevitably we raise
the question of a "canon" of literature. The establishment of
canon is a historical question that has not been adequately inves-
tigated, though Ernst Robert Curtius, in *European Literature and
the Latin Middle Ages* (1948), has an excellent chapter on the
emergence of the modern canon of classical authors with glances
at the French, Italian, and German situation. It raises the whole
question of what is a "classic" and how a classic has come about
to be one. A process of selection is going on with criteria that
vary from age to age, from country to country. The establishment of Dante, Petrarch, and Boccaccio as the Italian classics
seems a straightforward process but even Dante was for a time
under a cloud. The selection of the great French classics, Corneille, Racine, Molière, was obviously related to the dominance
of France under Louis XIV while the exaltation of Shakespeare

and Milton in England was achieved by quite different processes, independently from immediate political concerns. In Germany the emergence of Goethe as the classic was a slow process of the nineteenth century and the relative positions of Schiller and Lessing are still in doubt. Empirical research on these questions is barely beginning.[4] The reasons and ways in which only five English poets of the Romantic age—Wordsworth, Coleridge, Byron, Shelley, and Keats—survived are complex and somewhat obscure. I believe, however, that the canon of literature is far more firmly established, at least for the more remote past, than many skeptics allow. Attempts to depreciate Shakespeare, even when coming from such a classic in his own right as Tolstoy, cannot succeed.

Sainte-Beuve, in one of his earliest essays, protested against this idolatry of the very great and professed his interest in secondary writers as a matter of justice,[5] and there have been many attempts to rescue minor and minimal writers from oblivion. In France, Daniel Mornet, in Germany, Josef Nadler, and Van Wyck Brooks in the United States, with very different assumptions, have made it a principle of literary-history writing. But they cannot fully succeed to obliterate distinctions of rank. The idea often propounded today, that quality is not inherent in the objects themselves and is simply imposed by the reader, is surely misguided, however important we may feel the role of the audience may be.

There are good arguments for the study of subliterary genres, colportage, kitsch, pulp fiction, *Trivialliteratur*, or whatever we call it, but they are arguments for the social importance of subliterature as a reflection of popular taste. There are no doubt borderline cases and within the subgenres distinctions of quality can be made. We can grade detective stories, science fiction, Gothic romances, Westerns, even pornography, and any other current genre by aesthetic, social, and moral criteria. There was and is a constant interchange between high literature and "subliterature." High literary forms descend to popular forms; for instance, chivalrous romances were transformed into chapbooks, and upperclass literature has often been in need of "rebarbarization." The impact of folksong and folk ballad at the end of the eighteenth century is an obvious example, but it can also be ar-

gued that, for instance, Dostoevsky lifted the French sensational
novel into the higher realm of supreme fiction. E. D. Hirsch's
definition of literature as "including any text worthy to be taught
to students by teachers of literature"[6] either begs the question in
the word "worthy" or seems to endorse the practice of even
reputable American universities where Tarzan, *The Wizard of Oz*,
Mickey Spillane's *The Big Kill*, and the *Story of O.* are included in
literature courses. We cannot get around the question of quality,
which is the central question of criticism.

If we define literature as imaginative literature, poems, plays,
and novels, we are faced with the problem of how to distinguish
it from literature in the wider sense. It has been answered substantially in two ways: literature is fiction or literature uses language in a special way. In *Theory of Literature*, I have tried to
combine the two answers and have been criticized since, especially by Bennison Gray, for embracing two incompatible definitions. "Fictionality" is a new term for the difference between art
and life, for a recognition of art as make-believe. Fiction means a
denial of a truth of immediate correspondence with reality. Fiction tries to build a world of illusion and does so by distancing,
by framing. In most arts there has been a tug of war between the
necessity of realizing that art is art and the attempt to persuade
us that art is continuous with life and has to tell us something
about it. The old anecdotes about the sailor who climbed the
stage in order to rescue Desdemona from Othello or about the
medieval audience beating up the actor playing Judas show the
urgent need of distancing. The pull toward identification with a
fictional hero or heroine and their fate can be so strong as to
change lives, suggest elopements, adulteries, crimes, and even
suicides.[7] More recently an opposite attitude has become a men-
ace. Literature is considered to be only about literature, words
about words, a game with no relation and no contact with life.

I am content to understand fictionality in the broad sense of
"semblance," *Schein*, illusion (which is not deception), as a man-
made, intentional world which draws on the real world and sends
us back to it. In this view there is no need to worry about the fact
that much literature does contain factual statements and propositions. They still lose their status of literal truth of correspondence the moment they enter into a fictional context. Nobody

can, of course, dispute the fact that we find in fiction statements that can be sometimes verified, references to specific localities and events, to real persons living today or in history. Anybody who knows Paris will be able to identify streets and buildings in reading Balzac's *Cousine Bette*, Flaubert's *L'Education sentimentale*, or Zola's *L'Assommoir*. The Cathedral of Rouen is evoked in *Madame Bovary*. A Londoner may check the novels of Dickens with his knowledge of landmarks, some still visible and some documented by lithographs or old photographs. Examples could be endlessly multiplied and also complicated by the deliberate concealment of actual localities by some authors by invented names. Proust calls Illier Combray, Cabourg Balbec.

Real people are depicted by many writers, novelists, and satirists so accurately that the descriptions were recognized and sometimes have become actionable. Dryden in *MacFlecknoe* ridiculed a living person, Thomas Shadwell; Alexander Pope in *The Dunciad* pilloried a horde of scribblers by name. James Sutherland in his edition of the poem has not only laboriously identified the targets but accumulated from many obscure sources information about them much of which could not have been known to Pope himself and hardly to any single person at that or any other time.[8]

Novels may convey information about, say, the weather at a specific date or describe institutions, tools, costumes, and customs accurately. Balzac at the beginning of *Lost Illusions* gives a lengthy account of the equipment, the staff, the techniques, and the vicissitudes of a print-shop under the Revolution and Napoleon, which we can assume to be substantially correct. In all of these cases the truth-claim is beyond doubt, and the truth of the statement of information could be verified.

The question becomes much more problematical when we consider the historical novel or drama. Herbert Lindenberger in his *Historical Drama* (1975) has discussed some of these problems perceptively. Shakespeare, Voltaire, Schiller and Shaw refer, to take a striking instance, to a historical personage, Joan of Arc. Today we can read a transcript of her trial and are fairly well informed about her life. But Shakespeare treated her as witch; Schiller wrote a "romantic tragedy," *Die Jungfrau von Orleans*, in which she is killed in battle rather than burned at the stake; and in Shaw's *Saint Joan* she appears as an argumentative British young lady disputing with her judges on nationalism and religion. In Voltaire's comic epic, *La Pucelle*, she is a target of lusty men bent on depriving her of her certified virginity until she joyfully succumbs to the enticements of the royal Bastard.[9] I would conclude that in each case her figure is purely fictional, that it is functioning within a structure only very obliquely related to what we conceive to have been historical reality.

There are many mixed cases. In Tolstoy's *War and Peace*, historically documented scenes are described such as the meeting of Napoleon with the Tsar Alexander I on a raft in the river Niemen at Tilsit and the arrival of a French officer, Savary, on October 17, 1805, to call on the Tsar in Vyshkov, a little town in Moravia. At other times we find that Tolstoy maliciously transferred a description of Napoleon's elaborate toilet from an account dating to his years at St. Helena to the morning of the battle of Borodino, and we have the word of an eyewitness that the Tsar did not, as Tolstoy describes it, munch cookies and distribute them to the crowd in Moscow from a balcony.[10] All this gives rise to scholarly detective work or possibly may yield insights into the creative process, but I shall be content to say that the question of accuracy does not matter in fiction, that Napoleon and the Tsar are as fictional figures as Natasha Rostov or Pierre Bezukhov who, in their turn, may draw features from actual people: Tolstoy's own sister-in-law and his own life experiences.

All these references to reality should be distinguished from propositions in fiction which claim to be truth or state a true belief of the author or his mouthpiece. To give often quoted examples: Browning is supposed to be saying "God's in His Heaven—/All's right with the world" (though actually in the play, *Pippa Passes*, this pronouncement is put into the mouth of the girl Pippa who soon is to experience that much is wrong with the world). Leopardi, in his poem, "A se stesso," tells us, on the contrary, that "il mondo è fango" and we know that he means it, as much of his poetry is a cry of desolation and despair. Innumerable such generalizations from the most general to the most trivial can be found throughout fiction. Shall we discuss optimism versus pessimism or Balzac's statement that "ignorance is the mother of all crimes"?[11] What shall we say to the first sentence of *Anna Karenina*: "Happy families are all alike: every unhappy family is unhappy in its own way"? Shall we produce instances showing that not all happy families are alike and should we rather recognize that the statement functions as introducing us to the household of the Oblonskys where Kitty has just discovered her husband's affair with the French governess?

There is now an enormous literature on these questions. Logicians, semanticists, aestheticians have mulled them over and made subtle distinctions. Gottlob Frege, Roman Ingarden, Monroe Beardsley, John Searle, and more recently, in German, Gottfried Gabriel in *Fiktion und Wahrheit* (1975) and Käte Hamburger in *Wahrheit und aesthetische Wahrheit* (1979) have analyzed the role of factual statements, propositions, and assertions in detail.[12] I want to dismiss these problems as irrelevant to literary criticism. The historical personages, the actual places and buildings, even the propositions function quite differently in a fictional context. The relation to a specific external reality ceases to matter. We need not know whether the Tsar actually munched cookies in 1805 on his balcony or whether Napoleon had his back rubbed with *eau de cologne* on the morning of the battle of Borodino. We need not even worry that Joan of Arc dies in battle in Schiller's play. Nor does the professed intention of the author matter. His sincerity in trying, for instance, to hurt, to ridicule and humiliate living human beings such as Thomas Shadwell, Lewis Theobald, and Colley Cibber is not in doubt but the accuracy of the allegations or the effect on the victims and their contemporaries are questions completely extraneous to any critical concern. Actually in reading *The Dunciad* we experience the sense of a swarm of insects, we receive an impression of anonymity, triviality, and inconsequence despite the apparent concrete singularity of the names. As Austin Warren commented: "The context provides the categories, while the proper names are annually replaceable."[13] Even satirical poetry illustrates the old idea of the universalizing power of art. Sutherland's labors have only an antiquarian interest.

Nobody can, of course, prevent anybody from debating the question of whether "all's right with the world" or whether "the world is mud," but extracting these statements from their contexts reduces them to propositions that could be also stated in a philosophical treatise, a moralist's tract, or even by a proverb. Literature can be a source for all kinds of documentation, can serve as evidence for opinions, psychological states of mind, social conditions, and so on. It can be used as a source for the history of a city, of law or medicine, or of printing, as a work of literature is an assembly of diverse statements and values that cannot be all aesthetic. But to be a work of imaginative literature, of literature as fiction, as art, it must be dominated by the aesthetic function.

This view should not be considered aestheticism, art for art's sake, or a denial of the reference of art to life. The reference, however, is oblique and arises from the contemplation of the imagined world in relation to ordinary reality, by analogy. Only the totality of the work of art conveys its meaning, not individual references to the real world. The total meaning of a work of art is a social and historical fact: it is itself part of man's created reality.

Still we must not shirk the age-old problem of the truth of literature. It is entangled in the very different senses in which truth is conceived. It may mean simply adequacy to extraliterary states of affairs or objects, the claim that forms the basis of realism. It may be logical truth, internal coherence, convincingness, plausability that we require even of the most fantastic fiction; it may be a term for sincerity, genuineness, authenticity with which the work renders the experiences of the author; or finally it may be the truth of revelation of some mystery behind the appearances of the world, a claim that can be made in terms of traditional religious truths or in the sense of Being required by Heidegger. While one cannot deny that art conveys much information and knowledge, I argue (as many before me) that truth of correspondence, realism, "reflection of reality" is not an aesthetic requirement but only one style of art; nor is logical truth or sincerity or truth of revelation indispensable. Still I would side with those who recognize that art gives knowledge that is not merely information or discursive argument. Knowledge is understood as realization, as bringing home, as making us aware as when we say: "I did not know that this is so until I

saw it with my own eyes, experienced it myself." Literature thus
gives us knowledge of the quality of life and nature, of its particularity, of the "world's body," to use J. C. Ransom's striking
phrase. But it also suggests the possibilities of life, its permanent
features, the universals of man and nature. It is the old answer
that literature combines the particular and the universal, yields a
"concrete universal," the Hegelian term recently revived, or presents an "icon," an image, a metaphor of the world. We can
express this function in many more or less precise ways. It seems
preferable to use these terms than the old tag about "utile et
dulce," instruction and entertainment. What we have said about
the truth of literature is a reformulation of the *utile* that stressed
the moral truths, didacticism. The *dulce*, the aesthetic experience is, however, still the inescapable condition of all art. It must
not, however, be confused with pleasure as the Latin "sweet"
suggests. Pleasure is far too general a term: every experience is
either pleasurable or unpleasant. To define art by pleasure is, as
Croce said wittily, like trying to define fish by the water in which
they swim.[14]

In denying the one-to-one relationship of literature to external facts or truths, we ignored the problem of doubtful cases.
Defoe's *Journal of the Plague Years* and his *Memoirs of Cavalier*
were for a long time considered historical documents. Even the
anonymous *Robinson Crusoe* was read by contemporary audi-
ences as a factual travelogue. *Gulliver's Travels*, soon afterward,
could not have been read that way: it must have been recognized
as fiction in spite of its pretense, an old fictional device, to record
the truthful narration of an honest captain. In this century the
worship of the document has suggested many attempts to produce hybrid forms such as the "factography" of the Russians
in the twenties, Truman Capote's *In Cold Blood*, and Norman
Mailer's *Armies of the Night*, reportages to my mind which use
fictional devices but which claim to be either a "nonfictional
novel" or a "collective novel," paradoxical names for fictions
based on documents or personal experiences, two sources that
are as old as the hills. Documentary dramas such as Rolf Hoch-
hut's *Der Stellvertreter* remain plays even though they may put
documented statements into the mouths of their figures, whether

Pope or commoner. These hybrid forms show our thirst for facts or possibly the drying up of imagination, the assimilation of much literature to journalism, reporting or historiography.[15]

The same process can be observed in historiography as it also, more justifiably than fiction, has been invaded by the scientific ideal. In history writing the share of invention has varied greatly with different writers and periods. The speeches in Thucydides are openly invented but *The History of the Peloponnesian War* quite rightly claims historical truth and reproduces the actual course of events that we can sometimes verify from other evidence such as archeological sources. Modern historians shun this method but often fall victim to the inventions of diplomats, earlier historians, and eye-witness accounts. But the recent attempts to eradicate the distinction between fiction and works of history which make a claim to truth, such as Roland Barthes's propagating the all-inclusive term *écriture* or calling anything in print *text*, merely postpone the problem. At most these terms serve as a strategy to elevate history and criticism to the status of creative writing, to defend a criticism that has become not only personal as it was quite consciously in Friedrich Schlegel or Sainte-Beuve, but fictional, even completely arbitrary, proclaiming misunderstanding, misreading, misprision to be positive virtues. It would mean the end of scholarship and criticism as it denies the existence and challenge of a determinate object.

A different attempt to assimilate historiography to fiction, Hayden White's *Metahistory* (1973), also fails to convince. White examines the ruling metaphors of the great nineteenth century historians (Macaulay, Carlyle, Michelet, Ranke, Burckhardt) perceptively with a scheme modeled on Northrop Frye's *Anatomy of Criticism* but cannot obliterate the distinction between historiography and fiction, however skillfully he shows the use of metaphors and other aesthetic devices in the writing of narrative history. It seems to me best to return to Sidney's phrase "The poet nothing affirmeth and therefore never lieth."[16] The historian and biographer may conceal and sometimes deliberately lie. The poet does not and cannot.

The attempt of Käte Hamburger in her *Logik der Dichtung* (1957) to split the realm of literature into two kinds: fictional and nonfictional, cannot convince, either. One kind is what she calls lyrical, existential, "real utterance" while the other is mimetic or fictional. The dividing criterion is the speaker. In the lyric the poet speaks, in the epic and drama he makes others speak. The novel in the first person (*der Ich-Roman*) is resolutely grouped with real utterance, undistinguishable, for instance, from a letter. The division leads, however, to insoluble dilemmas. She has to make awkward concessions to the dramatic monologue (*Rollenlyrik* in German) and the ballad and cannot handle such questions as Dostoevsky changing the first-person confession of Raskolnikov to a third-person narrative. As I have argued at length elsewhere[17] she can arrive only at a commonplace: some poems and novels use "I" as a speaker, while other poems and novels use "he or she." It is the ancient division of poetry by speaker which dates back to Plato's *Republic*. It cannot take the lyric and the first person narrative out of the realm of fiction. "Fictionality" remains a distinguishing characteristic of all imaginative literature, even the worst novel.

The other promising way of defining literature seems to be its relation to language. Nobody will deny that language is the medium of literature, and hence the idea to look for linguistic characteristics that set off literary language from the other uses of language, colloquial and scientific, seems an obvious one. But attempts at establishing a special literary language have failed. They can succeed only with certain types of poetry in which the language can be described as deviation from ordinary language, describable in sound patterns, grammatical and syntactical peculiarities, and differences of vocabulary. But nobody has succeeded in showing that deviation is a necessary condition of all poetry, not to speak of all literature, particularly the realistic novel. One even can point to good poems written in straightforward everyday language in no way deviating from plain prose. Examples from Wordsworth, Pushkin, and the French verse tradition have been quoted.[18] The attempts of I. A. Richards and his follower Thomas C. Pollock[19] to draw a distinction between emotive language reserved for literature and referential language or between connotative and denotative language are too crude and can be easily refuted if we think of the emotions displayed in a quarrel or a lovers' conversation, the connotations and subtle shades of meaning or associations, and even the verbal play of puns in daily conversation.

A much more promising answer than deviation is the view that "literariness" is "the capacity of the sign to point to itself and not to something else" to use the formulation of Tzvetan Todorov which seems to me preferable to the contradictory term "the autonomous sign" favored by the Prague Linguistic Circle. This self-reflexivity promotes the palpability of the sign and thus deepens "the dichotomy between signs and objects."[20] It is a good description of what happens in much modern poetry. A poem by Gerard Manley Hopkins asks us to realize the "inscape" of a landscape, a person, or a bird by focusing on specific words, and there are poems by Mallarmé and Khlebnikov, and many others since, which are almost enclosed displays of verbal art. But self-reflexivity fails to define literature and most poetry, and it is completely refuted by the novel in which words may become almost transparent. No verbal analysis, even in such a densely written play as *King Lear* can account for the effect of a simple phrase like "Undo this button" in the last scene (5. 1. 309). Literature is not only language and is not merely self-reflexive. It evokes a world of its own through language. I thus cannot accept the fashionable talk about the "prison house of language."[21] Literature does refer to reality, says something about the world, and makes us see and know the external world and that of our own and other minds.

Also purely formal criteria, organization, unity in variety, and coherence, are not enough to distinguish literature from nonliterature. We need to interpret organization very loosely to cope with much modern and ancient literature, and we must recognize that organization, coherence, and unity, however desirable, are intellectual concepts that are often satisfied by a good piece of philosophy, scholarship, or scientific exposition.

The only satisfactory way of setting off literature in the sense of high imaginative fiction is to say that literature is characterized by the dominance of the aesthetic function. The objection will be immediately made that nobody can define the aesthetic function but, I think, a little reflection will show that there is an aesthetic experience induced by a work of art and that we can recognize its dominance in a text. "Beauty" is a term now out of fashion as it seems limited to the agreeable and formally pleasing, but it is surely a definite describable experience in the contemplation of men, women, animals, plants, landscapes, sky-scapes, and seascapes and in the experience of the arts. To give examples of obvious beauty: listen to a Mozart concerto or look at a picture of Titian. Similarly in literature, the experience, wider and more varied to my mind than that of music or paint-ing, yields a state of contemplation, of intransitive attention that cannot be mistaken for anything else. One can search for the hundreds of attempts to define beauty. The newest calls it "a property of qualitative degree."[22] This reaching out in aesthetic experience is pleasurable, is *dulce*, and we should not shirk the idea of aesthetic enjoyment. But it can also be upsetting, shock-ing, moving, and cathartic even in its negativity as Theodor Adorno has argued impressively.[23] In this experience, which seems to me as self-evident as the color of snow or the sensation of pain, is implied a reaching toward an object that has this inherent quality. The object is by its nature value-charged, an object of value and imposing value. The term "value" is ad-mittedly and deliberately broad as it tries to cover the enor-mous variety of values in literature. It suggests that, in discrimi-nating among works of literature, we need a theory of value, an "axiology," in short, criticism in the old sense of evaluation, discrimination.

We have come to distinguish four fields of meaning for the term "literature." There is literature without distinction of sub-ject matter but with the implication of quality, aesthetic, intellec-tual, moral, or political. Below it, we may say, are all writings, historical, political, philosophical, critical, and didactic, that do not reach the level for inclusion in a national literature. I am afraid that the writings of most scholars and critics belong to this second category. Then there is the other meaning of literature as imaginative literature, which I would set off by the concept of "fictionality" and confess the failure of making the distinction one of a special literary language. This descriptive meaning in-cludes bad fiction, or whatever we call subliterature, which is well worth study as a social document for the history of taste. It fulfills a social function that we may deplore as escapism or welcome as satisfying human aesthetic urges. And finally there is the realm of imaginative literature in which the aesthetic function dominates.

A consciousness of these issues, clarity of terminology, seems to me one of the main *desiderata* of any community of scholars and students and thus in any advance of understanding and cooperation among them. It is most urgent in the study of literature.

Poetics, Interpretation, and Criticism

GEORGE WATSON, in a little book, *The Literary Critics*, has told us that the history of criticism is "a record of chaos marked by sudden revolution." "The great critics do not contribute: they interrupt,"[1] he says strikingly. At the risk of confirming Mr. Watson's view that I belong to the "Tidy School of Critical History," I shall argue that the case is not that desperate. Even in England, which Mr. Watson had primarily in mind, one could hardly deny that Dr. Johnson learned from Dryden and that T. S. Eliot learned from Coleridge and Arnold. There *are* continuities. The history of criticism is rather like a long drawn-out debate about a few contested concepts.

We can see today and in history the conflict of two endeavours: the search for poetics, for laws, or at least for rules or constants in literature, for a universal matrix on the one hand, and the unending attempts to interpret individual works or minds of authors on the other. We might recognize that these are both legitimate tasks and they they correspond to age-old distinctions in the workings of the human mind. Poetics or theory of literature aims ultimately at the establishment of a science of literature that many today would like to make over into a social science on the model of linguistics, using even such tools of quantification as statistics. The interpreters want to get at the hidden meaning of a text, unmasking its mysteries with the assumptions of Freudian psycho-analysis or Jungian archetypal anthropology or, more recently, with existentialist ambitions of identifying with the mind of an author. It is, to put it in gross terms, the old conflict between rationalism and irrationalism, or simply the contrast of concern for either the universal or the individual. It might be, shifting the emphasis slightly, the concern for the self

The Presidential Address of the Modern Humanities Research Association read at University College, London, on 4 January 1974 behind or below it. It is the contrast between interest in crafts-manship and technique versus a glad or resigned admission of the incomprehensible, the ineffable in the inspiration of the poet, which we have rechristened the workings of the uncon-scious.

We could call Aristotle the father of both of these strands. Besides the *Poetics* he wrote also *peri hermeneias*, a major treatise in the *Organon*. Both poetics and hermeneutics carry his stamp even today. We deplore, however, the uses to which Aristotle's *Poetics* was put during the Renaissance and after when his au-thority (combined with Horace's *De arte poetica*) gave rise to long and dreary wrangles about the unities in tragedy and the proper machinery in the epic. But the general neoclassical enterprise of searching for a scheme of literature, a table of genres, standards of imitation and ideals for the correct structure of a work of art and the right response of the right reader can be defended as basically sound. It assumed, one should admit, too easily a stable psychology of human nature, a fundamental set of norms in the work, a uniform working of human sensibility and intelligence. Still, in its best formulations, particularly after empiricism has eroded the rigidity of seventeenth-century authoritarianism, it shied away from a universal, totally exhaustive rational scheme that would lay claims to validity for all times and places. For instance, Lord Kames in his *Elements of Criticism* (1762) expounds the standard of taste but sees the paradox that we must exclude many classes of men. "Those who depend for food on bodily labor are totally devoid of taste"; Orientals, people in the dark Middle Ages, Germans, and Russians do not count. Ruefully he has to admit that the "exclusion of classes so many and numer-ous, reduces within a narrow compass those who are qualified to be judges in the fine arts," while he still clings to his faith in a "wonderful uniformity among the emotions and feelings of different individuals."[2] If we look at eighteenth-century genre theory, we see that such an authoritative writer as Hugh Blair, in his *Lectures on Rhetoric and Belles Lettres* (1783), does not even attempt to argue for any precise principle of classification nor pretend to any completeness in his heterogeneous list of literary kinds: he discusses "Descriptive Poetry" along with the "Poetry of Hebrews" and then turns, in complete orthodoxy, to what he calls "the two highest kinds of poetical writing: the Epic and the Dramatic."[3] But soon, particularly in Germany, with Herder, these two highest kinds were displaced by a general concept of lyrical poetry, of "song," and Herder was also one of the first to proclaim that no "theory of the beautiful in all the arts and sciences is possible without history."[4] Literary history arose, in Italy and England and later in Germany, and with it poetics fell into desuetude.

In England nothing was written that could be called poetics throughout the nineteenth century, if we ignore two exceptions: Coleridge and the little-known Eneas Sweetland Dallas. But both these writers can be, on this point at least, described as echoes of the Germans. There, in a surprising turn with the advent of Kant, poetics became attached to dialectics. Schiller's treatise *On Naïve and Sentimental Poetry* (1795) arrived at a scheme of the relationship between man and nature which is at the same time a philosophy of history and a theory of genres. Friedrich Schlegel rang the changes on subjective and objective poetry. Schelling, particularly with his oration "On the Relation of the Plastic Arts to Nature" (1807), supplied Coleridge with the idea of art as "mediatress between, and reconciler of, nature and man,"[5] while August Wilhelm Schlegel yielded the formula for organic versus mechanical poetry.[6] Dallas rather followed Wilhelm von Humboldt's and Jean Paul's coordination of the main kinds of poetry with the dimensions of time: associating the play with the present, the tale with the past, and the song, somewhat mysteriously, with the future.[7]

Only in Russia did Alexander Veselovsky try undauntedly to construe a historical poetics, a universal evolutionary history of poetry in which the history of poetic devices, themes, forms, and genres would be traced through all literatures, oral and written. No wonder that his project remained incomplete.

But poetics revived in the twentieth century on a grand scale. The first were the Russian formalists, who, shortly after 1914, focused sharply on formal devices, using linguistic tools to analyse the language of poetry as a special language. They also were the first to attempt a strictly formal study of the types and procedures of fiction, though Henry James and the expounder of his views, Percy Lubbock, in the *Craft of Fiction* (1921) had attempted something analogous with the different perspective of James's own novelistic practice.

In France, Paul Valéry initiated the revival of poetics with conceptions often surprisingly similar to those of the Russians, of whom he could have known nothing. He also believed in a special language of poetry and the predominance of form. Valéry occupied a newly established Chair of Poetics at the Collège de France from 1937 until 1945.

In England, I. A. Richards, with his *Principles of Literary Criticism* (1924), was the first to propose an original theory of poetry after its long dormancy, but with its assumptions of a neurological psychology, allowed the bridge between reader and work of art to collapse completely. "The balanced poise" achieved by art, Richards says expressly, "can be given by a carpet or a pot or a gesture as unmistakably as by the Parthenon, it may come about through an epigram as clearly as through a Sonata." Thus it is "less important to like 'good' poetry and dislike 'bad' than to be able to use them both as a means of ordering our minds."[8] Poetry is reduced to mental therapy, to a beneficial harmless drug when the character of the object (pots, carpets, gestures) or the quality (good or bad poetry) ceases to matter. Fortunately, Mr. Richards's practice belies his theory: he was able to analyze poems as objects open to inspection. What as theory of poetry amounts to a grandiose confusion of poetry with all value judgments, with our commitments and beliefs, surprisingly yielded sensitive interpretations of single poems. Poetics, with Richards, becomes theory of interpretation, *hermeneutics*.

But many others have not given up poetics. On the contrary, recent years have seen the most inclusive and ambitious theories of poetry propounded for a century and more. Thus Emil Staiger's *Grundbegriffe der Poetik* (1946) declares time to be the form of poetic imagination and aligns the main kinds or rather modes —the lyrical, the epical, and the tragic—with the three dimensions of the time concept. The lyrical is associated with the present, the epic with the past, and the drama, oddly enough, with the future. Heidegger's analysis of time is invoked to claim an exhaustive scheme for all poetry. In Staiger time reigns supreme. In Northrop Frye's *Anatomy of Criticism* (1957) the cycle of nature rules over all literature. The book does much more than the title seems to promise. It is a theory of literature as "existing in its own universe, no longer a commentary on life or reality, but containing life and reality in a system of verbal relationships" and a new theory of genres of which there are only four: comedy, romance, tragedy, and satire; and these correspond to the four seasons: spring, summer, autumn, and winter, the rhythm of nature. The literary universe is in Frye's conception a "universe in which everything is potentially identical with everything else."[9]

In the meantime, the example of Saussure's linguistics with its emphasis on system and structure combined with the discovery of Russian formalism led in France to the broad movement known as structuralism. Vladimir Propp's *Morphology of the Folk Tale* (1927) impressed Claude Lévi-Strauss. Roman Jakobson, who had been a member of both the Moscow and the Prague Linguistic Circles and became a Professor at Columbia and at Harvard, provided a personal link. A Bulgarian settled in France, Tzvetan Todorov, translated an anthology of the Russian formalists into French.[10] In 1970 a periodical, *Poétique*, was founded, which proudly announced a revival of poetics. It was to include not only "studies of poetic language, structures of narration, rhetorical figures, systems of genres but to expand into discussions of all language games, folklore, mass communication, and even the language of dreams and madness, down to the humblest productions of texts and the most fortuitous encounters of words."[11] Todorov, in many writings, particularly a survey of poetics (which, in practice, draws almost all of its examples from prose) in a symposium entitled *Qu'est-ce que le structuralisme?* (1968), advances the claim of the new poetics to establish an exhaustive, complete system or science of literature on the analogy of a linguistic system. Literature, as in Frye, is considered a part of language, self-enclosed as all language is purely arbitrary, in no relation to reality. Roland Barthes, the presiding spirit of the group, for whom Todorov wrote his doctoral dissertation,[12] asserts that "all writing is a narcissistic activity. Reality is always only pretext. Writing (*écrire*) is an intransitive verb. It cannot explain the world. Rather it neutralizes the true and the false. It is the irreal itself."[13] Todorov thus can announce a kind of involution. The aim of poetics "is not so much a better knowledge of the object but the perfecting of scientific discourse."

"The object of poetics is precisely its method."[14] "The method is the object of science and its object, the method." A *reductio ad absurdum* is achieved. The object, poetry and literature, has disappeared. There remains only a disembodied methodology.

Still, one may question the theoretical bases of this whole enterprise. One need not even raise doubts about Saussure's doctrine of the complete arbitrariness of language (a dispute begun with Plato's *Cratylus* and by no means settled completely even today) to question the applicability of the model of a linguistic system to the totality of literature. I am not convinced that linguists have established the system of language beyond the phonemic level, but even if they could succeed, as Chomsky's transformational grammar claims, in arriving at a few universal language principles, I doubt whether such an enterprise can establish a system of literature. Literature is not a single system of internal relations but an enormous developing, changing manifold spreading over huge stretches of time and space. As I have argued elsewhere, literature is not only language: "Motifs, themes, images, symbols, plots, and compositional schemes, genre patterns, character and hero types, as well as qualities such as the tragic or the comic, the sublime or the grotesque, can be and have been discussed fruitfully with only a minimal or no regard to their linguistic formulations. The mere fact that the great poets and writers—Homer, Virgil, Dante, Shakespeare, Goethe, Tolstoy, and Dostoevsky—have exercised enormous influence, often in poor and loose translations that hardly convey even an inkling of the peculiarities of their verbal style, should demonstrate the comparative independence of literature from language."[15]

The attempts to express narrative themes and situations in linguistic terms, as Todorov does in writing a *Grammar of the Decameron*, seem to me, at best, only witty analogizing. The love passion, he tells us, "may be seen as optative of sexual intercourse, while renunciation may be thought of as its negative optative; the conditional frequently takes the form of tasks familiar in fairy tale or medieval romance: while the subjunctive of injury might be expressed as a simple threat."[16] The whole doctrine of man's imprisonment in language should be doubted: we must assume that language itself is in an ontological relation to reality, as all older philosophers of language and even Heidegger assert. There is, after all, a perceptual life of man: personality and self (*pace* Gilbert Ryle) cannot be reduced to language relations. Even deaf-mutes find their way around the world. This does not deny that civilization as we know it is possible only because of the development of language or that linguistics can throw light on many questions of literature. It only denies the view of the prison-house of language with the nihilistic consequences drawn by the prophets of the death of literature.

Interpretation, one would think, is the remedy or the antidote to such poetics. It has, at least, as long a history, if we recall the allegorical interpretations of Homer in antiquity and the tradition of biblical exegesis that began very soon after the rise of Christianity as it had to define its relationship to the Old Testament and interpret it for its users. Erich Auerbach has done much to make us understand the use of *figura*. Nor should one ignore the age-old enterprise of legal interpretation, of legal codes, and legal texts. In the Renaissance the interpretation of classical authors became codified and was soon, in a process which I believe has never been studied, transferred to vernacular texts. I need only allude to the history of textual criticism of Shakespeare in the eighteenth century or to Richard Bentley's freakish edition of *Paradise Lost*. It is still largely confined to conjectures about printer's errors and studies of variants, but it soon expanded into commentary and comparison. To give only English examples: Thomas Warton's *Observations on the Fairie Queene* (1754) or Walter Whiter's *Specimen of a Commentary on Shakespeare* (1790), which studies images and imagery in the light of associationist psychology, show how far literary interpretation was advanced in the eighteenth century without much theoretical foundation.

Rules and procedures for interpretation were formulated rather in biblical and legal exegesis. The revival of the Greek term *hermeneutics* seems to be due to a book by J. C. Dannhauser, *Hermeneutica sacra* (1654), but for the later development Johann August Ernesti's *Institutio interpretis Novi Testamenti* (1761) seems to have been the authoritative book that confronted Schleiermacher when he gave a new turn to hermeneutics.[17] What had been a technique of textual exegesis became with him a doctrine

of total understanding (*Verstehen*). While Schleiermacher recognized the role of grammatical and comparative exegesis, he
subordinated it to what he called the "divinatory" method: to
empathy, to identification. The sources, as Karl Otto Apel has
shown,[18] go back to Protestant pietism, of which Schleiermacher
was a disciple, and finally to mysticism: to Jakob Böhme, Eck-
hart, and Tauler. Dilthey, at least in his early stage, resumes
Schleiermacher's theory of understanding to make it the basis of
his contrast between the natural and the moral sciences. (The
term *Geisteswissenschaften* occurs first as a translation of "moral
sciences" in the German version of John Stuart Mill's *Logic*.[19])
The scientist "explains," looks for causes; the humanist "understands," enters another man's mind. Dilthey later modified his
psychological approach. Understanding, he argued, means not
merely entering another man's mind but rather an interpretation
of man's expressions, of the shapes and forms in a tradition, of
documents and monuments, which he designates with a Hegelian term, the "objective spirit." Here is the source of German
Geistesgeschichte, which must rely on the concept of *Zeitgeist* and
emphasize the differences between periods and man's attitudes
and conceptions in different ages. In Dilthey and many others it
led to historicism and ultimately to a resigned relativism. Hans-
Georg Gadamer, in *Wahrheit und Methode* (1960), the most influential book of modern hermeneutics, gave a new turn to the
concept under the influence of Heidegger. Gadamer rejects the
psychologism of Dilthey and develops rather the view that interpretation is a fusion of our own horizon, our own historicity
clearly recognized as such, with the horizon of the past. What is
needed is *Wirkungsgeschichte*, a tracing of the effects of a work of
art on its readers, a study of the audience rather than of the
author. All this led to a complex debate that far exceeds literary
scholarship; Emilio Betti, an Italian legal historian, and E. D.
Hirsch, in *Validity in Interpretation* (1967), have criticized Gadamer for what seem to them the subjectivist consequences of his
analysis. Hirsch has revived the concept of the intention of the
author, which since Wimsatt's "Intentional Fallacy" had been
considered irrelevant, and has argued for an approach through
genre to assure the correctness of interpretation.

The effect on concrete literary study of hermeneutic speculation was profound, at least in Germany and France. Emil Staiger, in *Die Kunst der Interpretation* (1955) has most strongly defended and skillfully exemplified the assumption that "the criterion of feeling is also the criterion of scholarship."[20] The category of causality is useless in literary studies. What matters is the discovery of my harmony with the object and of the harmony in the object, if it is a genuine work of art. *Stimmigkeit* has served Staiger well in his many interpretations of German poems. It also made him condemn all modern literature as disharmonious in a speech that provoked the protest of his friend Max Frisch.[21] Staiger is in harmony only with Goethe and the German romantics.

The French interpreters have different, though still romantic tastes: their heroes are Rousseau, Baudelaire, and Proust. Georges Poulet, who oddly enough is considered the head of the "Geneva school" though he has taught at Edinburgh, Johns Hopkins, and Zürich, has been the main theoretical expounder of interpretation in French. Poulet argues that a work of art is not an object but a pattern of meanings behind which a consciousness is to be discovered. "The literary critic needs to forget the objective elements of the work and elevate himself to the apprehension of a subjectivity without objectivity." In ever new variations Poulet expounds the view that the critic has to find "the sentiment of self" of an author, which he calls his *cogito*. It must not be confused with the psychology of the writer. It is inherent in the total work and can be reached only by an act of identification. "The same I must operate with the author and the critic."[22]

In practice, Poulet studies the act of self-awareness or the struggle to achieve identity by examining the use of time and space in the total work of an author, as time and space are the tools of his vision. In a later book, *Les Métamorphoses du cercle* (1961), Poulet uses the circle as symbol for existential coherence. In a letter addressed to me in 1956, he granted that this kind of criticism "seems to destroy and neglect the formal aspects of works. In our studies it is as if there were no poems, no novels, or plays with their particular meaning; everything becomes a continuous medium in which forms have only an indicative role like everything else. This is the most serious limitation of such criticism, and the one which makes it differ the most from criticism as it is understood in Anglo-Saxon countries today. In these countries, what is most important is the structural—and consequently objective—reality of isolated works; however, in France (with Du Bos, Marcel Raymond, Béguin, Bachelard, the early Sartre, Blanchot, Richard, Jean Wahl, and myself), as also, I believe, in Germany, in the schools derived from Dilthey, what is most important is the organizing consciousness, which can be attained only by lifting the mask of structures."[23]

That this is done with complete disregard for the meaning of an individual work was demonstrated by Leo Spitzer in a paper on Poulet's interpretation of Marivaux's *La Vie de Marianne*.[24] Marivaux, according to Poulet, is a kind of eighteenth-century Mallarmé: nothingness, pure confusion, surrender to the moment, pure succession characterize his mind. "Nothing survives except a sort of vaporous memory of all that has happened. And it is that sort of time along the length of which the novels of Marivaux finally evaporate." But "by a singular turn, the writer who seemed pre-eminently the writer of the instantaneous, can also depict a continuous flow of time in the manner of Bergson. Marianne is precisely both this and that: the point and the line; a point that extends out and prolongs itself, and is transformed into a line: an instant which exceeds and lengthens itself, and which is tranformed into time."[25]

Spitzer has little trouble in showing that this is sheer fancy, that the abrupt, broken style (*style coupé*) cannot change into a Bergsonian flux, just as a point cannot change into a line. Spitzer can show that the quotations from *La Vie de Marianne* are torn out of context: Poulet ignores the fact that Marianne is a courageous, stable, virtuous woman who triumphs over adversity. There is nothing to support Poulet's view of Marivaux as disintegrating the rational order and embracing a moral nihilism. Poulet would presumably have answered that he does not care for the character of Marianne or even for the novel of which she is the heroine but merely for the consciousness behind all the novels and plays of Marivaux, which he tries to reconstruct or rather divine from anything at hand.

Recently I had occasion to examine Poulet's pronouncements on Charles Du Bos and was surprised to discover that he did exactly the same thing he did to Marivaux, using passages out of their context to prove that Du Bos was a completely passive being, negative, totally receptive, with no personal life of his own. Poulet even applies to Du Bos passages from Du Bos's *Journal* speaking of Bergson and Proust, as if they were written about Du Bos himself.[26] The actual point of view of Du Bos's criticism, his early ranking by spirituality and later by Catholic orthodoxy, is completely obscured.[27] Poulet's method has opened the door to sheer arbitrariness, to caprice, or, simply, to uncontrollable intellectual games.

"Interpretation" does exist also in Anglo-Saxon countries, in spite of Poulet's sharp contrast to what is going on in French and German criticism. I am not thinking only of the effect of Poulet's and his friends' own writings in the United States today. J. Hillis Miller's books, particularly the book on Dickens dedicated to Poulet, *The Disappearance of God*, and *Poets of Reality*, can be described as applying Poulet's method to English and American texts, while Geoffrey Hartman has learned rather from Blanchot, though he uses also other methods: historical or structuralist. But I am thinking rather of anticipations of Poulet's concern, particularly by G. Wilson Knight. *The Wheel of Fire* (1930) considers each of Shakespeare's plays as "a visionary whole, close-knit in personification, atmospheric suggestion, and direct poetic symbolism." The final plays are "mythical representations of a mystic vision." Interpretation is to Knight a "reconstruction of vision."[28] In practice, Wilson Knight—while starting from image clusters and such oppositions as tempest and music—becomes an allegorizer who extracts from Shakespeare and many others a philosophy which is neither original, clear, nor complex. It amounts to a reconciliation of Eros and Agape, of order with energy, and so on with other pairs of contraries. All real poets bring the same message. As Austin Warren commented years ago: "After decoding of each, one is left with a feeling of futility. Poetry is revelation, but what does it reveal?"[29] T. S. Eliot wrote an introduction to Wilson Knight's book, praising his attempt to elucidate the pattern in Shakespeare's carpet: "to read character and plot with an understanding of a subterrene or submarine music." But he concludes not very happily that "if we lived [the work of Shakespeare] completely we would need no interpretation."[30] It sounds like saying, "If we were God, we would need no theology." Elsewhere Eliot complained that interpretation makes a pretence of conveying some insight into another author but "instead of insight," he protests, "you get a fiction."[31]

We might feel this way about some of the most widespread methods of interpretation, the psychoanalytical and the mythic. They are both systems of decoding or unmasking: of the neurotic personality behind the work, such as Kafka's, dominated by his father; or the complexes motivating a fictional figure, such as the Oedipus complex of Hamlet. Myth criticism is a kind of allegorizing: critics look for disguises of the sacrificial death of God, the rebirth in Spring, and for versions of the quest of the Holy Grail even in a fishing trip. A whole group of medievalists in the United States have tried, mainly under the influence of D. W. Robertson, to interpret Chaucer, the *Pearl* Poet, and Langland as allegorists (which they were in part) who recommended a single Christian virtue, Charity, under many disguises. A renewed interest in the fourfold levels of meaning expounded in Dante's letter to Can Grande (and in the *Convivio*) has led to an exclusive emphasis on the anagogic meaning at the expense of the literal. We seem to revive the kind of interpretation that made the *Song of Songs*, obviously an erotic poem, into an allegory of Christ's love for his Church (the feminine *Ecclesia*). One can, however, defend allegorical interpretation by saying with Northrop Frye that "all commentary or relating of the events of a narrative to conceptual terminology is in one sense allegorical interpretation."[32]

Many have begun to doubt the assumptions of modern interpretation. Morton Bloomfield has pointed out that according to Thomas Aquinas the literal sense is the only one in secular writing while the fourfold levels are reserved for the Sacred Writ.[33] But today the great classics have become sacred writs: they are read for their supposed mysteries: in English literature, Shakespeare, Milton, Blake, Shelley, and more recently even Yeats and Wallace Stevens are treated as sacred texts. Spitzer in many contexts has argued that the modern commentator "is enabled, by his training and studiousness, to approximate and perhaps restore the original meaning of a work of art composed at another time and place." For Spitzer there is "only one meaning which must be isolated with an energy bent on discrimination."[34] Others like Susan Sontag have simply rejected interpretation as concerned with items of content. "In the place of a hermeneutics we need an erotics of art," she concludes her well-known essay *Against Interpretation*.[35] Still, erotics seems merely to revive the old, sensible but hardly new recommendation of enjoyment, and thus, in critical discourse, of arbitrary pronouncements of taste, of impression. Even Roland Barthes, whom we think of as the prophet of structuralism and who in practice was often a sociologist of *bourgeois* mythologies and feminine fashions, comes, in a late piece, "Science versus Literature," published in the *Times Literary Supplement*,[36] to the conclusion that writing is subversive of the scientific discourse with its claim for reference to the world and truth. Writing is pleasure and pleasure-giving: a rather surprising conclusion for Barthes, developed in his recent little book, *Le Plaisir du texte* (1973). *Jouissance*, with explicit sexual overtones, appears here utterly individual and unforeseeable. Science and scientism are rejected.

Still, as students and scholars we cannot throw up our hands in despair at the enterprise of trying to understand literary works and even to theorize about literature in general. Even if we grant the aberrations of poetics and interpretation and recognize the impasse to which the two methods have come recently, we must not see them simply as incompatible. We must not make neat choices. F. R. Leavis, for instance, simply denied the need for theory in an exchange with me as far back as 1936. He could not be drawn out to define the underlying principles of his practice, and when I confronted him with literal quotations of his *obiter dicta* on theory, he dismissed such summarizing as "intolerably clumsy and inadequate." He took me simply as a representative of the philosophical approach, which is abstract, while his own is concerned with the concrete. "Words in poetry invite us not to think about and judge, but to feel into or become."[37] George Watson admits only descriptive criticism as legitimate and flourishing. Legislative and theoretical criticism are considered dead and sterile.[38] This excess of empiricism seems particularly the danger of the English, who might be confirmed in their distrust of theories when confronted with the current structuralist and existentialist speculations in France and Germany. Northrop Frye has taken the other extreme position. Only theory (his "criticism") counts. Everything else belongs "only to the history of taste, and therefore follows the vacillations of fashionable prejudice."[39] Still, it is possible to mediate the conflict. Gérard Genette, to my mind the best critic among the French structuralists, formulates the possibility of a synthesis very well: "In looking for the specific I find the universal, and in wanting to have a theory serve criticism I make criticism willy-nilly serve theory. This paradox is that of every poetics. And no doubt also that of all knowledge, always torn between two inescapable commonplaces: the particularity of all objects and the generality of all science. Reassurance comes from the less familiar truth that the general is at the heart of the particular, and thus—contrary to common prejudice—the knowable at the heart of mystery.[40] Georg Lukács, in his two-volume *Aesthetik*, has, in spite of his obsessive preoccupation with the "mirroring of reality" argued for a category of the aesthetic he calls "specificity" (*Besonderheit*), located between the universal and the individual. Lukács restates what Hegel had called the concrete universal, a term revived by Josiah Royce and more recently by William K. Wimsatt.[41]

Here, in these terms that reconcile the universal and the particular, is already concealed the transition to the third unavoidable task of criticism: judgment, ranking, the decision about art and nonart. Most of the methods discussed, poetics or interpretation, pretend or aim to be value free. The theorists of poetics aim at scientific objectivity; the interpreters surrender judgment in the act of identification. But all students of literature do judge, whether they select their texts by tradition and reputation or whether they do it in an individual act of sympathy or enthusiasm. William K. Wimsatt has argued in a paper "Explication as Criticism" (1951) that explication, or what I here call interpretation, "rises from neutrality gradually and convincingly to the point of total judgment." He sees the difficulty of an escape from the "two extremes of sheer affectivism and of sheer scientific neutralism." "The extreme theory of explicative criticism cuts apart understanding and value just as much as the avowed theory of effects—and that is another way of saying that our main critical problem is always how to unify understanding and value as much as possible, or how to make our understanding evaluative."[42] It does seem a desirable solution, but it has its practical difficulties. One may believe with I. A. Richards that the problem of value "nearly always settles itself; or rather, our own inmost nature and the nature of the world in which we live decide it for us."[43] But I cannot share this optimism: the erosion of values has gone too far, the argument for relativism has become rampant. The theorists of the sociology of knowledge have argued for a complete historicity of the observer, his imprisonment in his time and place. The critic, we are told, should constantly take into account his own place in history, criticize his own point of view, know that he is a transient being with the tastes of his own time and place. But surely complete relativism is untenable, not only on the logical ground that it asserts the absolute truth of "everything is relative" but also on pragmatic grounds. It would lead to a complete anarchy of values, to the acceptance of the old saying: "de gustibus non est disputandum." I believe that the parallel of ethics and logic applies also to the arts. There are crimes—such as wanton murder—that are indefensible; there are logical and mathematical truths such as two plus two are four (despite the Underground Man's wish that two plus two were five), which are irrefutable, and there are aesthetic standards that are coercive. There are minimal distinctions between art and nonart, value and disvalue, distinctions of quality between, say, Shakespeare and trash. Relativists always shirk the issue of thoroughly bad poetry and move always in the region of great and near-great art, where disputes are frequent because a work of literature is not only an aesthetic object but an assembly of often heterogeneous values. It can be valued for different reasons by different people because it is not something neutral out there but is charged with values, is a structure of values inseparable from its qualities. What we need is an axiology, a science of literary values. In short, we need criticism, a kind of criticism, in which I believe the English critical tradition has been particularly rich, with its array of poet-critics: Dryden, Pope, Johnson, Wordsworth, Coleridge, Arnold, and T. S. Eliot. They were all molders of taste, creators of values.

Criticism as Evaluation

IN many contexts, for many years, I have called for a return to criticism in the original sense of judging, to criticism as evaluation. Both main trends in the history of criticism, revived and redefined in this century, poetics and interpretation, have given up the problem of judgment, of ranking, of the decision about art and nonart. The scientists and would-be scientists, the statisticians and the devotees of text grammar and even, in theory, most of the French structuralist critics assembled around the magazine *Poétique* cannot make any value distinctions; they think that making them would violate their ideal of scientific objectivity. Since they are interested in devices and regularities, they can plead that these can be observed even in trash or subliterature, kitsch and colportage. Also Northrop Frye, a critic quite apart from this scientific trend of linguistic poetics, argues in the "Polemical Introduction" to his *Anatomy of Criticism* that "the study of literature can never be founded on value judgments."[1] He conceives of literature as a system of fictions in which there is no qualitative difference between a fairy tale or a comedy of Shakespeare. Evaluation is relegated to the history of taste that, like the stock exchange, registers only whimsical fluctuations. What Frye calls "criticism" is a system, an all embracing timeless scheme in which any and all productions, good and bad, significant and trivial, have to find their place. The new interpreters, particularly the so-called Geneva school, have to come to a similar conclusion as they ask for complete identification with a consciousness behind the work, for an exchange of egos, for an "adhesion so total" to quote Jean Rousset, "that it precludes all judgment."[2]

But the task of evaluation is unavoidable as all students of literature *do* judge, whether they select their text by tradition and reputation or whether they do it in an individual act of sympathy or enthusiasm. But even after the selection of a text from the millions of books accessible today, constant decisions have to be made as to which of its innumerable traits or relations are to be selected for attention. Choices, explicit and implicit, are everywhere involved; what to exclude and what to ignore, what to single out and what, inevitably, to appreciate and to value. The description of value cannot be divorced from evaluation. A work of literary art cannot be perceived, let alone understood, except as an object of value. Immanuel Kant, in the *Critique of Judgment* argued long ago that meaning is inseparable from value in the aesthetic transaction.[3] The ideal of a neutral scientific objectivity in literary studies is simply a chimera, a delusion.

Many literary historians recognize that evaluation is inevitable but argue that evaluation is a historical process resulting in the "verdict of the ages," the formulation of a "canon" that can be studied like any other historical phenomenon. Thus Ernst Robert Curtius's immensely erudite *European Literature and the Latin Middle Ages* (1948) has made an impressive beginning in tracing the establishment of the canon of classical writers. No doubt, we can describe, say, the fluctuations of the fame of Dante who, for a time in the eighteenth century was, for instance, dismissed by Horace Walpole as "extravagant, absurd, disgusting, in short a Methodist parson in Bedlam."[4] Even Shakespeare's fame was not always secure: in spite of the high praise of Ben Jonson and of Dryden, Thomas Rymer could ridicule *Othello* as a "bloody farce without salt and savour"[5] and Voltaire could call Shakespeare a "village clown," a "drunken savage" though he admitted that he had found "some pearls in his enormous dunghill."[6] In recent years, the history of reception, *Rezeptionsgeschichte*, has been touted in Germany as the panacea for literary history. It seems to me only a reasonable plea for many old things: a history of criticism, a study of audience expectations and reactions. Its novelty is the use of Gadamer's theory of interpretation, of the idea of a "fusion of horizons," of the interplay between texts and recipient in which the text is assumed to be transformed by the reader. Hans Robert Jauss, its learned proponent, argues that the attitude of author to his public can be reconstructed not only from addresses to the reader or external evidence but implicitly: through the assumption, for instance, in *Don Quijote* of a knowledge and concern for chivalric romances.[7] But I do not see how

Jauss can bridge the gap between the implied audience in a work and the actual reactions of an audience in history. His method is only a refinement of the history of taste which leads to the old relativism.

The view is widespread that we simply have to study the critical situation of bygone ages and have to recognize that there are so many diverse types and styles of literature that no rational choice among them is even possible. Every time had its own poetry and criticism justified in its place. Poetry cannot go wrong and apparently even criticism that is only a reflection or justification of contemporary taste. Frederick A. Pottle in his *Idiom of Poetry* (1941) propounded the view that there are profound "shifts of sensibility" in history and that there is thus a "total discontinuity" in the history of poetry.[8] Mr. Pottle thought mainly of what he considers the irreconcilable taste for either Alexander Pope or Wordsworth. This view would split the history of literature into a multitude of different periods and areas of sensibility if we push Pottle's idea to its logical conclusion and apply it on an international scale and in the whole extent of historical time. We end with complete relativism, with the "whirligig of taste" (the title of a book by E. E. Kellett published in 1929), the tyranny of flux.

Some erudite scholars have been content with this resigned solution. My late colleague at Yale University, Erich Auerbach, the author of *Mimesis*, formulated this historistic creed eloquently in a review of the first two volumes of my *History of Modern Criticism*. He argued there that we should not fear extreme relativism. "The historian does not become incapable of judging; he learns what judging means. Indeed, he soon ceases to judge by abstract and unhistorical categories; he even will cease to search for such categories of judgment.... It is from the material itself that he will learn to extract the categories or concepts that he needs for describing and distinguishing the different phenomena. These concepts are not absolute: they are elastic and provisional, changeable with changing history."[9] He and others want the critic to see himself historically, in his own limited space and time. The so-called "sociology of knowledge" propounded by Karl Mannheim, in *Ideology and Utopia*, has pushed self-consciousness furthest. But this merely raises the question of all knowing, it leads to universal skepticism, to theoretical paralysis. The case of knowledge and even of historical knowledge is not that desperate. The genesis of a theory does not necessarily invalidate its truth. Men can correct their biases, criticise their presuppositions, rise above their temporal and local limitations. I agree with Eliseo Vivas that value, aesthetic or otherwise, is "present only in a certain psychological perspective but it is still present *in* the thing for those endowed with the capacity and training through which alone it can be perceived."[10] Judgment refers to an objective character that is open to inspection. There are, in a work of literature, meanings that I would call obligatory, while other meanings may be only potential or even purely facultative, the additions and associations of the recipient. Most of the disagreements among evaluations are due to the fact that a literary work of art is an assembly of values that are not purely aesthetic. A work belongs to literature at least in the sense of imaginative literature, of *belles lettres*, because the aesthetic value is dominant. But this does not preclude the presence of other values for which it has been appreciated and praised. They may be moral, political, religious, national and of course intellectual values. Thus often differences of opinion are not due so much to different responses but simply to the selection of different values in the work.

I have called this view "perspectivism"—possibly a mistaken choice as the term is preempted by the different use by Ortega y Gasset—which must not be confused with relativism. I recognize the impossibility of upholding a rigid absolutism in view of the historical changes of taste and styles but I also reject relativism, which has been considered the necessary consequence of these changes. "Perspectivism" is suggested by the analogy of our seeing, say, a house, very differently from different angles while we still must admit that there is a house out there of definite dimensions, layout, material, colors, and so on, which can be ascertained accurately and objectively.

Often differences of opinions are due to shifts in the vocabulary of description and evaluation. Thus when in older periods critics did not call certain works of art beautiful or refused to think of the Alps as beautiful, they assumed a narrow concept of the beautiful as the pleasant and agreeable. In the nineteenth century the term beauty took over functions previously reserved for the "sublime," a word that seems to have almost disappeared from our critical vocabulary.

One should also realize that there is a recognition of value that may not agree with one's feeling of relevance to oneself. I might admire a work of art, value it even very highly, but feel that it does not say anything to me, personally, in my immediate situation or mood.[11]

As Roman Ingarden[12] has shown convincingly, a literary work of art must be conceived as a schematic construct that has places of indeterminacy, "white spots," that will be filled out differently by different readers. Ingarden speaks of "concretizations" or more simply of the "life" of a work of art, its accretions of meaning in the course of history. But this does not preclude the objective character of this construct and the conviction that ideally interpretations can be correct. If all interpretations or readings were equal we could not differentiate among them. But it is surely the experience of every teacher that he can and must reject wrong interpretations and that he even can, in concrete cases, refute a wrong interpretation by an appeal to the text or an appeal to the totality of a work while the perverse interpreter may have fastened on some detail or distorted the meaning of a phrase. The concept of adequacy of interpretation leads clearly to the concept of correctness of judgment. Evaluation grows out of understanding; correct evaluation out of correct understanding. I have argued this so many times that I am ashamed of repeating myself. Logic, ethics, and, I believe, even aesthetics cry aloud against complete relativism. It would lead to a dehumanization of the arts and a paralysis of criticism.

If we look at criticism in this century we soon discover that it has not given up the task of evaluation. In what follows I should like to show how critics in this century have judged and by what criteria and shall attempt to provide a provisional classification of the criteria actually in use.

Much criticism judges by extra-aesthetic criteria: moralistic or political and social in the widest sense weighing the presumed influence of a work of literature on society or the kind of ideal of life that can be judged for its usefulness or rightness. Thus moralistic ideas inspired the American neo-humanists who be-

lieved in a sharp division between natural and moral man, between humanism and humanitarianism. Irving Babbitt and Paul
Elmer More rejected Rousseau and romanticism, modern subjectivism and naturalism. Naturalism is to them an all inclusive
term that allows them to condemn almost all modern literature.
More's essay on Joyce speaks of the "moral slough" of *Ulysses*, its
"weary and ugly art," its "philosophy of the inane" and even
Proust is treated as a mere naturalist.[13] The article "The Cleft
Eliot" belabors the dichotomy between the obscure poet, the
"lyrical prophet of chaos," and the solid orthodox critic.[14] But
we may judge with our hindsight that Paul Elmer More was not
so far wrong in protesting against the overrating of such writers
as Sinclair Lewis, John Dos Passos, and Joseph Hergesheimer.[15]

Also Yvor Winters—even though he contributed to the anti-
humanist symposium and has very different modernist tastes in
poetry—judges by moral standards. "Moral," however, is used
by him in a very broad sense: it often means discrimination, a
sense of truth and falsehood and not only a sense of right and
wrong. Poetry achieves a unity of thought and feeling, but,
Winters insists, it is achieved only by an act of moral judgment.
Winters tells us over and over again that "the ethical interest is
the only poetic interest."[16] Criticism is a judgment of the judgment pronounced by the poem. It will and must appeal to constant principles, to a conception of absolute truth and rightness.
The primary function of criticism is thus evaluation. "Unless
criticism succeeds in providing a usable system of evaluation it is
worth very little,"[17] says Winters strikingly and proceeds to sup-
ply us if not with a system, then with many examples of his own
opinions that such and such a poem is better than that one or
even that this stanza, this line, this metaphor or even this word is
better than an alternative. Ranking is Winters's main and, among
American critics, almost unique preoccupation. Winters has rewritten the whole history of English and American poetry from
his point of view, severely condemning anything he considers
primitivism or decadence. The romantics, including Emerson,
Poe, and Whitman are on his blacklist. Yeats cannot be taken
seriously as he holds absurd philosophical and political views,
and Robert Frost, an "Emersonian romantic," is labeled a "spiri-
tual drifter."[18] Winters has the courage of his opinions, an amaz-

ing self-confidence in distributing precise praise and blame. But one wonders often why he praises a particular poem or line. One runs up against a final obscurity: the ipse dixit of Winters.

If we glance at France, moralistic criticism is there prevalent too but it is often more definitely combined with political standards. Thus Julien Benda diagnosed what he considered the decadence of French literature as moral and political decadence and as the triumph of unreason. France is byzantine. The Bergsonian philosophy of flux, Gide, Valéry, and the surrealists, their worship of the dream and the unconscious, all serve to support the central thesis. A very different group of critics around the *Action française*, now discredited because of their flirtings with nazism, illustrate the combination of moral and political criteria best. Charles Maurras, their leader, proclaimed himself the champion of order against barbarism, also in literature. T. S. Eliot sympathized with Maurras and increasingly applied the standard of social order and later of religious orthodoxy though he admitted that it should be invoked only after the aesthetic judgment has done its work. A distinction between "artness" and "greatness" with greatness decided by moral and religious criteria led to a return to the old distinction of form and content and introduced the problem of belief. To what extent, asks Eliot, must the reader share the beliefs of an author in order to appreciate him? Eliot answered his question by stating that we can give "poetic assent" only to poets whose views we can consider "coherent, mature, and founded on the facts of experience,"[19] a criterion that allowed Eliot to disparage Shelley and D. H. Lawrence. It is finally a moralistic, didactic judgment: Shelley and D. H. Lawrence would not be good for the society Eliot envisages as ideal.

An early admirer of Eliot, F. R. Leavis, the most influential practical critic of the century in England, has developed also largely moralistic criteria based on an advocacy of tradition which is conceived as centered on Old England, civilised but still basically rural. "Maturity," "sanity," "discipline" are Leavis's key values, which somewhat surprisingly are in his later writings modified by a worship of Life. Life, with a capital L, is understood in the sense of the Life force of D. H. Lawrence, considered the greatest writer of the century, the devastating critic of modern industrial civilization. Lawrence, we are told, "belongs to the same ethical and religious tradition as George Eliot."[20] The appeal to this incongruous pair allows Leavis to condemn almost all modern art: Joyce, Wyndham Lewis, Auden, Dylan Thomas, and many others. He clings to the discoveries of his youth: Conrad, Lawrence, Gerard Manley Hopkins, and the early T. S. Eliot.

If we now glance briefly at Germany we must conclude that ultimately didactic criteria inspired the criticism of the George circle though they are usually considered to be complete aesthetes. Friedrich Gundolf, in all his books, appeals to an ideal of sublime, heroic greatness, to discipline and order.

Marxism, in Russia and elsewhere, in so far as it is not merely descriptive and explanatory, must also be considered a form of didacticism. It requires "partisanship," it always judges whether a work or an author has contributed to the coming of socialism, either by being "progressive" in its or his time or by supporting the cause of Revolution today. Authors are asked not only to reflect reality but to depict it as anticipating the future. More subtly, Georg Lukács, the Hungarian Marxist, judged writers in relation to the historical process: they are valued for their insights into the structure of a society and its movement toward the socialist future. Lukács can, for instance, appreciate Sir Walter Scott because he supposedly saw the right turning points of history even though his professed political opinions were conservative.

Moral, political, and religious criteria are often loosely bound up with nationalist ideas. We see this most clearly in the Germans. Max Kommerell, originally a disciple of Stefan George, wrote the most extravagant exaltation of the German classics as leaders of their nation (*The Poet as Leader in German Classicism,* 1928). Reading it one would not guess that Klopstock was a Christian or that Herder was a clergyman. The whole group of the German classics is subjected to a process of strange rarefication. Particularly Goethe and Hölderlin are treated with religious awe. Hölderlin is a seer who will create a new nation. "His poetry alone assures us that the same Fate rules over us [Germans] as over the Greeks."[21] During the Nazi period orgies of self-glorification coupled with a denigration of anything considered non-German were celebrated even in serious erudite works.

In other countries nationalism is also often a main standard of criticism. The whole classicist trend in French criticism is oriented toward an ideal French spirit that contrasts with Nordic and Slavic murkiness. In Spain it is often assumed that *hispanidad* is a value demonstrated in its great writers as is the Latin or Italian spirit in Italy. This kind of argument Leo Spitzer has called "national tautology," as it implies the assertion that a Spanish or Italian work is great because it is genuinely Spanish or Italian and that it is genuinely Spanish or Italian if it is great.[22] England is comparatively immune, in its self-assurance, to the search for "Englishry" (a rare word), but some Americans have, for a time, cultivated "nativism" and judged works of literature for their specifically American flavor. Van Wyck Brooks attacked Mark Twain and Henry James as "defaulters from America." Even Marxist criticism, international in theory, manages often to appeal to the concept of nationhood (*narodnost*) that in the Slavic languages can easily be confounded with the people and even with the suppressed classes. The Czech Academy has sponsored a large scale *History of Czech Literature* that constantly exploits these ambiguities.[23]

Confronted with the many nationalisms one might appreciate the movement of "comparative literature," which has tried to overcome the limitations imposed by the study of a single national literature. Ironically enough, particularly in France, "comparative literature" often led, however, to a kind of bookkeeping in which the power of a nation for influencing others is exalted, or, more subtly, one's nation is praised for its receptivity to this or that great author of another nation. Still, with "comparative literature" and more generally with the growth of cosmopolitanism, a consciousness of the unity of Western literature seems to be slowly spreading. Ideally, a universal poetics that would encompass all nations, Asian and African included, can be envisioned. Concrete work on a truly universal scale is, however, still very rare outside of folklore. The Chadwicks' three volumes, *The Growth of Literature* (1932–40) and Sir Maurice Bowra's *The Heroic Tradition* (1952) may serve as examples.

Such a universal theory of literature, "poetics," will inevitably appeal to aesthetic criteria. Criticism cannot be satisfied with even the most benign nationalisms, local moralisms, religious commitments or specific political ideals. But the isolation of the aesthetic factor presents a difficult philosophical problem. The Gordian knot was cut (though hardly untied) by Benedetto Croce when he appealed to intuition, to an almost instinctive recognition of what is poetry and what is not. In practice, his criticism is often a sensitive anthologizing, an apodictic selection of poetic moments, buttressed by a clearly formulated classification of the kinds of poetry ejected from the inner sanctum: oratorical, didactic, philosophical but also sentimental, confessional, poetry exploiting raw emotion. Croce displays in practice a specific taste that could be called a moderate classicism (he speaks of *classicità*), distrustful of the Baroque (considered a form of ugliness), the decadent, and the experimentally modern. Moral and even political criteria easily fuse with his definitions of the leading sentiment of an author.

Most other critics in this century have developed criteria based on preference for specific historical types and styles of literature. Thus we can speak of a new classicism in this century: in France it was usually combined with political conservativism, with an appeal to order and thus was violently anti-romantic, as in France Romanticism is identified with the revolution and with Rousseau. Even André Gide spoke of his classicism, which he interprets as a principle of modesty and understatement,[24] and Paul Valéry, whatever his practice as a poet, lauds classicism as discipline, purity, restraint, submission to even completely arbitrary conventions. Thus, he says, "the demands of a strict prosody are the artifice that confers on natural language the qualities of a resistant matter."[25] The "dance in fetters" allows the poet to achieve the ideal artwork, unified, nontemporal, imperishable, beyond the decay of nature and man, absolute. In England—partly under the influence of the French but also drawing on native sources such as Matthew Arnold and the neo-humanists—T. E. Hulme and T. S. Eliot proclaimed a new classicism. In Hulme it is combined with a contradictory enthusiasm for Bergson and flux while classicism was to him also admiration for abstract, unorganic art: for cubism and Epstein. Eliot's classicism is mainly ideological. He defines it "as a tendency toward a higher and clearer conception of Reason, and a more severe and serene control of the emotions by Reason"[26] and in support appeals to a heterogeneous list of names: Sorel, Maurras, Benda, Hulme, Maritain, and Babbitt. Not a single poet is included. In practice Eliot hardly ever discusses any classical or neo-classical author with the exception of Virgil whom he interprets as a forerunner of Christianity, as an *anima naturaliter Christiana*.[27] In English literature Eliot cares mainly for Dryden in preference to Pope and declares expressly: "My opinion is, that we have no classic age, and no classic poet in English."[28] Eliot's classicism seems almost more a matter of cultural politics than of aesthetic preferences as his taste rather prefers Dante, the metaphysicals and the symbolists.

German academic criticism has been largely romantic in taste. Emil Staiger's *Grundbegriffe der Poetik* (1946) assumes as a matter of course that the German romantic mood lyric and the confessional poetry of Goethe provide the standard of true poetry. In asides he admits that "The Italian when he speaks of the lyric thinks of Petrarch" and that Horace could not be fitted into his categories.[29] Max Kommerell, a critic who grew up in the George circle, was one of the few Germans who raised doubts about these dogmas. He recognised that long ages of poetry and criticism got along without invention, spontaneity, lived experience, and the other shibboleths of romantic criticism. He came to appreciate highly stylized, conventionalized art and devoted his last efforts to a study and translation of Calderón.

In England and America, under the impact of Pound's and Eliot's disparagement of Victorian and romantic poetry, romantic taste declined. F. R. Leavis and the American New Critics shared and developed Eliot's anti-romantic views more systematically and often more violently. Particularly Shelley suffered an eclipse compared to his exalted position in the Victorian age, with Swinburne and many others. But in recent years a new reaction has set in which has reinstated the English romantic poets by emphasizing their "visionary" power, their striving for a reconciliation between man and nature, subject and object. The writings of Northrop Frye on Blake, the books of Meyer Abrams, Harold Bloom, and Geoffrey Hartman have done most for this rehabilitation, which seems, however, confined to American academic circles.

A taste for realism and particularly for the realistic novel of the nineteenth century informs other critics widely scattered over many countries. Lukács is the main exponent of this taste, based as it is on his firm commitment to a concept of literature as a reflection of social reality and a conviction that modern art, in rejecting realism, reflects only the decadence of the West. Realism in Lukács is sharply contrasted with naturalism, which is concerned with the surface of everyday life and with the average while realism creates types which are both representative and prophetic. Officially in Russia "socialist realism" is touted as "the fulfillment of all art and literature."[30] It requires adherence to a political ideology but also prescribes the use of the specific methods of realism and forbids the use of others though some Marxist schoolmen have interpreted socialist realism so broadly that it allows them to include Mayakovsky, Aragon, and Brecht among its practitioners. Harry Levin, in *The Gates of Horn: A Study of Five French Realists* (1963) has, in agreement with historical usage, discussed the realistic novel as a critical commentary on the greatness and decline of the bourgeoisie while Erich Auerbach in his *Mimesis: The Representation of Reality in Western Literature* (1946) has widened the concept to include Homer and the Bible at least in certain scenes. But also for him the culmination point of realism is the nineteenth century in France. Stendhal and Balzac are properly realistic, that is, both historistic and social. Though Auerbach thinks of himself as a historian and philologist closely involved with his texts and is averse to theory and criticism, he actually has a definite standard of realism. It must not be comic, it must not be didactic or ethical or rhetorical or idyllic. The Russians are excluded as didactic, the Germans (or rather Austrians and Swiss) of the later nineteenth century such as Adalbert Stifter and Gottfried Keller, as idyllic. Realism must not even be only tragic. It must be tragic with a peculiar concreteness and historical particularity. It could be called existential realism, which combines two elements: tragic depth and historical concreteness.[31]

To many critics classicist, romantic and even realistic tastes will, in this century, appear old-fashioned. Much criticism has been deliberately in the service of the new movements of the twentieth century. In the English-speaking world the abrupt, unargued pronouncements of Ezra Pound and the often epigrammatic essays of T. S. Eliot have most resolutely broken with the immediate past and created a new taste for the metaphysicals, the French symbolists and, slowly, for their own poetry. Pound also propagated those then little-known regions of world literature which he found compatible with his imagism: Propertius, Anglo-Saxon poems, the Troubadours, the *dolce stil nuovo*, Elizabethan translations, and Chinese poems. The role of the surrealists in France (in particular, of André Breton) and their manifestoes, of the expressionists in Germany, the futurists in Italy, and the very different futurists in Russia needs only to be alluded to. We may think also of Robbe-Grillet who rejects the realistic and the psychological novel as dead ends. All these movements often brusquely repudiate the past and exalt their particular brand of writing to the center of the literary stage. Sometimes, however, they looked for a pedigree in the past. The French surrealists found forerunners in Nerval, Lautréamont, and Rimbaud; the German expressionists in the *Sturm und Drang* and in Georg Büchner; the Russian Futurists in anyone who could play the game of language, from Edgar Allan Poe to Mallarmé and Khlebnikov.

Today we are confronted not only with critics who reject the past in order to create and justify the future or rather their own brand of poetry, but we have to face a new nihilism, picking up motifs from Marinetti's futurism and Dada. Vociferously the death of literature is being declared as imminent both here and in France. Logically silence is now being recommended as an ultimate solution of all critical problems: by George Steiner as when he asks, "Is the poet's verse not an insult to the naked cry?"[32] and by Ihab Hassan when he denounces, with a quotation from D. H. Lawrence, the green dragon, the evil-smelling *Logos* and rhapsodizes on Pop and Op art, John Cage's music of silence, Rauschenberg's empty canvases, in order to advocate a new critical language that would somehow expand man's consciousness of the ineffable and the inexpressible.[33] It is all very modish, vague and elusive, almost "psychedelic"; and finally almost comically paradoxical as all these apocalyptic prophets of the death of literature and eulogists of silence continue writing and publishing.

What cannot be dismissed in all of these extravagances is the general revolt against aesthetics which makes anything like agreement on criteria or even on the nature of art impossible. The very existence of the aesthetic response or experience has been denied in recent decades. The theory of empathy that reduced aesthetic feeling to the physical action of inner mimicry; John Dewey's *Art as Experience* (1934) and I. A. Richards's writings on literary criticism are just a few examples of this trend. I. A. Richards argues, for instance, that "when we look at a picture, or read a poem, or listen to music, we are not doing something quite unlike what we are doing on our way to the Gallery or when we dressed in the morning." But his abolition of the difference between art and life, between kinds of behavior— looking at pictures, listening to music, reading a poem and walking to the Gallery or dressing in the morning or, to continue in this vein, eating breakfast, doing sums, and so on—cannot surely satisfy anybody who has had the experience of art and who wants to clarify its nature. Even Richards has to invent a quantitative difference between art and life, to ascribe it to a "greater number of impulses which have to be brought into coordination with one another" in order to achieve "the resolution, inter-animation and balancing of impulses"[34] he considers the proper effect of art. He lands in extreme psychologism. The whole state of mind, "the mental condition *is* the poem,"[35] he tells us. In theory at least, the way is open to individual caprice, to complete arbitrariness.

But the existence or rather experience of the aesthetic state seems to me undeniable. Its negation seems to me like ignoring the existence of the color red or denying that snow is white. It is immediately evident and it can be and has been described phenomenologically as "the constitution of a structured self-sufficient, qualitative whole."[36] In this description is already implied a universal criterion: "unity" or "organicity" which must not, however, be interpreted narrowly as merely an endorsement of classicist standards. It is not merely coherence, harmony, the congruence of form and content or "style," even in the sense of Goethe, as above objective imitation and subjective manner. It must be seen as a unity that allows a supercession and organization of opposites. We may remember the *discordia concors* that Dr. Johnson sees in John Donne, the union of opposites of Coleridge and his sources, and more recently the views of the New Critics exalting the tensions and paradoxes within a work of art, or even Adorno's view that "the idea of harmony is expressed negatively by embodying contradictions, pure and uncompromised, in its innermost structure."[37]

Still, one could object that a criterion that merely identifies a minimal requirement for what is art is insufficient as a standard of value. We may even wonder whether a higher organization, a tighter cohesion, necessarily constitutes greater artistic value. I believe, however, this is so in almost all cases. The multiple relations we discover in a great work of art, the implications and complexities *are* a measure of value. Criticism, particularly of the last fifty years, has done much in uncovering such relationships even in apparently simple works.

But one should grant that there may be other universal criteria though it seems difficult to arrive at any one on which there is universal agreement. The frequently invoked criterion of sincerity, or its modern version, authenticity, genuineness, remains romantic in implication and derivation: it excludes much stylized, conventionalized art. "Intensity," "local quality," the poetic moment do not get much further. The standard of truth to reality—even if understood widely—seems to exclude most fantastic, symbolic, allegorical, and Utopian art, as well as the purely decorative and playful. However difficult it has proved to isolate the quality of art, the specific "literariness" in literature, we cannot and must not dispense with the problem of artistic value. All relativism breaks down when we are confronted with the difference between very great poetry and pretentious trash, kitsch. We should admit that the appeal to universal criteria, while justifiable and necessary in theory, is in practice constantly obviated by the critic's individual procedures of discovering value and of formulating evaluation. It is an encounter that often need not even lead to an expressly formulated conclusion. Still, it is a discovery of values, a value response that will be necessarily specific and must vary from work to work. Very little has been done to study the actual process by which great critics have arrived at their valuations of specific works of art. A study could be made of critics and criticisms which might throw light on this process in concrete instances while I have been here content to move on the level of general criteria: aesthetic and extra-aesthetic. The relativistic argument that we enjoy the art of all ages and peoples can be turned against the defenders of critical anarchy. The fact that we can admire neolithic cave paintings, Chinese landscapes, Negro masks, Gregorian chant, and Béla Bartók, Homer, and James Joyce, merely demonstrates that there is a common feature in all art which we recognize today more clearly than in earlier ages, more encumbered by the burden of the past, more restricted by inherited prejudices and limiting tastes. A proper historical sense should not lead to relativism at all: it rather should enable us to perceive the fullness and variety of the world of art. There is a common humanity that makes all art, however remote in time and place, accessible to us. We can rise beyond the limitations of traditional tastes into a realm, if not of absolute, then of universal art, varied in its manifestations but still amenable to description, analysis, interpretation, and finally, inevitably, to evaluation.

The Fall of Literary History

SOME thirty years ago I wrote a book, *The Rise of English Literary History*.[1] Today one could write a book on its decline and fall. Hans Robert Jauss begins his paper *Literary History as a Provocation of Literary Scholarship* by saying that "Literary history has in our time not undeservedly fallen into disrepute. The history of this venerable discipline shows, during the last hundred and fifty years, unmistakably a course of steady decline."[2] George Watson, in *The Study of Literature*, speaks of "the sharp descent of literary history from the status of a great intellectual discipline to that of a convenient act of popularization."[3] Christopher Ricks, in a review of Watson's book even doubts that "literary history is a worthwhile activity" and that it ever was "a great intellectual discipline."[4] Ricks cannot think of any literary historians who would represent the "tradition of confident historiography of literature," except perhaps Saintsbury and Oliver Elton. It never occurs to him that literary history might have been written elsewhere than in England. There *is* a great tradition of narrative literary history, in Germany beginning with the Schlegels, in France with Villemain and Ampère, in Italy with De Sanctis, in Denmark with Brandes, in Spain with Menéndez y Pelayo, in Russia with Veselovsky. Among nineteenth-century Americans, George Ticknor and Moses Coit Tyler wrote important narrative literary histories whatever their shortcomings. Ricks ignores also the fact that literary history need not necessarily cover the whole of a literature or a very long span of time as Elton's six volumes do. It might be a history of a genre, such as comedy, epic, or ode; it might be the history of a technical device, such as prose-rhythm or the sonnet; it might be the history of a theme or themes, such as classical mythology in English poetry; or it might be the history of a mode, such as allegory, humor, or the grotesque. I cannot see why the history of ideas in literature should be excluded from literary history. Examples could be found in plenty.

Still, whatever we may advance against Mr. Ricks's dismissal of literary history or however much we may deplore that Louis Kampf, 1971 President of the Modern Language Association of America, could issue a premature death certificate of all "academic literary study,"[5] we can hardly help agreeing that something has happened to literary historiography which can be described as decline and even as fall. Particularly in the interval between the two world wars widespread dissatisfaction with literary history was voiced in almost every country. It was directed against several related features of established literary historiography which should nevertheless be kept separate. One was the general dissatisfaction with what could be called the atomistic factualism of much literary scholarship and the resultant inconsequential antiquarianism, still with us; the second target was the uncritical scientism that pretends to establish causal relationships and provide causal explanation by a listing of parallels between works of literature or by correlations between events in the life of a poet with the themes or figures of his works. Thirdly it was widely felt that literary history suffered from a lack of focus, that it surrendered its central concern to general history, a trend which, in the United States, was endorsed in Edwin Greenlaw's *Province of Literary History.*[6] I like to quote Roman Jakobson who, in 1921, compared the literary historian to "police who are supposed to arrest a certain person, arrest everybody and carry off everything they find in the house and all the people who pass by chance in the street. Thus the historians of literature appropriate everything—the social setting, psychology, politics, philosophy. Instead of literary scholarship we got a conglomeration of derivative disciplines."[7] Literary history was (and often still is) the *Allerleiwissenschaft* taught by Professor Diogenes Teufelsdröckh. The national limitations and nationalistic commitments of much literary history, particularly in Germany and France, excited some dissatisfaction that found expression in the newly constituted discipline of comparative literature. One particular strand of nineteenth century literary history—the attempt to emulate the evolutionism of Herbert Spencer and Darwin—fell, however, almost silently into oblivion.

I shall not try to rehearse this debate. One of my earliest articles in Czech was a demolition of the evolutionary theory behind Legouis-Cazamian's *Histoire de la littérature anglaise*.[8] In severe reviews of Herbert Grierson's *Critical History of English Poetry*[9] and of the collective histories of English and American literatures edited by Albert C. Baugh and Robert E. Spiller,[10] I criticized the mixture of biography, bibliography, anthology, information on themes and metrical forms, sources, attempts at characterization and evaluation sandwiched into background chapters on political, social, and intellectual history which is called "literary history." Many others, independently, have voiced similar misgivings. Harry Levin, for instance, has well exposed the failure of *The Oxford History of English Literature*.[11]

The dissatisfaction and the reasons for dissatisfaction are thus obvious enough: We must rather ask what can be done to reform literary history and what proposals have been made to do so. I suggest that they can be discussed under three headings. Some advocate the abolition of literary history; some propound its absorption or subordination to some related discipline, mainly general history or sociology; and finally some try to define a specific method of writing literary history.

The main argument for the abandonment of literary history comes from those who deny the pastness of literature. As early as 1883 W. P. Ker, later an eminent literary historian, stated that a work of literature is not a link in a chain and is above the world of movement.[12] In a late lecture[13] he elaborated the contrast between literary history dealing with an everpresent matter that it can point to, as a guide in a gallery points to the pictures, and political history that has to reconstruct a vanished past. In a fragment, published as late as 1955, Ker asserts that "literary history is like a museum; and a museum may be of use even if ill arranged: the separate specimens may be studied by themselves."[14] Mr. Ricks echoes Ker when he points to the radical difference between literary study and military, social and political history, "not least in this that you cannot have an edition of the battle of Waterloo or of George III's madness."[15] Most insistently Benedetto Croce, in a paper written in 1917[16] and since in many contexts, argued that works of art are unique, individual, immediately present and that there is no essential continuity between them. There is none, for instance, except an external technical sequence between Dante, Boccaccio, and Petrarch. In a letter in which he summarized a conversation I had with him in the year of his death (1952), Croce says expressly that "one can write only little monographs and critical essays and if one asks that these essays be put into some order, the answer is that everyone can put them into any order he pleases."[17] Croce's assumption sounds almost neo-Platonic: "A work of art is always *internal*; and what is called *external* is no longer a work of art."[18]

Without Croce's idealistic presuppositions the American New Criticism has said substantially the same. Allen Tate, for instance, told us that "the historical method will not permit us to develop a critical instrument for dealing with works of literature as existent objects" and that "the literature of the past can be kept alive only by seeing it as the literature of the present. Or perhaps we ought to say that the literature of the past lives in the literature of the present and nowhere else; that it is all present literature."[19] In England, F. R. Leavis said it with his customary violence: "Literary history . . . is a worthless acquisition; worthless for the student who cannot as a critic—that is, as an intelligent and discerning reader—make a personal approach to the essential data of the literary historian, the works of literature."[20] In German scholarship the same reaction against literary history brought about the dominance of "interpretation," most strikingly expounded and exemplified by Emil Staiger. The introduction to *Die Zeit als Einbildungskraft des Dichters* (1939) formulates the rejection of literary history most clearly. One cannot explain a work of art. One can only exhibit its traits. A "phenomenology" of literature is the only fruitful method of literary study.[21] I need only allude to the more recent vogue of "phenomenology" in France. The possibly oversharp distinction between extrinsic and intrinsic methods that organizes the order of the chapters in my and Austin Warren's *Theory of Literature* may have contributed to the singling out of the work of art as an isolated object outside history even though the last chapter of our book is expressly devoted to a program of literary history.

Even more widespread and successful have been the attempts to absorb literary history into general history, particularly the attempts to reduce it to a mirror of social change. I need only allude to the oldest systematic scheme of this kind: Hippolyte Taine's triad of *milieu-race-moment*, which is, however, misunderstood if interpreted as a version of positivistic determinism. I have tried to show that Taine was rather something of a Hegelian.[22] Harry Levin, particularly in his *Gates of Horn*, fruitfully developed the idea of literature as an institution.[23] Renato Poggioli has proposed an application of Pareto's sociology to literary historiography, using terms such as "residue" and "derivation" for a new periodization of literature.[24] Poggioli's *Theory of the Avant-garde* analyzes a master-current sociologically. He believes in the imperative of the period. The artist dwindles to the dimension of a victim of social forces.[25]

Obviously, Marxism has been by far the most influential in interpreting literary history as a reflection of social and economic forces. Literature becomes "ideology," overt or implied statement about class situation and consciousness. To give an example with which I am intimately acquainted: the *History of Czech Literature*, published by the Czechoslovak Academy of Sciences, reduces Czech literature to a commentary on the social and national struggles of the Czechs, minimizing religion and neglecting the art of poetry almost completely.[26]

Outside bureaucratic Marxist history-writing more sophisticated versions were produced. Georg Lukács knows of the "specificity" of literature, of the oblique and often distant relation between literature and the "substructure" but he also reduces literature to a species of knowledge, to a "reflection of reality," a term repeated with obsessive frequency in the first volume of the *Aesthetik*. It occurs there no fewer than 1,032 times. Literary history is seen as a "moment" of general history, as an illustration of the struggle between progress and reaction.[27] The lyric and poetry in general are slighted as they do not yield the characters, types, and plots Lukács examines in novels and dramas. It would be easy to demonstrate the insensitive distortions to which he subjects Hölderlin, Eichendorff, Dostoevsky, Nietzsche, Rilke, and others in the interest of his ideology. "Content" in the brute sense of involvement in the progress toward communism is the main criterion even though Lukács, as a theorist, has insight into form and its function.

Lucien Goldmann is a follower of the early Lukács: he told me once that Lukács complained to him that Goldmann wanted him to have dropped dead at the age of thirty. Goldmann, in *Le Dieu caché* (1956), construes analogues between the economic conditions of the *noblesse de robe*, the theology of Jansenism and the tragic world view of Pascal and Racine, making Pascal sound like Kant and *vice versa*. Goldmann tells us at least bluntly that literary history is a "really non-existent subject," though in an earlier paper he admits that "sociological analysis hardly touches a work of art."[28]

All these attempts—and many more could be cited—to absorb literary history into social history raise such problems as the integration of human history and the interrelationship between the activities of man, the role of the individual in history and the nature of explanation of one activity by another. One has the impression that at least in the West the grand "philosophies of history" in the style of Hegel, Marx, Spengler, and Toynbee are discredited in sober scholarly thinking. I do not share Karl Popper's extreme view of *The Poverty of Historicism* but rather sympathize with Jacob Burckhardt's tolerant reference to "the centaur on the forest edge" of historical studies.[29] Also the more cautious schemes of social evolution with their pervasive metaphors of growth and decay have been subjected to much trenchant criticism: recently in Robert A. Nisbet's *Social Change and History* (1969). Others have shown that the different activities of man do not cohere as closely as general historians assume and that one may doubt the unbroken continuity of linear developments. Siegfried Kracauer in his posthumous *History: The Last Things before the Last* (1969) has argued in favor of special histories and their comparative independence from general history. Hans Blumenberg, in *Die Legitimität der Neuzeit* (1966) has tried to show that many assumptions about continuity in intellectual history are mistaken, that we can rather speak of breaks in the tradition and even of a spontaneous generation of ideas. The whole concept of the *Zeitgeist* which was basic to German *Geistesgeschichte* has been called in doubt. Certainly the very close parallelism of the arts presents great difficulties: the difference between the arts as to their relation to antiquity should make us pause. Much of the parallelism among the arts is only metaphorical analogizing. In Mario Praz's recent *Mnemosyne: The Parallel between Literature and the Visual Arts* (1970), for instance, the *Divine Comedy* is contrasted with the *Canterbury Tales*: the

Tales testifying to the decay of the Middle Ages merely because they are unfinished.[30] One can take refuge in the idea of different time-schemes as Henri Focillon and his pupil George Kubler have done. In *The Shape of Time: Remarks on the History of Things*, Kubler conceives of historical time as intermittent and variable, in difference from the continuous time of a human being or animal.[31]

It would be foolish to deny the implication of literary history in general history: any reflective person even centuries ago must have noted the changes in literature that came with the fall of the Roman Empire, the advent of Christianity or the Renaissance of the fifteenth and sixteenth centuries. Literary historians long before Marx or Taine noticed the differences, in medieval literature, between works written for a courtly audience, by clerics for the clergy or the laity, or by burghers for their fellow artisans. But what the attempts at social explanation fail to achieve is the causal explanation of a specific work of literature, its individuality, its pattern and value.

I have read in the amazingly large literature stimulated primarily by Carl G. Hempel's paper *The Function of General Laws in History* (1942).[32] Hempel, a neo-positivist close to the Vienna Circle, argues that historical statements appeal implicitly to general laws he calls "covering laws." Historians are by implication considered scientists even though they cannot verify these laws, cannot predict the future, are sometimes unaware of the laws, and are often content with what Hempel calls mere "explanation sketches." A whole series of analytical philosophers—Arthur C. Danto, William Dray, W. B. Gallie, Patrick Gardiner, W. H. Walsh, and Morton White, to mention only a few[33]—have either elaborated on Hempel's thesis or modified it or rejected it in favor of a concept of historical explanation that actually ceases to be causal. Some historians—often labeled "idealists"—reject all causal explanation and defend narration as the only proper historical method. R. G. Collingwood can say, "When the historian knows what happened, he already knows why it happened."[34] Michael Oakeshott speaks of "the continuous series model of explanation,"[35] suggesting that a historical event is explained if we narrate it with no lacuna as we might account for a collision between two cars by describing the exact course of their movements. Most of this enormous, often hair-splitting and logic-chopping discussion is concerned with questions of responsibility, ethical culpability, normal and abnormal human behavior, accidents such as sudden deaths in history and is completely oblivious of the very different problems of literary or art history. Questions such as "Why did Brutus stab Caesar?" or "Why did Louis XIV die unpopular?" are characteristic problem cases. Only Morton White discusses intellectual history.

Some of the distinctions between types of causal explanation made in this debate, however, are applicable to literary history. We can, for instance, speak of accidents such as the deaths of Shelley and Byron or we might think of the (possibly apocryphal) "person on business from Porlock" who interrupted Coleridge while writing down *Kubla Khan*.[36] We might try to distinguish between "standing conditions" and outside influences such as the effect of the French revolution or the sudden influx of German ideas and themes toward the end of the eighteenth century. We might speak of "proximate causes" for this influx in singling out Coleridge's trip to Germany in 1798 made possible only by the Wedgwood annuity. But all this concerns biography or large-scale historical trends that might be described as "conditions" but we never succeed in naming the cause or even a cause of a single work of art. Morton White gives examples of causal explanations for certain views of John Dewey[37] but does not produce more than psychological motivation: Dewey, for instance, wanted to defend ethical naturalism because he was a political liberal. It is difficult, however, to see in what sense his liberalism "caused" his naturalism: there were plenty of liberals not given to ethical naturalism. We can only guess at the workings of Dewey's mind, his reasons and arguments; we do not establish causes. Louis Kampf in criticizing my paper "German and English Romanticism: A Confrontation,"[38] complains of my neglect of "causal explanation" and comes up with the old idea (also discussed in my paper) of the "German artist's almost total separation from his society" but Kampf cannot suggest how this situation explains more than, at most, the preference for the lyric or the grotesque and fantastic, art-forms well represented in other presumably less alienated societies. Alienation cannot account for a single work of art: not even for *Heinrich von*

Ofterdingen or *Kater Murr* nor for their differences. Actually, some of the most fantastic and subjective German writers were, in their private lives, successful landowners or government officials such as Achim von Arnim or Joseph von Eichendorff. Novalis was a mining official; E. T. A. Hoffmann, a judge. Cause, in the sense as defined by Morris R. Cohen—"some reason or ground why, whenever the antecedent event occurs, the consequent must follow"[39]—is, we must conclude, inapplicable to literary history. A work of art need not to have caused another one. One can only argue that any work of art would be different if another work of art had not preceded it. Obviously if there had not been an *Iliad* or an *Odyssey* or an *Aeneid* or a *Divine Comedy*, subsequent literature would be different. We can speculate rather futilely on these eventualities but can never argue even that works of art as closely related as the pre-Shakespearean *King Leir* and Shakespeare's *King Lear* or *Hamlet* and the German *Bestrafter Brudermord* are connected causally: we can only say that Shakespeare knew the earlier play and can describe the use he made of it and we can show that the German play is ultimately derived from *Hamlet*. One work is the necessary condition of another one but one cannot say it has caused it.

The so-called laws of literary history boil down to some vague psychological generalities: action and reaction, convention and revolt, the "form-fatigue" formulated by a German architect Adolf Göller in the 1880's.[40]

Cause may, it should be granted, be used loosely and widely. R. S. Crane in a paper "Principles of Literary History," which was published in the year of his death (1967) and has, I believe, received no attention, uses cause in the fourfold meaning derived from Aristotle. He constantly speaks of causes in Aristotle's fourth sense of "purpose" or "aim." He considers the "causes in the work which condition its effect on readers" when we would more clearly speak of traits, characters, or qualities of a work or he speaks of "causes in the author which condition his acts of composition," which seem nothing other than his motives or intentions.[41] We must concede the final inexplicability of a great work of art, the exception of genius. Long ago Emile Faguet objected to Taine's method that it may account for a burgher from Rouen in the 1630s, and even for Thomas Corneille, but not for the genius of his brother Pierre Corneille.[42] The art historians who more commonly deal with collective styles and anonymous works than literary historians have often come to the same conclusion. Thus Henri Focillon who studied *The Life of Forms in Art* reflects, in the context of the rise of the Gothic style in architecture, that "the most attentive study of the most homogenous *milieu*, of the most closely woven concantenation of circumstances, will not serve to give us the design of the towers of the cathedral of Laon. . . . It emerges with a highly efficient abruptness."[43] Like Focillon we might argue that even if we knew the life of Shakespeare in the greatest detail, knew the social and theatrical history of the time better than we know it now, and studied all the sources, we still could not predict the peculiar shape and physiognomy of a play like *Hamlet* or *King Lear* if we did not know the text or imagine it would have been lost. Causal explanation as deterministic scientific explanation by deduction from a general law or demonstration of a necessary efficient cause fails if applied to literature.

The absorption of literary history into general history, the determinism of social explanation, has been opposed not only by the proponents of criticism but by theorists who proposed the idea of an internal evolutionary history of literature. Its earlier version, dependent heavily on Darwinian evolutionism, has been generally abandoned. The Russian formalists, however, worked out a restatement that avoids the analogies with biology and adopts rather Hegelian (and Marxist) dialectics as the model. The parallel to similar attempts in art history, particularly Wölfflin's *History without Names*, must have been also in their mind. But they developed it in a literary context as they could appeal to the example of Alexander Veselovsky who tried to write collective developmental literary history largely drawing on folk material and as they, with their sympathies for Russian Futurism, could think in terms of poetic revolutions and completely new starts. They interpreted literary history largely as a wearing out or "automatization" of conventions followed by an "actualization" of new conventions using radically new devices. Novelty is the only criterion of change. "A work of art will appear as positive value when it regroups the structure of the preceding period. It will appear as a negative value if it takes over the structure without changing it,"[44] says Jan Mukařovský, the main theorist of the Prague Linguistic Circle who adopted the concepts of the Russians. In a paper criticizing Mukařovský's history of Czech versification based on this idea of internal evolution, dating back to 1934 and substantially repeated in "The Theory of Literary History" (1936),[45] I made an attempt to reconcile this concept of evolution with a theory of criticism. Mukařovský (and the Russians), I argued, are unable to answer the basic question about the direction of change; it is not true that evolution proceeds always in opposite direction. The single criterion of novelty would make us value initiators more highly than the great masters, to prefer Marlowe to Shakespeare, Klopstock to Goethe. We are expected to forget that novelty need not be valuable, that there may be after all, original rubbish. The very material of literary history, I argued, must be chosen in relation to values, and structures involve values. History cannot be divorced from criticism. Criticism means constant reference to a scheme of values that is necessarily that of the historian. The mere selection of texts out of hundreds and thousands surviving is an act of judgment and the selection of the particular traits, details, or qualities that I choose to discuss is another act of judgment that is inevitably performed with the conceptual tools the historian is able to apply. This is not advocacy of anarchical subjectivism. We still must require submission to the texts, respect for their integrity, "objectivity" in the sense of a desire to overcome personal prejudices and to criticize one's own standpoint. Nor can the recognition of the inevitability of a personal or temporal point of view—what Lovejoy has called the "presenticentric predicament"—mean simply surrender to skepticism, sheer relativism, as we would then have to doubt the possibility of all knowledge. I cannot adequately discuss this problem here: it has worried me and many historians.

Still, whatever its difficulties, I cannot see why one reviewer of my *History of Modern Criticism*, Bernard Weinberg,[46] denied me even the title of a historian because I believe that the history of criticism should "illuminate and interpret our present situation" and because I single out theories by Lessing and Friedrich Schlegel with approval. The unargued assumption seems to be, in the words of his mentor, Ronald S. Crane, that a "history without prior commitments as to what criticism is or ought to be ... history without a thesis"[47] is the only legitimate way of writing history. I am surprised to hear that my attention to anticipations of modern theories or my references to contemporary poetic theory "invalidates my *History* as history." Judged by such a criterion Bosanquet's *History of Aesthetic*, Croce's history of aesthetics in *Estetica*, Saintsbury's *History of Criticism* and, on analogous grounds, almost all literary, philosophical, and political historiography would be "invalidated." I prefer to side with Croce, Meinecke, Troeltsch, Huizinga, Collingwood, Carr, and many others who have argued that "historical thinking is always teleological,"[48] that "history properly so called can be written only by those who find and accept a sense of direction in history itself."[49]

I am not alone with the emphasis on criticism as value judgment: long ago Norman Foerster cogently formulated the view that "the literary historian must be a critic in order to be a historian."[50] Though sketchily, English literary history has been rewritten with new value judgments in the essays of T. S. Eliot, in F. R. Leavis's *Revaluation*, in Cleanth Brooks's "Notes for a Revised History of English Poetry," and in Yvor Winters's *Forms of Discovery* (1967).[51]

Still, the idea of an internal evolution of literature has fallen on deaf ears. I myself, in a paper, *The Concept of Evolution in Literary History* (1956),[52] modified (and as I see now implicitly rejected) my earlier view. I argued that an artist, as any man, may reach, at any moment, into his remote past or into the remotest past of humanity. It is not true that an artist develops toward a single future goal. What is needed is a modern concept of time, modeled on an interpenetration of the causal order in experience and memory. A work of art is not simply a member of a series, a link in a chain. It may stand in relation to anything in the past. It is not only a structure that may be analyzed descriptively. It is a totality of values that do not adhere to the structure but constitute its very nature. The values can be grasped only in an act of contemplation. These values are created in a free act of the imagination irreducible to limiting conditions in sources, traditions, biographical and social circumstances.

I have read the two numbers of the new periodical *New Liter-*

ary History which contain valuable articles, but no new ideas of
literary history beyond the traditional study of periods, genres,
and influences are suggested. D. W. Robertson, for instance,
restates historicism that asks us to reconstruct the situation of
the writer in the past; Hallett Smith defends his approach to
Elizabethan poetry through genre tradition; Robert Weinmann
rehearses Marxism; W. K. Wimsatt discusses imitation in English
eighteenth-century poetry. Geoffrey Hartman's piece called expressly *Toward Literary History*[53] comments on the idea of the
progress of poetry from ancient Greece and Rome to England
with the apparent aim of emphasizing again the national tradition of poetry. Wimsatt's and Hartman's papers corroborate
W. J. Bate's *Burden of the Past* (1970), which speaks eloquently of
the English poet's sense of the crushing weight of tradition and
the way of overcoming it not merely by escaping or denying it
(as much modern art does) but by reaching into the past: Wordsworth going back to Milton, Keats to Spenser, Milton and, above
all Shakespeare.[54] A history of Renascences is suggested: a sense
of the presence of the whole past, as it was suggested in T. S.
Eliot's "Tradition and the Individual Talent." All these three
items buttress my rejection of linear development, the conception of a free reaching into the past.

One more proposal for immanent literary history has come
recently from Germany: the "Rezeptionsgeschichte" advocated
by H. R. Jauss.[55] This is not merely a demand for a history of
readers' reactions, of criticisms, of translations—first voiced, I
believe, in the now forgotten book, *Critique scientifique* by Emile
Hennequin in 1888—but assumes, with Gadamer and Heidegger, a "fusion of horizons," a necessary interplay of text and
recipient in which the text is assumed to be transformed by the
reader. Jauss argues that the attitude of an author to his public
can be reconstructed not only from addresses to the reader or
external evidence but implicitly: through the assumption, for
instance, in *Don Quijote* of a knowledge and concern for chivalric
romances. Lowry Nelson, in a paper "The Fictive Reader and
Literary Self-Reflexiveness,"[56] has made, independently, concrete suggestions on different types of this relation. Jauss's criterion is still the same as that of the Formalists: "novelty" though
he shifts its meaning from technical, artistic innovation to a

change in consciousness: to a history of the effect (*Wirkungs-geschichte*), the success and influence of works of art. One must welcome emphasis on hitherto unexplored aspects of literary history but in practice "Rezeptionsgeschichte" cannot be anything else than the history of critical interpretations by authors and readers, a history of taste that has always been included in a history of criticism.

The new literary history promises only a return to the old one: the history of tradition, genres, reputations, less atomistically conceived as in older times, with greater awareness of the difficulties of such concepts as influence and periods but still the old one.

Possibly, this is a good and right thing. The attempts at an evolutionary history have failed. I myself have failed in *The History of Modern Criticism* to construe a convincing scheme of development. I discovered, by experience, that there is no evolution in the history of critical argument, that the history of criticism is rather a series of debates on recurrent concepts, on "essentially contested concepts,"[57] on permanent problems in the sense that they are with us even today. Possibly, a similar conclusion is required for the history of poetry itself. "Art," said Schopenhauer, "has always reached its goal."[58] Croce and Ker are right. There is no progress, no development, no history of art except a history of writers, institutions, and techniques. This is, at least for me, the end of an illusion, the fall of literary history.

Science, Pseudoscience, and Intuition in Recent Criticism

WHEN Austin Warren and I published *Theory of Literature* late in 1948, we thought of it as an attempt to formulate the assumptions on which literary study is conducted but also as supplying information on European developments such as stylistics, German *Geistesgeschichte*, Russian formalism, Polish phenomenology, and Czech structuralism, trends at that time almost totally unknown in the English-speaking world. We were appalled at the lack of any discussion of fundamentals in literary theory and by the general lack of awareness even of the need for literary theory. Things certainly have changed in the twenty-five years since the publication of our book. Here on this continent and in Europe there has been an enormous explosion of interest in literary theory. *Theory of Literature* must have met some contemporary demand as it has been translated into twenty languages, but today it is sometimes dismissed as a "conservative" introduction. Still, for instance, our proposals for the reform of graduate study[1] recommended a turn to the study of the theory of criticism as well as to comparative literature at the expense of philological research and the compartmentalization of literature along national lines, which was and still is radical in the American academic context. So was the thesis that literary study should aim at a body of organized knowledge of literature in general, though we were careful not to claim for literary theory the status of an exact science.

When we look at the present situation in Europe (with some echoes and repercussions in America), we see that on the one hand, the ambition of literary theorists to make the study of literature an exact science has increased a hundredfold and that, on the other hand, the ideal of an organized knowledge has been completely abandoned by others in favor of intuition, vision, and even an obscure act of identification. To put it crudely, literary theory has split into two factions: science or would-be science versus intuition; those who want to construe a universal and universally valid scheme or matrix of literature and those who plunge into the mind or consciousness of a poet by procedures that are confessedly purely personal, unrepeatable, not subject to any control by laws of evidence.

One can argue that this split is based on the divergent types of interest motivating these two contradictory procedures. Either we are concerned with universals, with regularities or possibly laws of literature, or we care for the uniqueness or at least the particularity of a work of art and for our experience of it, which is necessarily subjective and even existential. Morton Bloomfield, in a fine paper entitled "Two Cognitive Dimensions of the Humanities,"[2] has traced this conflict back to St. Thomas Aquinas's distinction between two types of knowing: either *per cognitionem* or *per connaturalitatem*. He illustrates this wittily by the contrast between Leporello and Don Giovanni. Leporello lists the thousand and three conquests of his master, while Don Giovanni enjoys the women. If Leporello is meant to represent "science," he is, I am afraid, decidedly the worse off, though Mr. Bloomfield could have reminded us that Don Juan at the end was carried off by the devil.

Let us, in the meantime, grant the justice of both aspirations: the scientific and the intuitive. What has happened to them in recent years? Science, in theory, believes in the demand memorably formulated by René Descartes: "Whatever is doubtful is not part of science. Only that which can be ascertained without any doubt is part of science."[3] With the dazzling success of mathematics and statistics in mind, many have tried to make literary theory and particularly the analysis of style amenable to quantification. They seem to believe that nothing is true that cannot be measured. Some such methods have been proposed to us as far back as 1927 in Edith Rickert's *New Methods for the Study of Literature*, which will strike us today as elementary and even naïve compared to the sophisticated statistical methods developed in recent years. They have sometimes yielded concrete results. I think that Alvar Elegård, for instance, has made it statistically probable that the *Junius Letters*, a series of political pamphlets against George III and his ministers (1769–72), were written by Sir Philip Francis.[4] I am also convinced by Louis

Milic's work on the prose style of Jonathan Swift, in which he construes a "Swift profile" based on the frequency and distribution of seriatim and sentence-initial connectives,[5] by Josephine Miles's statistical studies of favored adjectives and modes of sentence-making over several centuries of English poetry,[6] and by some of the contributions to Lubomir Doležel and Richard W. Bailey's collection *Statistics and Style* (1969).[7] But I begin to wonder when I look at the colored graphs of Wilhelm Fucks in *Nach allen Regeln der Kunst* (1968) and am told (statistically) that the sentences of Immanuel Kant are longer than those of Ernest Hemingway and that Kant's sentences are on the average 94 percent more "compounded" (*geschachtelt*) than those of the other texts examined. What can one say when the metrical "linking" (*Bindung*) of texts ranging from Julius Caesar (at the lowest) to Byron's Elegies (at the highest) is calculated without regard to language, versification, or period, with Byron's Elegies (what could those be?) coming out on top. Look at the international symposium *Mathematik und Dichtung*[8] and discover that an enormous apparatus is brought to bear to establish that students agreed much more readily about the respective merits of some German sonnets when they were told the names of the authors than when they were shown them anonymously. A concordance coefficient is worked out. A Russian, G. Shengeli, is surprised that rhythmical variations in four-line stanzas selected from Russian poets are in no relation to the value of the poems; Pushkin is at the bottom, Severyanin at the top. There is another paper in the same volume by Gustav Herdan which proves with elaborate statistics that in Chaucer's *Canterbury Tales* the Latin vocabulary increases with the length of the tale studied. The author never asks whether this fact could not be explained easily enough by one's knowledge that the "Knight's Tale," the longest of the *Tales*, is a chivalrous romance based on an Italian source, whereas the much briefer "Miller's Tale," for example, is a coarse anecdote in colloquial English. I suggest that in all these cases the results are either nugatory or immediately apparent to simple common sense.[9]

Professor Fucks admits plaintively that "a fundamental difficulty with language consists in the fact that whenever we speak, write, read, or listen, whole swarms of associations and emotions accompany the reading, writing, or listening."[10] He has put his finger on the point at which statistical study fails or rather has to fail. He and many acute and diligent researchers who use vocabulary measures, sentence-level measures, calculate redundancy and entropy do not know that a work of literature is not an assembly or sequence of units, a series of quantities, but a qualitative whole, a value-charged totality. An entire book may be implicated in a single sentence.

Another very active group of theorists has got hold of Chomsky's transformational grammar and has tried to base text grammars upon it. The newest and most systematic work of this kind is Teun A. Van Dijk's *Some Aspects of Text Grammars* (1972), and a new magazine, *Poetics*, is filled with contributions of this orientation. I do not presume to judge transformational grammar, but I can say with confidence that the application to literature comes up with little except a new terminology. Thus we are told by Van Dijk that in a novel "the time of the event described precedes or coincides with the time of the utterance," portentous news that is represented by the notation $t_0 \geq t_1$. Mr. Van Dijk puzzles then over the logical possibility $t_0 < t_1$, that is, "can we possibly narrate future events?" "Empirically this is only possible of course under the dominance of such operators as *Irr*, *Neg Fact*, or *Poss*, and we actually find such narration in all science fiction, with Orwell's *1984* as a clear paradigmatic example, where $t_0 = 1948$ and $t_1 = 1984$. Here we have to deal with the problem to what extent nonreal time can be specified as present, past, or future, because—as irrealis—it seems rather to constitute a fourth, irreducible temporal category. In this case we must reject $t_0 \geq t_1$ as unsatisfactory and add as the only restriction that $t_0 < t_1$ is correct only if the narrative text is *Neg Fact* or *Irr*."[11] The text of *1984* begins: "It was a bright day in April and the clocks were striking thirteen"—or should it have begun: "It will be a bright day in April . . ."? If the "formalization of macrostructures," as Van Dijk calls this operation, achieves no more than such trivialities in Newspeak we might as well forget textual grammar. We must quote again Horace's "parturiunt montes, nascetur ridiculus mus."

But this would be entirely unjust to the group in Paris usually called structuralists, who aim at a total scheme of literature drawing not so much on Chomsky as on the Russian formalists and Saussurian and Jakobsonian linguistics. I think very highly of the work of Tzvetan Todorov, a Bulgarian settled in France who has analyzed narrative structures with great ingenuity.[12] Gérard Genette has gone even beyond him with his recent "Discours du récit," which, I am afraid, bristles with neologisms but does penetrate further into Proust's novelistic technique than any earlier study.[13] We all know the brilliant work of Roland Barthes, who in his little book on Racine combines psychoanalysis, anthropology. Marxism, and a schematic thematology. But even these ingenious men seem to me to be engaged in an impossible enterprise based on mistaken assumptions. I am not convinced that a language is a closed system of internal relations or, at least, that linguists have succeeded in demonstrating this beyond the sound stratum; I am, rather, sure that literature is not and cannot be a system of limited internal combinations. Literature is not a structured synchronic totality but an enormous, historically and locally diversified manifold. Literature, as I have argued before,[14] is not merely language and cannot be exhaustively described by linguistic means. The overlap with pantomime and the film alone shows that much in literature is nonverbal. But the French group not only believes that linguistics includes poetics but seems to assert often that all reality is linguistic, that we are caught in a language trap, in a prison-house from which there is no escape. They seem to deny our perceptual life and not to know about deaf-mutes finding their way around in this world. As language and sign systems are conceived of as entirely autonomous, capable of expressing only relationships, consciousness and personality are declared to be secondary phenomena determined by language. This destruction of the individual and his consciousness and conscience is, in the group associated with the review *Tel Quel*, put in the service of a revolutionary ideology that seems either anarchistic or self-styled Maoist. They proclaim the death of the subject, and hence the death of literature as it was understood before, and reduce language to language games. This view has been picked up in Germany by Helmut Heissenbüttel, who confidently declares that the "subject is only a bundle of speech habits. The self-conscious I turns out to be a fiction and dissolves into a field of relational points."[15] Literature is linguistic hallucination.

Few go so far, but for criticism the dire consequences are obvious. Roland Barthes has redefined the term *écriture* so that the distinction between scholarly prose and poetry is abolished. He has pleaded, against an obtuse attack by a conventional historical scholar, Raymond Picard, for complete liberty of interpretation[16] and has defined the critical proof as lying "not in the ability to *discover* the work under consideration but, on the contrary, to *cover* it as completely as possible with one's own language."[17] Something like a dialectical reversal has occurred. What had started out with the ambition to become a science has ended in sheer arbitrariness, caprice, and self-display. Criticism, at least as it has been conceived since Aristotle, is abandoned.

The same result, a final extinction of criticism, is oddly enough achieved also by the second trend: by hermeneutics, interpretation, the criticism of consciousness. Again the ambition seems to me originally right. Phenomenology, as developed in an acute analysis of the literary work of art by the Polish philosopher Roman Ingarden, allowed a rejection of psychologism, background studies, didacticism in favor of a concentration on the work itself. Heidegger's analysis of the concept of time gave tools to Emil Staiger when, in 1939, he proclaimed the turn to the individual work and rejected all causal explanation in favor of description, interpretation, understanding.[18] In the same year Max Kommerell, in *Geist und Buchstabe der Dichtung*, pleaded for a return to the "simplest, though not the easiest [task of criticism], the unbiased questioning of the object."[19] In German-speaking countries this movement must also be seen as a reaction against the disgraceful episode of nazism, which abused historical methods in its exaltation of *Deutschtum*. In the United States the so-called New Criticism was a similar healthy reaction against the old purely external historical scholarship. "Close reading" was the slogan, rather than literary history. Not "Spenser's Irish Rivers"—the topic of the first paper I had to write as a graduate student of English at Princeton—but the precise meaning of *Lycidas* or the "Ode on a Grecian Urn." In French-speaking countries the so-called Geneva school developed its methods of intense contemplation not only of a work but of an *oeuvre* and of the mind behind it. I can only allude to Marcel Raymond, Albert Béguin, Georges Poulet, and Jean-Pierre Richard and note that they have followers and admirers in the United States: Geoffrey Hartman, J. Hillis Miller come to mind. But in most of these writers, however successful their practice—they are men of sensibility—danger signals appear very early. They have also abandoned any respect for correct interpretation, for any laws of evidence, and have defended and indulged in not only overreading and misreadings but often deliberate distortions as well. Martin Heidegger can be cited for the defense: "A genuine explanation understands a text not better than its author but differently."[20] Heidegger speaks of the "overcoming of science," and this surely happens not only in his arbitrary readings of poems by Hölderlin, Trakl, and Rilke but also when a follower like Staiger introduces the totally fanciful concept of *Schlagfigur*, an obscure internal rhythm, into his interpretation of Goethe's life.[21] Poulet picks up the old metaphor of the interpreter wanting to enter the mind of his author, needing sympathy and empathy to push it to the extreme of identification. This identification is meant quite literally: "The same I must operate in the author and the critic."[22] An actual exchange of selves or *cogitos* is postulated. Taken literally, this theory of interpretation surely assumes a concept of mind that cannot be defended rationally. Identification can never take place except as a metaphor. As a prescription for criticism it is as preposterous as Croce's asserting in 1900, "When I penetrate the innermost sense of a canto of Dante's, I am Dante."[23] Croce later saw the impossibility and even falsity of this claim and concluded—wisely, to my mind —that criticism is rather a translation from the realm of feeling into that of reason and thought. Critics, he said, should be reminded of the warning posted in some German concert halls in his youth: "Das Mitsingen ist verboten."[24] Recent criticism has not heeded this poster. It has become for many an excuse for self-definition, for a display of one's ingenuity and cleverness in battering the object or, in ambition, a pretext for "vision," for the discovery of a supernatural reality. Poulet says candidly: "A critical essay of the twentieth century resembles most a devotional tract of the fifteenth or the seventeenth century."[25] Criticism becomes a substitute religion. It has its sacred texts: in English, the prophetic books of Blake, Wordsworth, Shelley, Yeats, and Wallace Stevens; in French, Nerval, Lautréamont, Baudelaire, Mallarmé, and Proust; in German, Hölderlin, Nietzsche, and Rilke, in parts. Criticism aims not so much at the characterization of a work as at the construction of a perceptual or ideological pattern in the mind of the author, and through it, at the discovery of some dark truth about the universe in accordance with Heidegger's cryptic saying that poetry is "das Sich-ins-Werk-Setzen der Wahrheit des Seienden."[26] Yet this truth is for Heidegger not a public truth but an orphic teaching about gods and the earth. In the Geneva school it is the dream of a magical universe where man ceases to feel at all different from things, or a version of Catholic spirituality. In the works of several Americans it has acquired overtones from Jewish mysticism; Martin Buber is evoked at times. Criticism becomes philosophizing on one's own, happily exempt from any checks from history, natural science, or logic. In an odd way the two trends of recent criticism converge; both have abandoned the old ideals of submission to a text, of correct interpretation, and both have rejected what seems to me to be the central task of criticism—evaluation. The scientists and would-be scientists cannot make any value distinctions: they think that this would violate objectivity. In practice they often have to accept the verdict of the ages, which is after all the accumulated opinions of others in the past. Since they are interested in devices and regularities, they can plead that these can be observed even in trash or in subliterature. The Geneva school is precluded from evaluation by the very theory of identification. In practice, of course, these critics study only authors whom they value; neither they nor anyone else can escape the problem of evaluation.

It is time to revive the reasoned traditional concept of criticism as knowledge aiming at the description, interpretation, characterization, and finally evaluation of works of art that challenge us by what Husserl called "a structure of determination"[27] that is there in the object to see, to feel, to comprehend, and to value. Criticism must not become—as it has often become in recent

years—a pretense for either the display of combinatory ingenuity or the indulgence in personal visions. One should take to
heart a saying of Goethe's: "Knowledge is kept back because
people are busy with what is not worth knowing or with what
cannot be known."[28]

The New Criticism: Pro and Contra

TODAY the New Criticism is considered not only super-seded, obsolete, and dead but somehow mistaken and wrong. Four accusations are made most frequently. First, the New Criticism is an "esoteric aestheticism," a revival of art for art's sake, uninterested in the human meaning, the social function, and effect of literature. The New Critics are called "formalists," an opprobrious term used first by Marxists against a group of Russian scholars in the twenties. Second, the New Criticism, we are told, is unhistorical. It isolates the work of art from its past and its context. Third, the New Criticism is supposed to aim at making criticism scientific, or at least "bring-ing literary study to a condition rivaling that of science."[1] Finally the New Criticism is being dismissed as a mere pedagogical device, a version of the French *explication de texte*, useful at most for American college students who must learn to read and to read poetry in particular.

I want to show that all these accusations are baseless. They can be so convincingly refuted by an appeal to the texts that I wonder whether current commentators have ever actually read the writings of the New Critics. Inevitably one must ask what the reasons are for this ignorance and these distortions, and one will have to come up with answers that allow a statement of the limitations and shortcomings of the New Criticism. Still, I think that much of what the New Criticism taught is valid and will be valid as long as people think about the nature and function of literature and poetry.

Before we enter into the merits of the case we must come to an agreement as to whom we should consider New Critics. The term itself is old. The Schlegel brothers, early in the nineteenth century, called themselves "neue Kritiker," and Benedetto Croce, when he did not want to use the pronoun "I," referred to his own views as "la nuova critica." Joel E. Spingarn, the historian of Renaissance criticism, took the term from Croce when he expounded Croce's theories in a little book, *The New Criticism*, in 1911. E. E. Burgum edited an anthology with this title in 1930, and finally John Crowe Ransom, the founder of the *Kenyon Review*, wrote a book, *The New Criticism*, in 1941 which seems to have established the term in common usage, even though the book was far from being a celebration of the New Criticism. Ransom discusses there not contemporary American criticism in general but only three critics: I. A. Richards, whom he criticizes sharply; T. S. Eliot, against whose views on tradition he makes many objections; and Yvor Winters, whom he rejects in the strongest terms. It earned him a virulent reply in Winters's *Anatomy of Nonsense*.

In 1941, when Ransom's book was published, the views and methods of the New Criticism were long established. One can best observe their gradual emergence by thinking of them as reaction against the then prevalent trends in American criticism. Without too much simplification we can distinguish four main trends in American criticism before the advent of the New Critics. There was, first, a type of aesthetic impressionistic criticism, "appreciation," ultimately derived from Pater and Remy de Gourmont, prevalent in the first decade of this century. James G. Huneker may stand here as the representative figure. Then there was, second, the Humanist movement, of which Irving Babbitt and Paul Elmer More were the acknowledged leaders. In 1930 there was a great public commotion around them, but this date is misleading. The main writings of both Babbitt and More appeared in the first decade of the century: the first seven volumes of More's *Shelburne Essays* between 1904 and 1910, Babbitt's *Literature and the American College* in 1908, *Masters of Modern French Criticism* in 1912. Then there was, third, the group of critics who attacked the "genteel" tradition, the American business civilization, the "bouboisie," and propagated the naturalistic novel, Dreiser's in particular. H. L. Mencken and the early Van Wyck Brooks were in the limelight in the twenties. Finally there were the Marxists or near Marxists who flourished during the Great Depression in the early thirties. Granville Hicks is their best-known spokesman, but the much more versatile critic Edmund Wilson was also deeply affected by Marxism, though his actual methods were rather revivals of appreciation or of historicism in the wake of Taine. None of these critics can be mistaken for New Critics.

The new methods, the tone, and new taste are clearly discernible first in the early articles and books of John Crowe Ransom, Allen Tate, R. P. Blackmur, Kenneth Burke, and Yvor Winters, and somewhat later in Cleanth Brooks, Robert Penn Warren, and William K. Wimsatt. A date such as 1923 when Allen Tate spoke of a "new school of so-called philosophic criticism"[2] cannot be far off the mark for the earliest stirring in the United States. The influence of T. S. Eliot was obviously decisive, to which later that of I. A. Richards should be added. Eliot's *Sacred Wood* dates from 1920, Richards's *Principles of Literary Criticism* from 1924.

If we look at this list of names we soon discover that the group was far from unified. Ransom, Tate, Cleanth Brooks, and R. P. Warren may be grouped together as Southern Critics. Burke and Blackmur stand apart, and Yvor Winters was a complete maverick. I could collect and quote a large number of their pronouncements violently disagreeing with their supposed allies and show that they hold often quite divergent and even contradictory theories. Even Ransom, the teacher in different years of Allen Tate, Cleanth Brooks, and R. P. Warren, holds views very different from those of his pupils. Burke and Blackmur later rejected the New Criticism in strong terms, and Winters never was happy with the association. The view that the New Criticism represents a coterie or even a school is mistaken. With the evidence of disagreements among these critics—which it would take too long to develop in detail—it may seem wise to conclude that the concept and term should be abandoned and these critics discussed each on his own merits. I have done so in the forthcoming fifth volume of my *History of Modern Criticism*, where I give individual chapters to each of these men. Some chapters, in preliminary versions—on Ransom, Tate, Blackmur, Burke, Brooks, and Wimsatt—have appeared scattered in various periodicals.

Still, something tells us that there is good sense in grouping these critics together. Most obviously they are held together by their reaction against the preceding or contemporary critical schools and views mentioned before. They all reject the kind of metaphorical, evocative criticism practiced by the impressionists. Tate, Blackmur, Burke, and Winters contributed to a symposium highly critical of the neo-humanists, and others voiced their rejection elsewhere. They all had no use for Mencken and Van Wyck Brooks, particularly after Brooks became a violent enemy of all modernism. Furthermore, they were almost unanimous in their rejection of Marxism, with the single exception of Kenneth Burke, who in the thirties passed through a Marxist phase and, anyhow, after his first book moved away from his neo-critical beginnings. What, however, in the American situation mattered most was that they were united in their opposition to the prevailing methods, doctrines, and views of academic English literary scholarship. There, in a way the younger generation may find it difficult to realize, a purely philological and historical scholarship dominated all instruction, publication, and promotion. I remember that when I first came to study English literature in the Princeton graduate school in 1927, fifty years ago, no course in American literature, none in modern literature, and none in criticism was offered. Of all my learned teachers only Morris W. Croll had any interest in aesthetics or even literary ideas. Most of the New Critics were college teachers and had to make their way in an environment hostile to any and all criticism. Only Kenneth Burke was and remained a free-lance man of letters, though he taught in later years occasionally at Bennington College and briefly at the University of Chicago. But he very early deserted the New Criticism. It took Blackmur, Tate, and Winters years to get academic recognition, often against stiff opposition, and even Ransom, R. P. Warren, and Cleanth Brooks, established in quieter places, had their troubles. Ransom's paper "Criticism, Inc." (1937) pleaded for the academic establishment of criticism, and thanks to him and others criticism is now taught in most American colleges and universities. But it was an uphill fight. I still remember vividly the acrimony of the conflict between criticism and literary history at the University of Iowa, where I was a member of the English Department from 1939 to 1946.

The New Critics with one voice questioned the assumptions and preoccupations of academic scholarship with different degrees of sharpness. The wittiest and most pungent was Allen

Tate. In a lecture, "Miss Emily and the Bibliographer" (1940), Tate exposed the vain attempts to emulate the methods of science by tracing influences conceived in terms of forces, causes and effects, or biological analogies of growth and development, or by applying psychology, economics, and sociology to literature. They all shirk, Tate argues, the essential task of criticism, "the moral obligation to judge," for "if we wait for history to judge," as they plead, "there will be no judgment." We must also judge the literature of our own time. "The scholar who tells us that he understands Dryden but makes nothing of Hopkins or Yeats is telling us that he does not understand Dryden."[3] As early as 1927 Tate said that "the historical method has disqualified our best minds for the traditional functions of criticism. It ignores the meaning of the destination in favor of the way one gets there."[4] Winters argues similarly. The superstition of a value-free literary history ignores the fact that "every writer that the scholar studies comes to him as the result of a critical judgment." The professors who engage in "serious" literary study— bibliography, philology, textual criticism, and related disciplines —not only hold criticism in contempt and do their best to suppress it in the universities, but also, Winters tells us bluntly, "were fools and where they still flourish they are still fools."[5] Blackmur also rejected the methods of what I shall call "extrinsic" criticism. Scholarship, he grants, is useful in supplying us with facts but becomes obnoxious when it "believes it has made an interpretation by surrounding the work with facts."[6] The mild-mannered Ransom could become caustic at the expense of "the indefensible extravagance in the gigantic collective establishment of the English faculties" that fail to teach criticism.[7] Many more voices could be added to a revolt against the positivism of nineteenth-century scholarship, which in the United States was vigorously stated as early as 1908 by Irving Babbitt in *Literature and the American College* and was widespread and effective on the continent of Europe, especially in the twenties.

Still, one should understand that this rejection of academic historical scholarship must not be interpreted as a rejection of the historicity of poetry. Cleanth Brooks has, in many contexts, mostly in interpreting seventeenth-century poems, shown that the critic "needs the help of the historian—all the help he can get." "The critic," he argues, "obviously must know what the words of the poem mean, something that immediately puts him in debt to the linguist (or rather lexicographer, the *OED*, I might add); and since many of the words are proper nouns, in debt to the historian as well."[8] In order to interpret the "Horatian Ode" of Andrew Marvell correctly we must obviously know something of Cromwell and Charles I and the particular historical situation in the summer of 1650 to which the poem refers. But historical evidence is not welcomed only as a strictly subordinate contribution to the elucidation of a poem.

Brooks and all the other New Critics reinterpret and revalue the whole history of English poetry. It was an act of the historical imagination (however prepared before) to revise the history of English poetry; to exalt Donne and the Metaphysicals; to reinstate Dryden and Pope; to sift and discriminate among the English Romantic poets, preferring Wordsworth and Keats to Shelley and Byron; to discover Hopkins; to exalt Yeats; and to defend the break with Victorian and Edwardian conventions as it was initiated by Pound and Eliot. Brooks's "Notes for a Revised History of English Poetry" (1939) sketches the new scheme clearly. Winters's books, particularly his last, *Forms of Discovery* (1967), do the same, with a different emphasis, more dogmatically. But it is not enough to refute the allegation of lack of historical sense by pointing to the interest in historical elucidation and even in literary history properly conceived. Rather I would agree that the New Criticism embraces a total historical scheme, believes in a philosophy of history, and uses it as a standard of judgment.

History is seen substantially in the terms of T. S. Eliot. There used to be once a perfectly ordered world, which is, for instance, behind Dante's poetry. This world disintegrated under the impact of science and scepticism. The "dissociation of sensibility" took place at some time in the seventeenth century. Man became increasingly divided, alienated, specialized as industrialization and secularism progressed. The Western world is in decay, but some hope seems to be held out for a reconstitution of the original wholeness. The total man, the undivided "unified sensibility" that combines intellect and feeling, is the ideal that requires a rejection of technological civilization, a return to religion or, at least, to a modern myth and, in the southern critics, allowed a defense of the agrarian society surviving in the South. The basic scheme has a venerable ancestry: Schiller's *Letters on Aesthetic Education* (1795) was the main source for Hegel and Marx. In the American critics, particularly in Tate and Brooks, the scheme is drawn from Eliot's view of tradition. In Eliot the "unified sensibility" comes from F. H. Bradley, who knew his Hegel. Brooks is confident in focusing on Hobbes as the villain; Tate singles out Bacon, Gibbon, and La Mettrie as the destroyers of the old world view. Ransom puts out a different version blaming "Platonism," which means presumably any generalizing abstracting view of the world. Tate praised Spengler's *Decline of the West*[9] and gave the scheme a peculiar twist in his practical criticism. He was most interested in poets who come at the point of dissolution of the original unity, who dramatize the alienation of man: Emily Dickinson and Hart Crane in particular. Tate sees poems always within history and echoes Eliot saying, in 1927, "My attempt is to see the present from the past, yet remain immersed in the present and committed to it."[10]

The role of criticism is great for the health of poetry, of the language, and ultimately of society. The charge of rejecting history, of having no "sense of the past" (voiced even by Lionel Trilling, in *The Liberal Imagination*) is easily refuted. Its refutation has already answered the other main accusation, that of aestheticism, of an art-for-art's sake view of literature. It is based on the insistence of the New Critics that the aesthetic experience is set off from immediate practical concerns: from rhetorical persuasion, bare doctrinal statement, or mere emotional effusion. The aesthetic state of mind can be induced only by the coherence and unity of a work of art. These views have an ancient lineage long preceding the art-for-art's-sake movement. The distinctions among aesthetic contemplation, scientific truth, morality, and practical usefulness were most elaborately drawn in Kant's *Critique of Judgment* (1790), and the idea of the coherence, unity, and even organicity of a work of art is as old as Aristotle. It was modified and amplified by the German critics around 1800, from whom Coleridge drew his formulas, and Coleridge is the most immediate source for English and American critics. One may raise doubts (as Wimsatt has) about the metaphor of organism if it is pushed too far in application to a work of art, but there seems to me a simple truth in the old view that a successful work of art is a whole in which the parts collaborate and modify one another. Much of the "close reading" practiced by Cleanth Brooks and followers demonstrates this truth even on recalcitrant material. But this insight is grossly distorted if it is supposed to lead to the conclusion that poetry is cut off from reality, is merely self-reflexive, and that it is thus only an inconsequential play of words. When Brooks combats the "heresy of paraphrase" he objects to reducing a work of art to a statement of abstract propositions, or to a moral message, or to any literal verifiable truth. But this emphasis on the specific "fictionality" of all art, its world of illusion or semblance, cannot mean a lack of relation to reality or a simple entrapment in language. Tate, for instance, emphatically condemned "that idolatrous dissolution of language from the grammar of a possible world, which results from the belief that language itself can be reality, or by incantation can create reality: a superstition that comes down in French from Lautréamont, Rimbaud, and Mallarmé to the Surrealists, and in English to Hart Crane, Wallace Stevens, and Dylan Thomas."[11] Poetry is turned to the world, aims at a picture of reality. It cannot be absolute or pure. It remains impure, like anything human, a theme eloquently developed in R. P. Warren's essay "Pure and Impure Poetry" (1942).

Both Brooks and Ransom uphold a version of imitation, of *mimesis*. Brooks asserts that the poem, if it is a true poem, is a "simulacrum of reality"[12] or "a portion of reality as viewed and valued by a human being. It is rendered coherent through a perspective of valuing."[13] In Ransom poetry is a display, a knowledge and restoration of the real world, a celebration of the beauty of nature, even a "representation of natural beauty."[14] None of the New Critics could have believed in the prison-house of language. This supposed consequence of any view of the unity, self-reflexiveness, and integration of a work of art has been debated thoroughly, for example, by Murray Krieger in *The New Apologists for Poetry* (1956) and by Gerald Graff in *Poetic Statement and Critical Dogma* (1970), but it poses a false dilemma. A poem may have coherence and integrity without losing its meaning or truth. The very nature of words points to the outside world. In *A Window to Criticism* (1964) Murray Krieger speaks of a "miracle," but such a gesture toward the irrational seems unnecessary unless we consider the reference of almost every word a "miracle." It points to or may point to an object in the outside world and at the same time is part of a sentence, of a phonemic and syntactical system, of a language code. The parallel to painting is obvious: a painting is enclosed in a frame, is organized by a relation of colors and lines, but simultaneously may represent a landscape, a scene, or the portrait of a real man or woman.

In the writings of the New Critics the coherence of a poem is not studied in terms of form, as the label "formalism" suggests. Actually the New Critics pay little attention to what is traditionally called the form of a poem. Brooks and Warren in their textbook, *Understanding Poetry* (1938), inevitably pay some attention to the role of meter and stanzaic forms, and Winters expounded his view on "The Audible Reading of Poetry."[15] But the New Critics reject the distinction of form and content; they believe in the organicity of poetry and, in practice, constantly examine attitudes, tones, tensions, irony, and paradox, all psychological concepts partly derived from Richards. The concept of irony and paradox is used by Brooks very broadly. It is not the opposite of an overt statement "but a general term for the kind of qualification which the various elements in a context receive from the context."[16] It indicates the recognition of incongruities, the union of opposites that Brooks finds in all good, that is, complex, "inclusive" poetry. Brooks has most consistently held a strictly organic point of view. Other critics abandon it. Thus Ransom draws a distinction between structure and texture which reverts to the old dichotomy of content and form. A poem, he says strikingly, is "much more like a Christmas tree than an organism,"[17] with the metaphors thought of as ornaments. Winters comes to a similar conclusion with a different emphasis. A poem is for him "a statement in words about a human experience."[18] The charge of formalism in any sense that is valid for the Russian school is completely off the mark. The New Critics are overwhelmingly concerned with the meaning of a work of art, with the attitude, the tone, the feelings, and even with the ultimate implied world view conveyed. They are formalists only in the sense that they insist on the organization of a work of art that prevents its becoming a simple communication.

The allegation that the New Critics want to make criticism a science seems to me even more preposterous. It might have emanated from those who felt hurt by their attack on "appreciation," on loose impressionism and mere self-indulgence in "adventures among masterpieces." More recently it often comes from defenders of a hermeneutics that assumes a mysterious identification with the author's *cogito* or rejects interpretation in favor of an "erotics of art," as Susan Sontag does in *Against Interpretation* (1964). Actually the New Critics are enemies of science. Science for Tate is the villain of history which has destroyed the community of man, broken up the old organic way of life, paved the way to industrialism, and made man the alienated, rootless, godless creature he has become in this century. Science encourages Utopian thinking, the false idea of the perfectibility of man, the whole illusion of endless progress. Tate says bluntly: "Poetry is not only quite different from science but in its essence is opposed to science."[19] Ransom, in particular, conceives poetry as the supreme antidote against science. He makes the conflict of art and science the leading theme of history. "In all human history the dualism between science and art widens continually by reason of the aggressions of science. As science more and more reduces the world to its types and forms, art, replying, must invest it again with body."[20] The investment with body, the reassertion of the particularity of the world against the abstractions of science, is Ransom's leading theme; the restoration of what he calls the "thingness" (*Dinglichkeit*) of the world is the aim and justification of poetry. None of the New Critics has any sympathy for the mechanistic technological views of the Russian formalists. The New Critics have completely shunned modern linguistics—the use of phonemics or of quantitative methods. If they sometimes spoke of criticism as a systematic, rational discipline they could not mean a modern value-free social science, for they always stressed the necessity of judgment, the qualitative experience poetry gives us. In the attempt to defend poetry against the accusation of irrelevancy, they put forward claims for the truth of poetry, for the knowledge conveyed which is conceived as superior to that of science. Over and over again Tate says that literature provides "the special, unique and complete knowledge," "knowledge of a whole object, its complete knowledge, the full body of experience."[21] This is not a claim like that of the Romantics for some visionary power, some special insight into a world beyond, which might lead to an obscurantist theory of double truth. It is rather a view of knowledge as "realization," as full awareness in the sense in which we can say, "You don't really know what it is like until you have lived through it." It is ultimately a version of the unified sensibility of T. S. Eliot, the union of feeling and intellect achieved in poetry. Criticism cannot be neutral scientism; it must respond to the work with the same totality of mind with which the work is created. But criticism is always subordinated to creation. Its humility contrasts precisely with the aggressions, the impositions of science.

None of the New Critics would have thought that their methods of close reading were "scientific" nor would they have identified criticism with close reading. Ransom, Tate, Blackmur, Winters, and Burke had developed their theories of poetry and their general point of view long before they engaged in anything like close reading. Tate's first excursion into close reading is the essay "Narcissus as Narcissus" (1938), a commentary on his own "Ode to the Confederate Dead." The examination of a poem apart from biography and conventional literary history became, no doubt, an important innovation in the teaching of literature in American colleges and universities. The turn to the text was mainly accomplished by the success of *Understanding Poetry* by Cleanth Brooks and Robert Penn Warren, which invaded the strongholds of philological scholarship in the early forties. The method of close reading became the pedagogical weapon of the New Criticism. One should grant that the proliferation of "explications" became later a dreary industry, but it is a mistake to consider close reading a new version of *explication de texte*. Close reading as practiced by Cleanth Brooks differs from *explication de texte* by offering critical standards, leading to discrimination between good and bad poems, resolutely pursued in the textbook and in many other articles since. The aim is understanding, "interpretation," which is the other name for the now fashionable term "hermeneutics." The method of the New Critics may

differ from the intuitive identification proposed by the phe-
nomenologists in the wake of Poulet or from the fusion of
horizons in the mode of Gadamer, but the aim is the same. It is
hard to see how a study of literature can get along without
interpretation of individual works and how one can be "against
interpretation," as Susan Sontag entitled her book, or declare
"interpretation" to be "the real enemy."[22] The view voiced by
Richard E. Palmer in his book on *Hermeneutics* that the New
Criticism has "a technological concept of interpretation"[23] mis-
takes its aim of suppressing irrelevant subjective preconceptions
or biographical explanations for an indifferent scientism. It
seems to me farfetched to bring in T. S. Eliot's belief in original
sin as Gerald Graff does[24] to explain the New Critics' emphasis
on impersonality. It comes rather from Flaubert's and Joyce's
desire for an objective art, "impersonality" meaning a rejection
of overt didacticism and confessional display. The New Criticism
surely argues from a sound premise, that no coherent body of
knowledge can be established unless it defines its object, which
to the New Critic will be the individual work of art clearly set off
from its antecedents in the mind of the author or in the social
situation, as well as from its effect in society. The object of
literary study is conceived of not as an arbitrary construct but as
a structure of norms that prescribes a right response. This
structure need not be conceived of as static or spatial in any
literal sense, though terms such as the well-wrought urn, or
Joseph Frank's spatial form, or Wimsatt's verbal icon suggest
such a misinterpretation. All these metaphors aim at a genuine
insight: although the process of reading is inevitably temporal,
as critics we must try to see a work as a totality, a configuration,
a gestalt, a whole.

I hope I have succeeded in refuting the common misconcep-
tions about the New Criticism, but I have studied the history of
criticism long enough to know that there must be reasons for the
fact that the New Criticism is currently so in disfavor that, for
instance, Geoffrey Hartman could not only entitle a book and an
essay *Beyond Formalism* but in it could quote Trotsky, of all people,
attacking the very different Russian formalists from his Marxist
point of view and then conclude that "there is good reason why
many in this country, as well as in Europe, have voiced a suspi-

cion of Anglo-Saxon formalism. The dominion of Exegesis is great: she is our Whore of Babylon, sitting robed in Academic black on the great dragon of Criticism and displaying a repetitive and soporific balm from her pedantic cup" and say that "Explication is the end of criticism only if we succumb to what Trotsky called the formalist's 'superstition of the word.' "[25] Hartman and others have tried to overcome this superstition either by appealing to a purely intuitive identification with the author behind the work or by advocating a complete liberty of interpretation in an attempt to exalt criticism to the status of art, to obliterate the distinction between criticism and creation for which Roland Barthes has adopted the convenient common term "*écriture.*"

But the objections to the New Criticism do not come only from this new apocalyptic irrationalism. They are much older and more serious. The New Critics were immediately attacked from two sides long before the new movements imported from France. The Chicago Aristotelians, who exalt plot, character, and genre, strongly disapproved of the New Critics' concern for language and poetic diction. Language according to the Chicago School is merely inert matter, a material cause of poetry, a view that seems to go back rather to the Renaissance scholar Scaliger than to Aristotle himself. The New Critics fared badly in their hands. R. S. Crane attacked Cleanth Brooks's "critical monism," deploring his preoccupation with paradox and his conclusion that the structure of poetry is the structure common to all literary works. Crane also criticizes the New Critics for their "morbid obsession with the problem of justifying and preserving poetry in an age of science,"[26] as this was no problem for Crane and his group. Crane accepts pleasure as the aim of art and imitation as its procedure in which we find pleasure and instruction. One must admit that the Chicago critics scored many points against the overreadings in R. P. Warren's study of *The Ancient Mariner* and the attempts of Robert Heilman to read *King Lear* as an almost spatial pattern of images. Still the Chicago Aristotelians were on some points the allies of the New Criticism. Crane was one of the first to defend and to recommend the study of criticism in the university.[27] The whole group advocates a rational systematic study of poetics even though their insistence on strict genre conventions and neutral analysis was unacceptable to the New Critics concerned with the nature of poetry in general and with criticism as evaluation.

The next, much more effective rejection of the New Criticism came from the so-called myth-critics. Myth as a system of metaphors or symbols is a central device in much of the New Criticism, but in the myth-critics it becomes the one overriding concern. Poetry is simply (and I think wrongly) identified with myth, and myth is used so broadly that it includes any theme, any story you can think of: Huck Finn floating down the Mississippi with Jim is a myth. Myth-criticism allows a discussion of content apart from the poem; it often became mere allegorizing. Every work of literature is a quest, or a version of the death of God and His rebirth. Still, one should recognize that Northrop Frye in his *Anatomy of Criticism* (1957) has not entirely discarded the achievements of the New Criticism, though he rejects criticism as judgment in theory (though hardly in practice).

The New Criticism was then totally rejected by the critics of consciousness, the so-called Geneva School and its followers in this country. Georges Poulet, their most articulate spokesman, does not want to analyze a single work of art, is uninterested in its form or specificity, for he is searching for the author's *cogito* behind his total *oeuvre*. The other French group that must not be confused with the Geneva School, the structuralists, who come from Saussure's linguistics and from Lévi-Strauss's anthropology, have some affinities with the New Criticism in their concern for a microscopic analysis of texts and a general poetics. Roman Jakobson was the link between the Russian formalists and the Paris structuralists, and all his recent work, hailed by I. A. Richards as the fulfillment of his own ambitions, demonstrates his concern and skill in interpreting individual poems. But Jakobson's methods are linguistic, attentive to the grammar of poetry, and pointedly ignore criticism as judgment or ranking. Still, there is one trend in Parisian structuralism, particularly the acute analyses of fiction or symbol practiced by the Bulgarian Tzvetan Todorov and by Gérard Genette, which is not incompatible with the ambitions of the New Criticism. Many others in France and here in the United States aim at an all-embracing structure of universal poetics and finally at a science of semiotics, an ambition beyond the ken of the New Critics. Their *ethos*, unlike the often religious motivation of the Geneva School, is scientific; the philosophy, implied positivistic or materialistic: some of the French group have embraced Marxism and even Maoism. The distance from the New Criticism is obvious.

Surely one of the reasons for the demise of the New Criticism is the distrust many feel toward the political and religious views of the main New Critics: toward T. S. Eliot's Anglicanism, which is shared for instance by Cleanth Brooks, or toward the Roman Catholicism of Allen Tate (a convert) or William K. Wimsatt, as well as toward the participation of three of the southern critics (Ransom, Tate, R. P. Warren) in the so-called Agrarian movement, formulated in the symposium *I'll Take My Stand* (1930). But the New Critics—unlike the later Eliot and the early Richards—never tired of rejecting the amalgamation of poetry and religion. Tate says expressly that "literature is neither religion nor social engineering,"[28] and Brooks and Wimsatt always kept the two realms rigorously apart in their critical practice. But one cannot deny that ultimately poetry with several of the New Critics turns out to be, if not religion, then a preparation for religion: it is assigned a role comparable to the imagination in Wordsworth and Coleridge. The poet and his reader are each brought back to the totality of being, are restored to their original humanity.

If one rejects this version of history, one can see the justification of a new turn in poetic taste. The revival of the English romantics as the Visionary Company centered in Blake and the current attempts to dismiss T. S. Eliot both as poet and critic and to reduce the role of all modernism imply a rejection of the New Criticism also in the everyday matters of selection and ranking of poets and poems.

Still even more profoundly the New Criticism is affected by the general revolt against aesthetics per se, by the whole rejection of any distinction between the aesthetic state of mind and any other activity. It goes back to the German theory of empathy, even to Benedetto Croce, wrongly suspected of aestheticism, though he abolished the distinction between art and any act of intuition; and to John Dewey's *Art as Experience* (1934), which denies all distinction between aesthetic and other experiences of heightened vitality; and paradoxically to the literary criticism of I. A. Richards, who had such an influence on the American New Critics with his book on *Practical Criticism* (1929) but propounded a behavioristic theory that ignores the difference between aesthetic and other emotions completely. Thus the very basis of any concern with poetry or literature as an art is undermined. The New Criticism has become a victim of the general attack on literature and art, of the "deconstruction" of literary texts, of the new anarchy that allows a complete liberty of interpretation, and even of a self-confessed "nihilism."

One limitation of the New Critics seems to me serious, possibly because of my commitment to comparative literature. They are extremely anglocentric, even provincial. They have rarely attempted to discuss foreign literature or, if they have done so, their choice has been confined to a very few obvious texts. Dante is discussed by Allen Tate; he also comments on passages in *The Idiot* and *Madame Bovary*. Winters admires the poems of Paul Valéry. Blackmur, late in his life, did write, often vaguely and obscurely, on Dostoevsky, Tolstoy, Thomas Mann, and Flaubert. A recent excursion of Kenneth Burke into Goethe seems most unfortunate.[29] That is about all. The justification of this preoccupation with texts in English is presumably the conviction of the critics that poetry is implicated closely in the language, and lyrical poetry, the nature of poetry in general, was their first concern. Still it *is* a limitation, considering the inexhaustible wealth of the world's literature speaking to us in many tongues, crying to be interpreted and judged.

I will not conceal my own conviction that the New Criticism has stated or reaffirmed many basic truths to which future ages will have to return: the specific nature of the aesthetic transaction, the normative presence of a work of art that forms a structure, a unity, coherence, a whole, which cannot be simply battered about and is comparatively independent of its origins and effects. The New Critics have also persuasively described the function of literature in not yielding abstract knowledge or information, message or stated ideology, and they have devised a technique of interpretation that often succeeded in illuminating not so much the form of a poem as the implied attitudes of the author, the resolved or unresolved tensions and contradictions: a technique that yields a standard of judgment that cannot be easily dismissed in favor of the currently popular, sentimental, and simple. The charge of "elitism" cannot get around the New Critics' assertion of quality and value. A decision between good and bad art remains the unavoidable duty of criticism. The humanities would abdicate their function in society if they surrendered to a neutral scientism and indifferent relativism or if they succumbed to the imposition of alien norms required by political indoctrination. Particularly on these two fronts the New Critics have waged a valiant fight which, I am afraid, must be fought over again in the future.

American Criticism of the Sixties

I N 1948 Stanley Edgar Hyman published a book on recent American criticism, called *The Armed Vision*, which was a veritable hymn to the achievement of the new critical movement in this country culminating in a glorification of R. P. Blackmur and Kenneth Burke as the "perfect critics." Recently Hyman confessed that the high hopes for the future of criticism he had entertained have not been fulfilled. "The distinguished generation of critics I celebrated has done little of significance since 1948, and their successors have done little more. . . . We live in the Age of Epigones, and we sing sad songs of the death of criticism."[1]

I should like to show today that this view is mistaken. On the contrary, even the critics whom Hyman had praised so highly but whose decline he is deploring were extraordinarily active in the sixties and often produced new and original work. The New Criticism has been replaced by new methods and new points of view that cannot, and should not, be dismissed as imitations, reactions, or even extravagances. New critics (not with a capital "N" but simply new) with new styles, temperaments, and ideas have emerged which make contemporary American criticism at least as diversified and exciting as it was in the forties.

I shall only briefly indicate what the established New Critics (the subjects of Hyman's *Armed Vision*) accomplished in the sixties. I. A. Richards—not an American but a leading figure on the American scene—has only restated his old doctrines. His new volume, *So Much Nearer: Essays toward a World English* (1968), contains an essay entitled "The Future of Poetry" (1960), which, in terms reminding us of Shelley and Matthew Arnold, voices a hope for poetry as a substitute for religion which I cannot help considering unrealistic and even undesirable. But then, Richards has long ago turned prophet rather than literary critic.

Kenneth Burke, another prophet among critics, has, however, consolidated, clarified, and expanded his teachings in his new book, *Language as Symbolic Action* (1966). It shows no decline in brilliance of mental acrobatics, in the skill with which Marx, Freud, Richards, and the pragmatism of Mead and Dewey are absorbed into a grandiose system of human motivation. In some of the essays Burke has returned to literary criticism proper when he discusses *Coriolanus*, *Antony and Cleopatra*, *Timon of Athens*, Goethe's *Faust*, Theodore Roethke and William Carlos Williams, often with his old perceptiveness and analytical vigor. But I for one am put off by Burke's obsession with scatological punning or "joycing" as he calls it. We are told, e.g., that Coriolanus has to do with "anus" and that Keats's "Beauty is Truth, Truth Beauty" contains a hidden meaning: Body is Turd, Turd Body. Burke must be taken for what he is: as something of an intellectual circus-rider, tireless, unaging, vibrantly alive, stimulating in the literal sense.

Richard P. Blackmur died in 1965. His posthumous volume, *A Primer of Ignorance* (1967), contains some older subtle essays on the American twenties, on Henry James and Henry Adams, but also new pretentious reflections on Europe and America which show how far Blackmur has gone into a private world of his own devising. The writing becomes so fuzzy and involved that it is impossible to preserve an interest in the solution of the meta-phorical riddles propounded or to care for the opaque mysteries that are barely hinted at. Still, the *Eleven Essays on the European Novel* (1964), for all their gropings and clumsy circumlocutions, contain insights into the moral problems of the main novels of Tolstoy, Joyce, Flaubert, Thomas Mann, and Dostoevsky.

Yvor Winters died in January, 1968. His last book, *Forms of Discovery* (1967), shows a further hardening of his position: the extravagance with which he speaks of Wordsworth, Coleridge, and Keats as bad poets and with which he exalts neglected fig-ures such as the Tudor poet George Gascoigne or the eighteenth-century satirist Charles Churchill has become so excessive that we may overlook the widening of his horizon to a total history of English poetry. The sentimentalism of the eighteenth century and the doctrine of the association of ideas appear as the villains who destroyed the great tradition of English poetry. His advo-cacy of the poem as a plain moral statement, rational, straight-forward, and sober (amusingly illustrated by his literal-minded

assault on Yeats's beliefs) remains, after all, an impressive dec-
laration of faith in reason, unique, apart, quite out of tune with
the main trends toward the irrational, ironical, and paradoxical
concepts of poetry prevalent in our time.

The chief expounder of complex, ambiguous, paradoxical
poetry, Cleanth Brooks, seems to have completely changed his
interests, approaches, and style. His book, *William Faulkner: The
Yoknapatawpha Country* (1963), could be described as exhibiting a
conversion from formal to thematic study. But Brooks very
carefully draws the line against sociology and symbol-mongering
and concentrates on what was always latent in his work: on the
religious and historical meaning of Faulkner's fiction, on the
myth of the South, without neglecting formal consideration of
the novels as novels.

We associate Brooks with William K. Wimsatt as they collaborated in *Literary Criticism: A Short History* (1956). But Wimsatt has
rather continued in his polemical pursuits, in his attempts to
expose the errors and fallacies of critics and thus to define their
true concerns. *Hateful Contraries* (1965), a new collection of his
papers, tellingly criticizes the Chicago Aristotelianism and the
myth criticism of Northrop Frye and restates his own emphasis
on the contraries or the tensions reconciled in poetry and the
theory of criticism. Wimsatt, with his learning, clarity of purpose, and polemical vigor seems to me the most eminent literary
theorist now active in this country. He focuses deliberately on
literary questions, while among the older New Critics, Lionel
Trilling has systematically gone beyond literature and even *Beyond Culture* (1966), as he called his last collection of essays.
Trilling is concerned with the effort of modern literature to free
itself not only from the ideals of the middle class but from
society itself. He admires this avant-garde literature but is upset
by its destructive consequences when put into practice and suf-
fers from the conflict between aesthetics and politics. In the two
main essays, "On the Teaching of Modern Literature" (1961)
and "The Two Environments" (1965), he complains that we
achieve "the acculturation of the anticultural, or the legitimiza-
tion of the subversive" and that "modern criticism has instructed
us in an intelligent passivity before the beneficent aggression of
literature." But under the impact of the events at Columbia in

1968 Trilling has seen that "what were once thought of as moral fantasies," such as the idea of violence, are now being acted out, that "the status of history and the historical sense" has deteriorated and that, in general, humanism—in the sense that it says "there are certain things fit for humanity and some which are not"—is being rejected. And he deplores this rejection.[2]

If we add the many graceful and sensible essays of Edmund Wilson so savagely denigrated by Hyman in *The Armed Vision* to a mere middleman, we have to acknowledge that the leading critics of the forties have not lapsed into silence. Nor can I see why their recent work, whatever its shortcomings, should be judged as necessarily inferior to their earlier writings. Critics are not poets: they gain by experience, grow in knowledge and wisdom, one hopes, with age.

The New Criticism has found many opponents. The harshest, polemically, have been the so-called Chicago Aristotelians who published in 1952 a large programmatic volume, *Critics and Criticism*. The Chicago group has not, however, been very effective in the sixties. I am not aware of any prominent adherent to its teachings outside the faculty of the University of Chicago. Their leader, Ronald S. Crane, died in 1967; a collection of his papers, *The Idea of the Humanities* (2 vols., 1967), consists largely of learned contributions to a history of ideas. Among the younger members of the group, Bernard Weinberg, a professor of French literature, was most productive. His *History of Literary Criticism in the Italian Renaissance* (2 vols., 1961), is an erudite compendium that draws on many manuscript sources. His *Limits of Symbolism* (1966) is, under this deceptive title, a series of close readings of some of the best-known poems of Baudelaire, Rimbaud, Mallarmé, and Valéry. In a preface to a book, *Types of Thematic Structure* (1967) by Eugene H. Falk, Weinberg attacked the new French criticism and reasserted the basic doctrines of the Chicago school: the emphasis on theme, plot, and genre rather than on language, metaphor, and symbol. Elder Olson wrote thin, dogmatic books on *Tragedy and the Theory of Drama* (1961) and *The Theory of Comedy* (1968). Wayne Booth, who joined the Chicago faculty only in 1962, has made a wider impact with his *Rhetoric of Fiction* (1961). He argues there persuasively against the dogma that the novelist must disappear behind his work. He shows that the interference of the author, for instance in Laurence Sterne's *Tristram Shandy*, does not necessarily damage the vitality of a novel as Flaubert and Henry James—reacting to too much moralizing, commentary, and addresses to the "dear reader"—thought it did. But Wayne Booth goes to the other extreme; he asks the novelist to take sides, to announce his verdict for a sane and sound morality, and condemns, for instance, Joyce and Céline for their moral indifference. Booth, though a fervent adherent of the Chicago school, has little in common with its basic doctrines except its distrust of irony and a generally conservative taste. To my mind the Chicago group has remained an ultra-academic concern. In the face of modern literature we simply cannot go back to Aristotle, however refurbished and updated.

Undoubtedly the most successful and widespread movement in American criticism since the New Criticism has been Myth Criticism, most influentially codified in Northrop Frye's *Anatomy of Criticism* (1957). Frye, since his main theoretical book, has collected his earlier essays as *Fables of Identity* (1963) and has published three series of lectures, respectively devoted to Milton's *Paradise Lost* and to the comedies and tragedies of Shakespeare. They are called *The Return to Eden* (1965), *A Natural Perspective* (1965), and *Fools of Time* (1967). They seem to me Frye's most attractive writings; the fearful symmetry of his system of modes, genres, symbols, and myths has receded into the background and Frye confronts his texts much more freely. In the newest book on Shakespearean tragedy, Frye argues, for instance, that the tragic vision is based on our being in time, on the sense of the one-directional quality of life which is then contrasted with the ironic vision, "an insight into the independence of the way things are from the way we want them to be."[3] The two visions somehow correspond to Nietzsche's distinction between the Apollonian and the Dionysiac element. These distinctions, in turn, are associated with the contrast or conflict, common in Shakespeare, between the wheel of fortune and the order of nature. Henry V, for instance, is considered a wheel of fortune figure who "starts in a Dionysian role of the madcap prince, with Falstaff, his Silenus tutor."[4] Falstaff is associated with a midsummer night's dream, with darkness and night.

Though Falstaff's company "go by the moon and the seven stars and not by Phoebus" (*Henry IV, Part I*, act I, scene ii, ll. 14–15), the Prince informs us that he is going to turn his back on their Dionysian role, "imitate the sun" (act I, scene ii, 1. 198) and become something more like the incarnation of Apollo.[5] And so it goes, amusingly, even wittily, associating and analogizing as Frye believes that "everything is potentially identical with everything else"[6] and that "literature like mythology is largely an art of misleading analogies and mistaken identities."[7]

Among Frye's more or less orthodox followers Angus Fletcher, with his book *Allegory* (1964), seems closest even though he makes symbol and myth disappear in a perversely broad concept of allegory. Robert Scholes and Robert Kellogg have written a history of fiction, *The Nature of Narrative* (1966), in which, very much in the wake of Frye, the modern social and psychological novel appears only as a symptom of the general decay of myth, legend, and fairy tale. Scholes's new book, *The Fabulators* (1968), exalts Barth, Burroughs, and other new rambling novelists as "fabulators" who return to the oldest forms of fiction.

Harold Bloom, in his writings on the English romantic poets, *Shelley's Myth-making* (1959), *The Visionary Company* (1961), and *Blake's Apocalypse* (1963), as well as in a recent essay "The Internalization of Quest-Romance" (1969), follows Frye in interpreting romantic poetry as a secular humanism expressed in a new myth. Bloom exalts Shelley and Blake. Their vision is interpreted as prophetic rapture transcending that of the nature-bound Wordsworth and Keats. Bloom minimizes the Christian and classical components of romanticism as he sees only the visionaries of the company. He differs from Frye by his interest in Martin Buber and Freud. More than anyone else Bloom has succeeded in restoring the romantic poets to their place from which they seem to have been dislodged by Eliot and Leavis. It is done with ethical fervor often at the expense of aesthetic judgment and correctness of interpretation.

On the whole, the myth criticism of Frye and his followers and precursors has, one should acknowledge, allowed a return to the "content" of literature, to its general human meaning. But myth and symbol have become terms so broad and vague that all distinctions are abolished. In Frye symbol is simply "any unit of

any work of literature which can be isolated for critical attention"[8] and with others myth is simply an honorific name for any
plot or action. Leslie Fiedler in *Love and Death in the American
Novel* (1960) wrote a history of that theme which is supposed to
prove that normal sexual and marital love is a failure in America,
and that a white and a black American male would rather flee
from civilization like Huck Finn and Jim on the raft down the
Mississippi. Fiedler calls this fictional situation a "myth" or
"archetype." Roy Harvey Pearce in *The Continuity of American
Poetry* (1961) construes a contrast between the "Adamic" and the
"Mythic" in the history of American poetry. He rates poets
according to their "visionary" or "prophetic" pretensions but
chides Whitman for not having attained true prophecy. He was
such a "humane poet." He did not achieve the inhuman heights
of the prophet. His poetry "projects not a world to which the
poet stands as witness, but one to which he stands as maker."[9]
Witnessing a revelation is apparently more important than
writing poetry. Oddly enough Pearce calls this myth-making
"The New Historicism"; it does not have anything to do with
what has been understood by that term as used by its proclaimer
David Friedrich Strauss in 1837 and now become suddenly
fashionable in America.

Myth criticism of all varieties from Frye to Pearce is basically
anti- and un-historical. It reduces all literature to a few myths.
Frye recently proclaimed that "all myths have two poles, one
personal, whether divine or human, and one natural: Neptune
and the sea, Apollo and the sun."[10] Others look for disguises of
the sacrificial death of the God, the rebirth in spring, and for
versions of the quest even in a fishing trip. Long ago Austin
Warren—who cannot be suspected of lack of sympathy for a
religious view of the world—formulated the objection from the
point of literary criticism: "As all the 'real' poets bring essentially
the same message, after decoding each one is left with a feeling
of futility. Poetry is 'revelation' but what does it reveal?"[11]

Myth criticism is closely allied with existentialism, at least in
America. Frye is highly admired. Irrationalistic presuppositions
make allies of the two. But the mood is obviously very different.
Frye is an optimist: something survived of the United Church of
Christ preacher in him. One cannot be sure how far American

critics have a proper grasp of the teachings of Kierkegaard, Heidegger, or Sartre. But they share the sense of absurdity and nothingness. Murray Krieger, the most articulate existentialist among American critics, began with a shrewd analytical book on the New Criticism, *The New Apologists for Poetry* (1956). But since then he has advocated "thematics" against the supposed "formalism" of the New Critics and has tried to defend a new dualism of form and content by the argument that it reflects a metaphysical dualism, "a vision of a final cosmic disharmony." In *The Tragic Vision* (1960) the protagonist of tragedy is deliberately taken out of the context of tragedy as dramatic structure. The tragic hero (or rather "visionary") is the man of the "sickness unto death," of modern nihilism. Even Dostoevsky's Idiot is assimilated to this concept, and there is less trouble with the heroes of Kafka, Camus, Thomas Mann, and Melville. Krieger's later books, *A Window to Criticism* (1964), which contains a tortuous reading of Shakespeare's Sonnets, and a miscellaneous volume, *The Play and Place of Criticism* (1967), attempt to build bridges to more traditional critical pursuits: the image of the moving jar is used to define the structure of a work of art as being both static and dynamic. "Contextualism," as Krieger calls the New Criticism, is defended against gross misunderstandings equating it with art for art's sake. With Krieger literature becomes "the only form of existential philosophy."[12] Philosophizing in existential terms, he asserts, is actually impossible. One can convey the existential vision only in fictional terms. It is all the more difficult, then, to see how it could be conveyed in terms of criticism.

These irrationalistic consequences are then drawn by George Steiner, in *Language and Silence* (1967), a collection of essays that range from Kafka to Marshall McLuhan, from Lukács to recent pornography. Steiner is obsessed with the theme of the devaluation of the word. Literature, he complains, surprised and shocked, does not humanize. Germans could read Goethe and Hölderlin and burn Jews. Language does not reveal reality. The only way to convey it is silence. "Is the poet's verse not an insult to the naked cry?" he asks but continues writing as does Ihab Hassan, who in a new book, *The Literature of Silence* (1967), exalts Samuel Beckett and Henry Miller as "the masters of an anti-literature," proponents of an irrationalist creed, without apparently seeing the gulf that divides the comic genius of Beckett from the vulgar and tawdry Henry Miller. Hassan quotes as his epigraph D. H. Lawrence denouncing the green dragon, the evil-smelling *Logos*, and rhapsodizes on Pop and Op art, John Cage's music of silence, Rauschenberg's empty canvases, etc., in order finally to advocate a new critical language that would somehow expand man's consciousness of the ineffable and inexpressible. It is all very modish, vague and elusive, almost "psychedelic."

Silence or rather "The Aesthetics of Silence" is also the theme of Susan Sontag's leading essay in her collection, *Styles of Radical Will* (1969). She reflects well on the paradox of a literature "noisy with appeals for silence" and its "coquettish, even cheerful nihilism." She recognizes that silence is "a metaphor for a cleansed, non-interfering vision," that "behind the appeals for silence lies the wish for a perceptual and cultural clean slate."[13] She sympathizes with this rebellion against the past, any past, and in the title essay of her earlier book, *Against Interpretation* (1966), attacks interpretation and hence all criticism as "the revenge of the intellect upon art,"[14] asking for "an erotics of art instead of a hermeneutics."[15] No wonder that she has written approvingly of "camp," the "love of the unnatural: of artifice and exaggeration," of kitsch, and in praise of the "pornographic imagination" that attempts "to drive a wedge between one's existence as a full human being and one's existence as a sexual being."[16] Her essay on style assumes that nobody has ever thought about the question. The past and academic scholarship are rejected as a matter of principle, as a deliberate pose, though Miss Sontag is far too sophisticated, knowledgeable, and intellectual really to believe in the instinctive mindlessness she advocates.

The French "critics of consciousness," sometimes spoken of as the Geneva School, have recently found adherents in the United States. The French critics grew out of existentialism and Husserlian phenomenology as well as the peculiar psychoanalysis of Gaston Bachelard. But they developed specific techniques of analyzing a poet's consciousness, his relation to time and space, the imaginary world constructed in his writings, and assume a history of these consciousnesses within a history of the human mind. J. Hillis Miller, who was a colleague of Georges Poulet at the Johns Hopkins University, can be described as his American disciple, but differs in being more religiously motivated than his master. His two books, *The Disappearance of God* (1963), which contains chapters on De Quincey, Robert Browning, Emily Brontë, Matthew Arnold, and Gerard Manley Hopkins, and *Poets of Reality* (1965), with essays on Conrad, Yeats, T. S. Eliot, Dylan Thomas, Wallace Stevens, and William Carlos Williams, elaborate a scheme of history; with the end of Romanticism, man (or rather the English poet) lost progressively belief in God while in the twentieth century he slowly finds his way back to God conceived as total being, the living presence of reality. *Poets of Reality* ends with the exaltation of William Carlos Williams whose writings, we are told, can be defined "to bring into existence, with silly words, an erotic space inhabited by a woman of the imagination. His works, taken all together, make a poem which is a woman."[17] Elsewhere he tells us of a little imagistic poem by Williams, "Young Sycamore," saying that "the poem is not a picture of the tree. It is an object which has the same kind of life as the tree. It is an extension of nature's process."[18] Fortunately Hillis Miller is not always that highfalutin. His book, *The Form of Victorian Fiction* (1969), discusses Thackeray and Dickens, George Eliot and Thomas Hardy in comprehensible terms; time, intrasubjectivity, the ontological basis of form, the narrator as general consciousness, the self and the community are some of its themes. A sense of works as totalities, as works of art, emerges which is usually missing in the critics of conscience. They break up the writings of every author into a mosaic of quotations without regard to context, drawing on letters, diaries, and jottings with equal freedom rather than on finished works, since they are not interested in the art of literature but in the doings within the mind of each poet, which must not, however, be confused with the mental events studied by psychology. They want to grasp the inevitable, inescapable individuality of the poetry itself.

Geoffrey Hartman is a critic somewhat more closely related to Maurice Blanchot, on whom he has written perceptively, than to Poulet. His book *Wordsworth's Poetry* (1964) gives a new reading of a poet usually considered simple and pellucid. The dialectic of nature and imagination is there analyzed with great subtlety as it is in several new essays on the general problem of romanticism which he sees as the attempt "to draw the antidote to self-consciousness from consciousness itself." In a wide-ranging collection of essays, *Beyond Formalism* (1970), Hartman dismisses the formalist's "superstition of the word," embraces with some reservations the view of Northrop Frye that literary works are a reflection of personal myths and communal dreams, welcomes the new French structuralism but goes then, if I understand him rightly and I am not sure I always do, his own way: in search of self-awareness, of authenticity, of a Heideggerian self-oblivion. Fortunately, Hartman can also engage in sensitive readings of poetry buttressed by great erudition or turn to the problem of literary history.[19] He can make much of the *genius loci* and the national tradition. An essay, "The Voice of the Shuttle,"[20] starts with the analysis of metaphor as analogy drawing on recent linguistics, proceeds then to a thematic analysis of a poem by Emily Dickinson and ends again, as so many contemporaries do, with the baffling aesthetic of silence. The wish to dissolve the medium, to intuit things directly, to achieve the unmediated vision (the title of Hartman's first book) is paramount.

The professional linguists who study literature make no such metaphysical assumptions and have no such misgivings. They are technicians, positivists, believers in scientific objectivity, often in quantification as the only scientific method. These ideas have come to the United States rather late but have found recently many adherents, particularly among students of metrics and style. Increasingly statistical methods are being applied to these questions: e.g., by Louis T. Milic in a book on the style of Swift (*A Quantitative Approach to the Style of Jonathan Swift*, 1962) or by Seymour Chatman to *Theory of Meter* (1965). More boldly, Samuel R. Levin, in *Linguistic Patterns in Poetry* (1963), has tried to extend linguistic patterns beyond the limits of sentence structures to forms such as stanzas. Recently attempts have been made to apply even Chomsky's transformational grammar to a study of style. Very high hopes are put on these methods and some proponents claim that all literary study should be absorbed by stylistics which, in turn, is only a branch of linguistics, a modern exact social science. Still, I should want to argue that there are central problems of literary study that will always elude quantitative methods, as a work of literature is not a neutral assembly of words but is, by its very nature, value-charged. One cannot escape the problem of criticism in the sense of judging. Discrimination, sensitive weighing of qualities, a simple recognition of what is art, will always be the main concern of criticism proper, however helpful quantitative methods may be for the establishment of au-thorship, the compilation of concordances, the analysis of meter and style or the registration of audience responses. Criticism will survive as it meets a human need. We want to understand and judge literature; we must know what is good and what is bad and why.

In this brief survey I have, intentionally, focused on academic criticism with interest in theory. I realize that I did not and could not discuss many fine books of critical importance about periods, genres, and individual authors. My survey would degenerate into a mere list if I should enumerate the many books that, happily, combine literary history with critical insights and judg-ment. Even thirty years ago such a personal union—the scholar-critic—was rare in this country. He occurs though less often than one would wish. I can only allude to three scholar-critics of different generations who do not easily fit into any single rubric: Austin Warren whose two recent books, *The New England Con-science* (1966) and *Connections* (1970), a collection of essays rang-ing from Donne to T. S. Eliot, celebrate the values and the virtues of "culture" and "tradition." Harry Levin whose *Gates of Horn* (1963) perceptively discusses the great French novelists from Stendhal to Proust with a theory of realism that is both sociological and linguistic. His new volume of essays, *Refractions* (1966), collects many items focused on general concepts—on convention, on modernism, on myth. And finally Peter Demetz, whose *Post-War German Literature* (1970) revives the art of critical portraiture in a social setting.

Surveying the enormous reviewing activity in this country is an almost impossible task. Still I should like to mention at least three sensitive poet-reviewers, the late Randall Jarrell (who died in 1965), whose *Third Book of Criticism* (1969) contains lively metaphorical criticism spiced with epigrammatic wit directed, for instance, at the ideological gyrations of W. H. Auden, or

James Dickey's *Babel to Byzantium* (1968), a series of vignettes of poets which culminates in the praise of Theodore Roethke as the greatest contemporary poet. But Dickey is hardly a critic. He can say of some lines of E. E. Cummings: "Yet when you come on a passage like this, what can you feel but silence, gratitude, and rejoicing?"[21] Howard Nemerov's *Poetry and Fiction* (1963) provides a nice contrast; his blend of irony and hard forthrightness shows affinities with the criticism of Eliot and Cleanth Brooks. He knows that criticism "is an art of opinion" but that poetry is allied to religion and that it draws "an intelligible world from the brute recalcitrance of things."[22] He ranges widely through history from Shakespeare to Thomas Mann, from Longfellow to Nabokov, writing rationally and lucidly, though with an acute sense of the difficulties of discussing poetry.

There are, besides, the reviewers, mainly in New York, who judge books—novels for the most part—by standards of verisimilitude, social relevance, and conformity to their political ideology. Norman Podhoretz, the editor of *Commentary*, distinguishes in an inordinately vain autobiography, *Making It* (1967), between three generations of the New York "family" that is characterized by a "commitment to left-wing anti-Stalinism and a commitment to avant-gardism."[23] Philip Rahv, the editor of the *Partisan Review*, is revered among the Founding Fathers. Recently Rahv has collected his essays under the title of *Literature and the Sixth Sense* (1969), the sixth sense being the historical sense. It contains few pieces written in our decade. I might single out the judicious downgrading of D. H. Lawrence as a critic and of F. R. Leavis's exaltation of Lawrence to the greatest writer of the twentieth century. Among the second generation of the New York "family" Alfred Kazin is the most distinguished critic: he is now writing reminiscences (*Starting Out in the Thirties*, 1965). His only recent volume of essays, *Contemporaries* (1962), collects largely older brief reviews, few of them of any direct literary interest. Irving Howe, who is a little younger than Kazin, worries in a new volume of his essays, *Decline of the New* (1970), about the unsettling moral and intellectual consequences of the breakdown of modernist culture. In the essay "The New York Intellectuals," Howe takes up the theme of Podhoretz's *Making It*, deploring with a fine ethical fervor the current abandonment of liberalism and of the norms of rationality and intelligence. Among the third generation, Norman Podhoretz is clearly the most gifted. He has something of the moral fervor of Lionel Trilling and F. R. Leavis, two of his teachers. He says courageous things about such topics as the New Nihilism, Jewish Culture and the Intellectuals, and the Negro Problem, but his collection of articles, *Doings and Undoings* (1964), does contain some strictly literary pieces: a long sympathetic account of Edmund Wilson and harsh reviews of Faulkner's *Fable*, Saul Bellow's *Adventures of Augie March*, and Updike's *Centaur*. Podhoretz has critical perceptions but they are subordinate to his social concerns. Literature becomes merely a pretext for social comment, one of the functions of criticism in a general sense but not of immediate concern in this context.

I should also say, I assume, something about recent theatrical criticism; it seems to be often, and quite rightly, deliberately unliterary and provincial, preoccupied with the ephemera of the Broadway or off-Broadway stage. I can only refer to the self-education, in public, of Robert Brustein, reflected in three books, *Seasons of Discontent* (1965), *The Theater of Revolt* (1966), and *The Third Theater* (1969).

I shall not deal with the burgeoning psychoanalytical criticism. It seems to me a dreary hunt for sexual symbols or an attempt to put a dead writer on the couch with inadequate means. Literature is here again used as a document, as an instrument for something else. This may be unavoidable as literature can and has been used for all purposes: it can serve as a source book for a history of law or medicine or natural science or what not. But the literary student must at some point decide what is his object: some general concern or a focus on the works of art which implies a challenge to understand them as they are. One might not agree with the solutions propounded, but modern "hermeneutics," as developed largely in Germany by Dilthey and more recently by Hans Georg Gadamer, asks the right questions as to the meaning of a work of art and the limits of subjectivism. We have now a good account of the movement: Richard E. Palmer's *Hermeneutics* (1969). An American, E. Donald Hirsch in *Validity in Interpretation* (1967), tries to establish criteria for objective interpretation of the author's original intention and the implied norms of a genre. He fails to convince me but he has raised again the central question that the criticism of the last ten years must make us feel more acutely than ever: what are the limits of arbitrariness? Is there no correct interpretation? Are there no eternal or at least constant standards?

I cannot try to answer this question today but I hope my survey has brought out the main trends and the main categories: the survival of the New Criticism, the languishing activity of the Chicago group, the expansion of myth criticism, the new vigor of existentialism and the related criticism of consciousness, the promise of the new linguistic methods, and the surprising absence of any Marxist criticism of consequence. My critical reservations should not obscure my genuine admiration for the brilliance, subtlety, and ingenuity of much recent American criticism. I have fulfilled my purpose if I have suggested the enormous variety of trends and personalities in recent American criticism which testifies to the undiminished intellectual life of the nation.

Russian Formalism

RUSSIAN literary criticism is of particular relevance for every student of criticism, for it provides far more than commentary on the history of Russian literature. Nowhere else have major critical positions been formulated so sharply and even extremely as in the Russia of the first quarter of this century. Nowhere else was the critical debate so lively, so acrimonious, so much a life-and-death matter (even literally so) as in the Russia of the second and third decade of our age.

Nineteenth-century Russian criticism was largely didactic, primarily a weapon of the liberal and, later, revolutionary opposition to the tsarist regime. Even politically conservative critics, such as Apollon Grigoriev, were concerned with an interpretation of literature in the service of an ideal "nationality." In Tolstoy, who went his own way rejecting both the utilitarianism of the radical democrats and the conservative ideology, we have a moralistic critic of the purest water and the boldest sincerity.

The change came in the 1890s: with the rise of symbolism, with Dmitrii Merezhkovsky and Valerii Briusov. For the first time, criticism became partly aesthetic, even *l'art pour l'art* in the French manner, exalting the "music" of verse, the "suggestion" of words, the personal mood of poetic themes. Another strand of criticism or rather literary theory became "mystical," claiming supernatural knowledge for poetry, "miracle-working," "theurgia." The most coherent spokesman for this second view was Vyacheslav Ivanov, who stated emphatically that art becomes religion by the magic of the symbol, that art is a revelation of a higher reality, which it achieves with the creation of a new mythology. This new poetic myth, he hoped, would transform not only society but all reality. The origin of these ideas in the history of Russian religious thought, particularly in Vladimir Solovev, is obvious. Farther back, they can be traced to the general tradition of neo-Platonic mysticism. Ivanov's formulations seem to me very close to Schelling's exaltation of a religion of art and his program for a new mythology. Symbolism, while representing a reaction against nineteenth-century realism and naturalism, must be thus considered as a revival of romanticism even though it had its own distinctive features. The differences between the two trends within symbolism, the aesthetic and the mystical, led, about 1910, to open polemics between the main exponents even though individual writers managed to balance themselves between the ideal of pure poetry and the claim of access to a supernatural realm. Shortly afterward the mystical pretensions of the symbolists were sharply challenged by poetic groups that assumed the rather absurd names of "clarism" and "acmeism." Their theories amount to little more than a restatement of classicism or rather Parnassism in their emphasis on clarity, objectivity, and concreteness often reminiscent of Western imagism. Moreover, all these theories were largely confined to a group of poets and their sympathizers and they were either ignored, attacked, or ridiculed by the bulk of the journalistic criticism both on the Right and on the Left. In addition, Marxist criticism was formulated in Russia during the years between the two revolutions, appearing in the writings of Georgii Plekhanov and the articles of Lenin. In practice Marxist criticism was a revival of nineteenth-century didacticism and a return to the taste of the middle of the nineteenth century for realism, for genre painting, for late romantic music.

The battle lines were thus drawn about 1910. Aestheticism, symbolism, Marxism confronted one another sharply. But it seems to me a mistake, or at least a blurring of distinctions, to minimize the change that came about just before World War I with the new avant-garde movements in Russia, usually lumped together under the terms "futurism" and "modernism." Modernism is an old and somewhat empty term dating back to the Middle Ages, revived in the debate between the ancients and the moderns—the Battle of the Books as it was called in England—and again revived in Germany and France under the new slogan "Classic versus Romantic." *Modernité* as a term occurs in Chateaubriand's *Mémoires d'outre tombe* in 1849 and is prominent in Baudelaire's discussions of modern art. The work of Constantin Guys, a mediocre pen-and-ink illustrator, became the occasion in 1863 for Baudelaire to celebrate "the ephemeral and fleeting beauty of modern life."[1] In Germany, after about 1887, the form *Die Moderne* became a slogan of writers whom we would classify today as naturalists. After all, *modo* in Latin means only "now," and you cannot prevent anyone who feels himself to be contemporary and in opposition to the past from calling himself "modern." But the term—used so widely, for instance, in Richard Ellmann and Charles Feidelson's anthology *The Modern Tradition* (1965), in Irving Howe's *Literary Modernism* (1967), and also, mostly pejoratively, in Soviet literary criticism—obscures the fact that symbolism is the culmination or possibly the "beautiful death" of the romantic tradition, continuous in every way with the past, while the new movements, ideas, and styles that precede World War I by a few years constitute a clean break with the great tradition. Futurism, cubism, Dadaism, surrealism, or whatever name was given to the new avant-garde groups represent a definite innovation, a real rupture with the past expressed rather badly by the military metaphor "avant-garde," used first by a little-known Saint-Simonian, Gabriel-Désiré Laverdant, in 1845.[2] I am thinking not only of the flamboyant proclamations of the futurists such as the Italian manifesto of 1909, which calls for setting the libraries on fire and flooding the museums, or of Mayakovsky's similar advice in the notorious "A Slap in the Face to Public Taste," signed by David Burliuk, Alexei Kruchenykh, and Velimir Khlebnikov in 1912, to "throw Pushkin, Dostoevsky, Tolstoy, and all the others overboard from the steamship of modernity."[3] I am thinking rather of their actual innovations in the practice of poetry and prose: the rejection of organic, biological, "beautiful" form in favor of abstract, geometrical, stylized art; the rejection, hence, of intimacy with nature in favor of the city and the machine, so loudly proclaimed by Marinetti and Mayakovsky; the replacement of symbolism by the realized metaphor or by allegory, obvious in Kafka, Camus, Čapek, Orwell, or Zamiatin; the withering of the faith in language as magic; its use as a means of persuasion or manipulation or as an autonomous sign devoid of any relation to reality, and, least of all, to a supernatural reality. While the symbolists thought of poetry as lifting us vertically into a higher realm, the futurists dreamed of a millennium or utopia that might be a socialist utopia, hence justifying their adherence to the revolution, or—as did Khlebnikov—they dreamed of a lost paradise even in the prehistory of mankind. Whereas the symbolists and acmeists believed in inspiration (and so did, for example, Marina Tsvetaeva), the new avant-garde thought rather about "how to make poems," as Mayakovsky called his little treatise in 1926.

I am aware that these distinctions are not always clear-cut: writers sometimes hold incompatible convictions or shift easily from one extreme point of view to another. Every time has its survivals and anticipations. In literary theory especially we are confronted necessarily with a limited number of issues historically debated over and over again, with "essentially contested concepts" which cannot be absolutely new. Still, the Russian Formalist movement that arose shortly after the great divide constitutes an enduring contribution to literary theory, an achievement of singular importance whose repercussions are felt even today. Viktor Shklovsky's *Voskreshenie slova* (Resurrection of the Word, 1914) is usually considered the first clear pronouncement, but, as a group appearance, the two small *Sborniki po teorii poeticheskogo iazyka* (Symposia on the Theory of Poetic Language), published in Petrograd in 1916 and 1917 and, after the revolution, the collection *Poetika*, printed in 1919, present something like a common front. The movement became institutionalized by the founding in October 1919 of Opoiaz (Society for the Study of Poetic Language).

The defense of futurism is explicit in Shklovsky's first prewar pamphlet, and it inspired Roman Jakobson's little booklet *Noveishaia russkaia poeziia* (The Newest Russian Poetry, Prague, 1921), devoted mainly to the poetry of Khlebnikov. The personal relationships of some of the formalists, particularly Osip Brik, Jakobson, and Shklovsky with Mayakovsky and Khlebnikov are a matter of literary history. But still it seems to me a mistake to reduce formalist theory to a mere echo, to a *post festum* apologetics of futurist poetry, as has been argued recently in Krystyna Pomorska's *Russian Formalist Theory and its Poetic Ambiance* (The Hague, 1968). Her thesis seems overstated. Criticism, formalist theory, in turn influenced the poets. The relation was, as we say today, "dialectical," though I would prefer to speak more modestly of interaction. This relationship cannot be decided a priori. It would be as futile an argument as the famous question of which came first, the chicken or the egg. We can show that some poets (Mayakovsky, in particular) accepted grate-fully, and, I think, sometimes with some puzzlement and sur-prise, the attention and the theories developed by academic or not so academic critics. They may have been emboldened in their experiments with language or at least made more fully aware of aspects of their practice, though it might be difficult to demonstrate this in concrete detail. The other relation is more easily proved: one can clearly see the influence of futurist prac-tice on the theories of the formalists, mainly in the defense of a free handling of words, their sound and their meaning, the new syntax, and free verse. But surely Russian formalism cannot and must not be reduced to mere apologetics for futurist practice. If this were so, Russian formalist theory would be a historical footnote of little interest outside of Russia except for students of Russian futurism. If it were so, we could not understand why Russian formalism should have had such repercussions in Po-land and Czechoslovakia in the 1930s and why, in a constellation of Russian poetry quite different from the years of World War I, it should again attract somewhat condescending attention in Soviet Russia today and increasingly also in the West. The ante-cedents of Russian formalism both in the history of Russian criticism and in Western thinking about literature are widely scattered and do not at all coincide with the antecedents of futurism. Even the sympathies of some formalists for futurism were far from total. Certainly, at least, Boris Eikhenbaum rather admired the acmeists, as his study of *Anna Akhmatova* (Peters-burg, 1923) shows convincingly. Yurii Tynianov, we are told, withdrew early from the orbit of futurism, and Viktor Zhirmun-sky—who from the beginning voiced reservations about some formalist doctrines—clearly cared most for symbolists and acme-ists. In every way the doctrine of the formalists, especially in its mature stage, eludes any reduction to a defense of futurism, even if we knew exactly what this term means. The prodigious research of Vladimir Markov has demonstrated that futurism was a blanket term for many warring splinter groups whose theoretical pronouncements amounted often to little more than the old pleadings for the freedom of the artist and his emancipation from the literary tradition. I shall try rather to describe the position of the Russian formalists without regard to the use to which their teachings were put by the poets or to the suggestions they may have drawn from futurist experimentation. Motivation or intention can never dispose of the actual content or value of a doctrine.

To give an accurate account of formalist teaching, it is necessary to make distinctions among the leading figures who differed sharply in background, temperament, and learning. The scale ranges from the brilliant but brash Viktor Shklovsky to Viktor Zhirmunsky, a cautious academic mind of great encyclopedic learning. Shklovsky (born in 1893) was the initiator, the gadfly, the first who formulated the central concepts most boldly. He collected his articles in a volume, O *teorii prozy* (On the Theory of Prose, 1925); Boris Eikhenbaum (1886–1959) began with the startling piece on Gogol's "Overcoat," "Kak sdelana 'Shinel' Gogolia" (How Gogol's "Overcoat" Is Made), elaborated a theory of the melody of Russian lyric verse (*Melodika russkogo liricheskogo stikha*, 1921), wrote a little book dissecting Mikhail Lermontov's poetry (1924), and gave a reasoned and even modest defense of the formal method in 1925. Boris Tomashevsky (1890–1957) was the specialist on prosody for the group. *Russkoe stikhoslozhenie* (Russian Versification, 1923) is the classic statement of their views, and in *Teoriia literatury* (Theory of Literature, 1925), Tomashevsky provided a summary and textbook of the group's doctrines. Yurii Tynianov (1894–1943) began with a study of Dostoevsky's parody of Gogol, published *Problema stikhotvornogo iazyka* (The Problem of Poetic Language, 1924), and devoted much effort and thought to the problem of literary evolution. The title of his collected essays, *Arkhaisty i novatory* (Archaists and Innovators, Leningrad, 1929), indicates his preoccupation with the seesaw of convention and revolt in the history of Russian poetry. Viktor Zhirmunsky (1891–1971), who began as a student of German romanticism, specialized in such questions as *Kompozitsiia liricheskikh stikhotvorenii* (The Composition of Lyrical Poems, 1921), and the theory and history of *Rifma* (Rhyme, 1923). He was also a comparatist, whose *Bairon i Pushkin* (Leningrad, 1924) handled a well-worn theme in an original manner. But the discussions of the formalist method in the collection

Voprosy teorii literatury (Questions of Literary Theory, 1928) show that even very early Zhirmunsky rejected the extreme statements of Shklovsky and Eikhenbaum. Viktor Vladimirovich Vinogradov (1895–1969) must be called a learned practitioner of stylistics rather than a theorist. His studies of Gogol and the early Dostoevsky laid the foundation for a history of Russian prose fiction culminating in his book *Evoliutsiia russkogo naturalizma* (The Evolution of Russian Naturalism, 1929). Roman Jakobson (born 1896) stands somewhat apart, though he was, as a very young student in Moscow, one of the initiators of the group and gave it the benefit of his linguistic training. But Jakobson left Russia in 1920 and his pamphlet *Noveishaia russkaia poeziia* (The Newest Russian Poetry, 1921) was published in Prague and the little treatise *O cheshskom stikhe* (Czech Versification, 1923), which proved important for comparative metrics, was published in Berlin in 1923. Most of his later writings were in Czech, French, and German. Also the linguist Grigorii Vinokur (1896–1947) published theoretical articles on poetic language in the 1920s and much later produced a fine study, *Mayakovsky novator iazyka* (Mayakovsky as Innovator of the Language, 1943). Osip Brik (1888–1938) apparently played a leading part in the organization of the group, but his published writings are scant; still his contribution on sound figures in the 1919 volume *Poetika*, and the studies of Lev Iakubinsky (died 1945) on the same question were important in the early phases of the movement. Boris Mikhailovich Engelgardt gave, in 1927, a very sympathetic descriptive account of the "Formal Method in Literary History" (*Formalnyi metod v istorii literatury*). Some scholars who were not strictly members of the group felt the stimulus of formalism. Grigorii Alexandrovich Gukovsky revolutionized the study of Russian eighteenth-century poetry (1927), and Vasilii Gippius wrote a book on Gogol (1924) which paid close attention to the problems raised by the formalists. Mikhail Mikhailovich Bakhtin (1895–1975), *Problemy tvorchestva Dostoevskogo* (Problems of Dostoevsky's Poetics, 1929), was deeply influenced by formalist methodology, though he tried to distance himself from the formalists quite sharply. Also Vladimir Iakovlevich Propp, whose *Morfologiia skazki* (Morphology of the Folktale, 1927) was a first attempt to tabulate and analyze narrative schemes in fairy tales, started with the formalist idea of functions as constant elements in folktales, even though Propp remained strictly a folklorist.

We should make distinctions not only between persons but between chronological stages: the early period of self-definition (from about 1916 to 1921), when a harshly polemical tone prevailed and the movement tried to set itself off sharply from the immediate past and attention was largely focused on a few problems of poetic language and prose composition; the middle period of expansion and consolidation (from about 1921 to 1928) subjected the whole complex of literary problems to reexamination (the shift to literary history is particularly marked at that time). Finally came the period of dissolution and accommodation (1928–35) when, partly under the pressure of the reigning Marxist dogma, some formalists recanted while others made compromises, attempted elaborate reconciliations between formalism and Marxism, or simply escaped into other disciplines and concerns. One need not ascribe this dissolution only to external pressure; people do change and shift their interests. Shklovsky developed an interest in the film and, as early as 1923, wrote a whimsical autobiography, ironically called *Sentimentalnoe puteshestvie* (A Sentimental Journey: Memoirs, 1917–1922). His later study, in 1928, of Tolstoy's *War and Peace* was a self-conscious attempt to combine formalist and sociological considerations. Since then some of his critical writings have become appallingly conformist and conventional, though a book on Dostoevsky, *Za i protiv* (Pro and Contra, 1957), shows some of his old spark. Eikhenbaum suffered the most harassment during the Zhdanov period in the late 1930s; he was singled out for attacks up to the time of his death, though in his prolific and erudite writings he had largely moved into literary biography. The three volumes on Tolstoy preserve only traces of his earlier concerns. The last unfinished volume on the 1870s and the new studies of Lermontov are heavily and even clumsily ideological. Tomashevsky devoted tremendous efforts to editing the Russian classics and wrote a large monograph on Pushkin, as well as *Stikh i iazyk* (Verse and Language, 1959). He became a learned textual and historical scholar. Tynianov wrote slightly fictionalized lives of the Decembrist poet Wilhelm Kiukhelbeker, the dramatist Alexander Griboedov, and Pushkin. His greatest success was the story *Podporuchik Kizhe* (Lieutenant Kizhe, 1930). Tynianov was the first of the brilliant group to die. Zhirmunsky engaged in most far-flung scholarly activities: a huge book on German dialects and a work on the Georgian epic suggest his range. Vinogradov became a prominent linguist: his books on the language and style of Pushkin (1941) are standard, as is his work on Russian grammar and the history of the Russian literary language. Jakobson spent eighteen years in Czechoslovakia, helped to found the Prague Linguistic Circle, and came to the United States in 1941. He is an outstanding theoretical linguist and Slavist. In recent years he has returned to problems of literary analysis, to the "grammar of poetry." His work is a bridge to the new French structuralism.

When we turn to the actual content of the teaching of formalism, we must be aware that some of these generalizations hold true only of certain authors, that there were shades and differences of opinion and even disagreements among them, and that what was propounded at one time may not have been propounded in a later stage. Still, we can try to sketch the formalists' general point of view.

The label "formalism" is misleading if applied to the mature teachings of the group. In the early pronouncements we do find formulations that sound like extreme aestheticism, a defense of "art for art's sake." Shklovsky goes particularly far: he can assert that all art is "outside emotion," that it is "without or outside compassion"; he often minimizes its social role, speaking resignedly or deprecatingly of its "harmlessness, its imprisonment, its lack of any imperative."[4] In *Khod Konia* (The Knight's Move, 1923) he deplores as an error the identification of revolutionary art with the social revolution and says extravagantly: "Art was always apart from life and its color never reflected the color of the flag that waved over the fortress of the city."[5] All subjects in art are equal. "Jocular, tragic, world-shaking and intimate works are all equal. The confrontation of a world with a world matters as much or as little as that of a cat with a stone."[6] Similarly, Jakobson ridiculed the ideological approach to art. "Why," he asks, "should a poet have more responsibility for a conflict of ideas than for a battle with swords or pistols?" Ideas in literature are like colors on a canvas, means toward an end. The usual confusion of life and art, Jakobson complains, turns us "into a medieval audience which wants to beat up the actor who played Judas."[7]

When Shklovsky says that "form creates content"[8] and when Jakobson defines the subject of literary scholarship "not as literature but 'literariness,' that which makes a work literary,"[9] we must understand that "form" is used so broadly by the formalists that it absorbs what is ordinarily called content. The old contrast between form and content is abolished. More wisely the formalists later spoke of "structure," a term that avoids the implication of form as an external husk enveloping the kernel of content. The mature teaching of the formalists distinguishes between elements of works of art that are indifferent aesthetically, are mere "material," such as words outside of their context or motifs in real life, and the way in which they acquire aesthetic effectiveness within a work of art. Form is the organization of pre-aesthetic materials. At their best the Russian formalists revived the old concept of the unity of a work of art, its integrity and coherence, though they have shunned the biological implications of the organism idea.

The Russian formalists consider form the result of two operations: deformation and organization. The term "deformation" has no derogatory implication; it means simply the changes imposed on the material, the effect achieved, for instance, by poetic language in contrast to the language of prose, the patterning by sound repetitions and figures, the nods and turns of a novelistic plot—in short, all the "devices ," "procedures," or "instruments" of art. But these devices must be applied in a systematic manner, must be organized, must harmonize with each other to achieve the totality of a work of genuine art, its specific shape or structure. Thus the Russian formalists studied (at first with great finesse) not only devices such as sound-patterns, meters, compositional forms, and genre conventions but also the aesthetic function of themes, motifs, and plots.

I cannot enter into an account of the work of the group on such technical questions as sound-patterns, the relation of metrical patterns to syntax or to intonation, or the role of word-boundaries in prosody. Much of this would have to be illustrated by Russian texts, though the main concepts, such as the stress on the whole verse rather than on the foot as the basic metrical unit, are applicable also to other languages. The rejection of the old graphic methods as well as methods based on an analysis by scientific instruments of oral recitation was a decisive step in freeing metrics from old superstitions. It revived a sense of the role of the conflict between the metrical pattern and the speech rhythm as the central fact of prosody. The formalists succeeded in restoring to metrics its necessary contact with linguistics and semantics.

The attack on the conception of poetry as "thinking in images"[10] was also very influential. The overemphasis on visual imagination seemed to the formalists refuted by much poetry that achieves its effects by sheer sound or sound figures, grammatical parallelisms and contrasts, or a rhythmic impulse and flow. Metaphor, they said, is a linguistic figure that need not be visualized. It need not be in any direct relation to reality. Realism rather uses metonymy, the figure of contiguity; it must be seen as another (and I suspect for them inferior) kind of art.

Some of the pronouncements quoted were directed against the didactic criteria imposed by the ideological tradition of Russian criticism—whether liberal, symbolist, or Marxist—and against the whole view that poetry serves as a kind of Salvation Army. But the formalists do not deny art its great social function; they rather broaden and redefine it. Over and over again they assert that "the purpose of art is to make us see things, not to know them. Art is there to awaken us from our usual torpor." They thereby rephrase an old motif of aesthetics known to Wordsworth or Joseph Conrad and prominent in Tolstoy. They remind us of John Crowe Ransom's insistence on the contrast of science and art, art being assigned the function of returning "the world's body" to us. The Russians analyzed the devices that make us see or rather "realize" this world. One such device forces us to slow down, to delay, to put on the brakes in order to focus on the work of art. "The way of art," says Shklovsky, "is a round-about way, a road that makes us feel the stones on it, a way which returns on itself."[11] Art is putting up hurdles, it is like a game of patience or a jigsaw puzzle. Frame stories, such as *The Arabian Nights* with their constant delays and disappointments, adventure and mystery stories, detective novels with their surprises and riddles, serve as examples. We may be somewhat puzzled by the attention that Shklovsky gives to the mysteries in Dickens's *Little Dorrit* or that Boris Eikhenbaum gives in a long essay to O. Henry, a writer of minimal importance in the history of American literature. Shklovsky consistently exalts Laurence Sterne's *Tristram Shandy* as the "typical" novel that makes us conscious of its form by frequent interruptions and digressions, by "laying bare" of its form, by a display of the technique of making, by a parody of the conventional novel. Sterne, according to Shklovsky, was the first to write a novel about the novel. Or to give another example of the method, Boris Eikhenbaum reinterpreted Gogol's "Overcoat"—which has been traditionally considered a humanitarian plea for the little man—as a grotesquerie aimed at displaying the art of storytelling. We hear the voice of the storyteller, an effect achieved by sound patterns, puns, comic illogical anticlimaxes, funny names such as the hero's, Akaky Akakievich, and such absurd events as the ghost's robberies of fur coats—a conclusion that is totally inexplicable and even jarring by the criteria of realism.

Formalism was at first deliberately and defiantly anti-historical. It coincided with the turn of philology away from historical studies of sound changes to a descriptive approach to living languages, away from the phonetic study of individual sounds to units of sounds as meaning, for which the term "phoneme" had been invented by Baudouin de Courtenay, a Pole of French descent who taught at the University of St. Petersburg. But the formalists soon saw that the wholesale rejection, futurist or Bolshevik, of the past was untenable and that the problem of literary history had to be reopened in new terms. They did this by postulating an internal evolution of art in which convention always alternates with revolt. They rejected the usual literary history as a ragbag of uncoordinated facts. As Jakobson said strikingly, "The old literary historians remind us of policemen who, in order to arrest a certain individual, arrest everybody and carry off everything from his lodgings, and arrest also anyone who passed by on the street. The historians of literature use everything—the social setting, psychology, politics, philosophy. Instead of literary scholarship, they give us a conglomeration of homegrown disciplines."[12] The formalists tried to change this by focusing on the art of literature, the evolution, say, of poetic diction, which they describe as a process of "automatization," of the wearing off of novelty, of felt strangeness and hence of aesthetic appeal that soon raises the desire for change. The revolt brings about an "actualization," as they call it, of new devices that in turn will wear out. But the formalists did not conceive of this process as a simple seesaw action and reaction. They knew that the evolution of the art of literature is closely bound up with shifts in the hierarchy of genres which are often due to social displacement. They showed how genres considered "low" have rejuvenated literature, how literature is in constant need of "re-barbarization." Dostoevsky lifted the French *roman-feuilleton* into the realm of high art; Blok exalted the gypsy song, and even Pushkin used the lowly album verse addressed to ladies for his noble love lyrics.

The Russian formalists, one should conclude, made a valuable and durable contribution to literary theory. They resolutely put the study of the actual work of literature into the center of scholarship and relegated biographical, psychological, and so-ciological studies to its periphery; they presented clearly the issue of "literariness" and overcame the old dichotomy of form and content; they boldly posed the problem of literary history as an internal dynamic process. All these are genuine contributions to which we should add the many technical refinements they made in the close analysis of sound patterns, meters, and compositional forms. They strikingly characterized the different styles of discourse, drew a sharp and fruitful distinction between fable and plot or what they called *siuzhet*, gave close attention to parody as reflecting the feeling of stylistic change, studied the different ways of storytelling, the role of the teller and his voice in the *skaz*, the *récit*, and examined the changing hierarchy of genres in literary history. Their attack on the predominance of the image as the main device of poetry seems to me convincing as was the emphasis on other poetic devices: the realization of metaphor, the role of grammatical and syntactical schemes, the sheer play of verbal art. All this and much more can and should be illustrated from their wide-ranging work, which is unfortunately often incomprehensible without a knowledge of the Russian texts discussed. Still their work is valuable not only as apologetics for avant-garde art or reinterpretation of the course of Russian literature but as a discussion, elaboration, and development of methods that arose in completely different contexts. Their theories are transferable and adaptable in other lands and times.

No theory falls from heaven and can claim absolute originality. The ancestry of the formalists is clear enough. Though the formalists rejected the metaphysical claims of the symbolists, their concern for the technique of verse and the analysis of poetry was anticipated by at least two of the important symbolist poets, Briusov and Bely. Particularly, Bely's large book on *Simvolizm* (Symbolism, 1910) with its statistical studies of Russian versification must have served as a stimulus. In 1917 a linguist, Sergei Kartsevsky, came back from Geneva after a year of study with Ferdinand de Saussure. I have alluded to the rise of phonemics. Zhirmunsky knew a great deal about the German interest in stylistics and the study of form: he refers to Oskar Walzel in particular. The basically phenomenological approach to literature may have been suggested not by reading Husserl, whose first volume of *Logische Untersuchungen* had come out in Russian translation in 1912 but rather by the work of a Russian philosopher, Gustav Shpet, who in *Iavlenie i Smysl* (Appearance and Meaning, Moscow, 1914) expounded the crucial difference between sense and meaning. The Russians knew the often fantastic suggestions of a pupil of Mallarmé, René Ghil, who had contacts with Briusov and from whom they drew the term "orchestration" (*instrumentirovka*) for the sound patterns of poetry. A little-known German book, Broder Christiansen's *Philosophie der Kunst* (1908), was translated into Russian in 1911. Such terms as *Differenzqualität* and *Dominante* are derived from him. I am not sure of the role of Bergson, whose collected works appeared in Russian just before World War I. He certainly speaks of the "devices" (*procédés*) of art, of its density, its texture (*faktura*). The idea of evolution is prominent in Alexander Veselovsky, the greatest Russian comparatist, whose work was focused on folklore. His basic conception of an internal history of art is paralleled in France in the writings of Ferdinand Brunetière, though the French scholar's *évolution des genres* presses the biological parallel far too hard.

Thus when Russian formalism attracted attention recently in the West, it could fortify analogous critical movements. An obvious parallel exists with the effort of the New Criticism in this country, though we must not minimize the differences in ethos and emphasis: the Russians are associated with revolution rather than tradition, their faith is in science rather than in interpretation. More recently, Russian formalism has been hailed as a precursor of the new French structuralism. Such an affinity is doubtless explained partly by a common adherence to the linguistics of de Saussure, but much of the stir caused by these claims seem to me based on a misunderstanding. The Russian concept of form or structure is always confined to a work of art or to groups of works of art and is not, as in Lévi-Strauss or Lucien Goldmann, an analogous large-scale social structure. With the Russians, structure is simply a term for the unity of the work of art. Only in a few late articles is the idea of a "system of systems," a general semiology, broached very tentatively. At most, they would speak of a dialectical relation to the other "series," to society and other arts.

Seen from a present-day perspective, the limitations of the Russian formalist doctrines are obvious to any student of criticism. I am thinking not so much of the extremism of some of their formulations, which can be corrected and has been effectively modified in the Polish and Czech movements inspired by the Russian formalists but of what, from the point of view of a literary critic, must appear as the major deficiency of the formalist point of view: the attempt to divorce literary analysis and history from value and value judgment. The formalists essentially chose a technical, scientific approach to literature which may appeal to our time but ultimately would dehumanize art and destroy criticism. It seems to me, for instance, an error to believe that "novelty" is the only criterion of value in the process of history. This would exalt an innovator such as Marlowe above Shakespeare. There is also original rubbish. Nor is the effect of art sufficiently described in terms of "realization," "visibility," "making strange," however rechristened. I have become also more and more skeptical of the concept of evolution in literature. The Russians are far too deterministic, far too trusting in some kind of necessity of an age, in a *Zeitgeist* that somehow prescribes the shape and direction of literature. One must take with a grain of salt a statement by Osip Brik that "if Pushkin had never been born, *Eugene Onegin* would have been written by itself,"[13] but even in less paradoxical formulations Eikhenbaum and the others speak constantly of art not as creation but as an act of discovery of forms that somehow pre-existed in a disguised state. The individual is slighted, a collective history is assumed, a history without names, a postulate propounded by Heinrich Wölfflin for the history of art. The concept of time that underlies such a formulation seems to me mistaken. An artist, like any man, may reach at any moment into the past of his own life or into the remotest past of humanity. It is not true that an artist develops toward a single goal. A work of art is not a member of a series, a link in a chain. It may bear relation to any number of ideas, events, or images from the past.

The formalists could not avoid the perils of historical relativism, which are anarchy and nihilism in aesthetics, and they embraced a concept of poetry that grossly overrates the mere virtuoso handling of language as sound or grammar, with the result that Poe, a truncated Mallarmé, and Khlebnikov appear as the central figures of modern poetry. In matters of taste they appear particularly time-bound, harking back, in spite of their rejection of mysticism and occultism, to the period of symbolism, to the ideal of "absolute" poetry, or to the view of poetry as game or puzzle. On the other hand, they have fortunately gone far beyond their temporal limitations and have raised and sometimes answered the great questions of literary theory and history, not only in Russia.

Mayakovsky, in "How To Make Verses," said: "Children (and young literary schools as well) are always curious to know what is inside a cardboard horse. After the work of the formalists the insides of cardboard horses and elephants stand revealed. If the horse is a bit spoiled because of this—we'll say: 'Forgive us.'"[14]

Reflections on my *History of Modern Criticism*

I must begin with an apology, or rather an explanation. I was asked by the organizers of this congress to speak on the basic ideas underlying my *History of Modern Criticism*. I agreed not because I want to advertise or even defend my *History* but because I consider it an opportunity to reflect on the writing of intellectual history and of a history of criticism in particular.

I have read in the vast new literature on historiography, which, at least in the Anglo-American world, is dominated by the methods of analytical philosophy, but I have come away disappointed, for practically all these books and papers analyze problems that are of little or no relevance to the writing of a history of criticism. Most of these discussions are concerned with questions of moral responsibility or culpability, with normal or abnormal human behavior, with accidents such as sudden deaths and assassinations. We are to consider such problems as "Why did Brutus stab Caesar?" or "Why did Louis XIV die unpopular?" Hardly anywhere are the very different problems of a history of criticism even raised. We must go elsewhere for parallels and possible models.

Obviously, the history of criticism differs profoundly from political, social, or economic history in one salient respect: the texts on which the history of criticism is based are immediately accessible, and they can be read, commented upon, interpreted, argued about, and criticized in turn, as if they had been written yesterday, even though they may have been written (like the *Poetics* of Aristotle) 2300 or so years ago. Thus the history of criticism is not history in the sense in which we write, say, the history of battles. The battle of Waterloo has to be reconstructed from recorded eyewitness accounts, from written commands or

Lecture delivered at the Eighth Congress of the International Comparative Literature Association, Budapest, 12–17 August, 1976.

depositions, or possibly from some physical remains, whereas texts such as Homer and Plato are present, just as the Parthenon is still present or the frescoes of Giotto in the Arena Chapel. Still, the history of criticism differs from the history of art or music or poetry by not being faced with the task of having to translate from one medium (or, as it is now fashionable to say, from one language or code) into another. In writing the history of criticism we use and have to use the same language (even if we translate from ancient Greek), the language of concepts. In short the history of criticism presents the same problems as all histories of ideas: the history of philosophy, the history of aesthetics, of political, religious, and economic thought, of linguistics, and many other branches of learning.

We thus have some help and models. Not much unfortunately can be learned from other histories of criticism. The only general history that preceded my books, George Saintsbury's dating from 1901–4, is a deliberately anti-theoretical, impressionistic history of literary taste. Saintsbury complains about the "error of wool-gathering after abstract questions of the nature and justification of poetry"[1] and hardly ever reflects on his method of writing, except to offer us an atlas and survey. More can be learned from R. S. Crane's review of J. W. Atkins's book entitled *English Literary Criticism: 17th and 18th Century* (1953).[2] Crane rejects Atkins's dull summarizing of doctrines and wants a chronological analysis of specific texts, a "history without prior commitments as to what criticism is or ought to be," a history "without a thesis," an aim I consider impossible to attain and undesirable.

More had been said about the writing of the history of philosophy. One can trace a history of the historiography of philosophy from Diogenes Laertius in the third century A.D. to the eighteenth-century compendia of Jakob Brucker (1742–67, five volumes) and Wilhelm Gottlieb Tennemann's twelve volumes (1798–1817) to Hegel's *Lectures on the History of Philosophy* (published in 1833–36 but based on manuscripts and transcripts by students sometimes dating back to 1815–16). All histories of philosophy preceding Hegel's can be called doxographies, i.e., summaries and expositions of the doctrines of philosophers, arranged either according to schools (Platonic, Sceptic, Epicurean, Stoic, etc.) or chronologically, with the ambition to do so neutrally, descriptively, though it is easy to detect the Leibnizian bias of Brucker or the Kantian of Tennemann. With Hegel the whole conception of a history of philosophy changed radically. In his introduction Hegel states resolutely that "the history of a subject depends closely on the concept one has of the subject." He admits that philosophy (and this would be even more true of criticism) has "the disadvantage compared to other sciences, that there are the most divergent views about what philosophy should and can do." But those who complain about the diversity of the manifestations of philosophy are, Hegel says with an unusual display of dry wit, like the man whom the doctor advised to eat fruit but who then refused cherries, plums, and grapes. "Diversity is thus not an impairment but an absolute necessity for the existence of philosophy. The study of the history of philosophy is thus the study of philosophy itself." The diversity of philosophy is conceived not as a random sequence but as "an organically progressive totality, as a rational continuity." Philosophy has a history that is "a necessary, consistent process." Every philosophy was necessary. None perished wholly. The newest philosophy, and he means his own, is the "result of all preceding philosophies." Hegel elaborates the paradox that in the "history of philosophy, though it is history, we still do not have to deal with anything that is past." "Truth," he says, "has no history, is not past."[3] For Hegel this implied the right and obligation of the historian to judge, to decide which ideas belong to the chain of development. The introductory reflections of Hegel's *History of Philosophy* are still pertinent today for a historian of criticism.

They raise the question I had to face. Is there such a subject as "criticism," which can be isolated from other activities of man, and does it show some kind of unity, focus, and continuity? I have answered "yes" to both of those questions, though, for instance, Benedetto Croce in his early pamphlet, *Critica letteraria* (1894) and Erich Auerbach in a review of my *History of Modern Criticism*[4] denied that criticism is a unified subject because of "the multitude of possible problems and crossings of problems, the extreme diversity of its presuppositions, aims and accents." I am content to answer that criticism is any discourse on literature. It is thus clearly circumscribed by its theme, as many other sciences are, and the multitude of problems and approaches is precisely the topic of my book. One of its tasks is the sorting out of the different ways of defining and regarding the subject. A history of the concept of criticism, literature, and poetry is at the very center of the book.

While Croce and Auerbach see only the cherries, plums, and grapes and seem to deny the existence of fruit, other historians have tried to abolish the distinction between fruit and the whole of plant life or, to drop the metaphor, the distinction between literary and other criticism, such as the criticism of art and music, and have even denied that criticism can be discussed otherwise than as a branch of general history. There is an undeniable truth to the view that reality forms a seamless web, that any activity of man is involved with all his other activities. Literary criticism is related to the history of literature and the other arts, to intellectual history, to general history whether political or social, and even economic conditions play their part in shaping the history of criticism. Attempts have been made to make criticism simply a mirror of a specific time and situation. Thus Bernard Smith, in *Forces in American Criticism: A Study in the History of American Literary Thought*,[5] states emphatically that "literary criticism seemed to me more clearly related to social history than are poetry and fiction." Criticism appears as "ideology"—not in the frequent sense of *Weltanschauung*—but as a false consciousness of reality, as a mere mouthpiece of specific literary or social trends. It becomes integrated into cultural history, becomes the expression of cultural change itself. We are confronted with the whole question of determinism, with the view that "everything must be treated not only as connected with everything else but as symptom of something else."[6] I have discussed this whole question several times elsewhere[7] and can here only repeat my conclusion. Cause—in the sense defined by Morris R. Cohen—as "some reason or ground why, whenever the antecedent event occurs, the consequent must follow"[8] is inapplicable in literary history or in the history of criticism. One work may be the necessary condition of another but one cannot say that it caused it. One must grant something to human freedom, to the decision of an individual. But we need not, in this context, move on this abstract plane.

As a historian of criticism I must make an attempt to describe the relationship of criticism to all the other activities of man without giving up the focus on the central subject. The relationship of criticism to the practice of writing must be constantly borne in mind. Sometimes there is the personal union of the poet-critic: most prominently in English literature, where poets such as Dryden, Wordsworth, Coleridge, Matthew Arnold, and T. S. Eliot are also landmarks in the history of criticism. Much criticism was written as a specific defense of a literary trend or school. I can only allude to the Schlegels as heralds of romanticism or to the Russian formalists as defenders of futurism. Criticism is closely related to aesthetics; it may be, as Croce argued, simply a branch of aesthetics, and I do discuss writers such as Kant, Schiller, Schelling, Ruskin, and Croce, though I try to steer clear of abstract speculations on beauty and the aesthetic response. Criticism is deeply influenced by philosophy. The empiricism of the British critics of the eighteenth century contrasts with the idealist and sometimes mystical assumptions of the German critics in the romantic period, as they differ from the positivists of the later nineteenth century in France. I could not ignore the impact of political history on criticism, when I discuss Madame de Staël expelled by Napoleon or the propagandist of liberal ideas, Georg Brandes, or the antitsarist fervor of the radical critics in the Russia of the 1860s. I do on occasion think of the economic basis of criticism, the different class origins and allegiances of the critics. The German professors of the early nineteenth century (including Hegel) differ obviously in lifestyle from a Parisian Bohemian such as Baudelaire or struggling journalists like the Russians: Belinsky, Dobrolyubov, and Pisarev.

All this is well and good, but we cannot get around the question raised in the quotations from Hegel. We must think of criticism as a relatively independent activity. No progress in any branch of learning has ever been made unless it was seen in comparative isolation, unless everything else was, to use the phenomenological terminology, "put into brackets." This isolation, which does not of course mean criticism for criticism's sake, is also a pragmatic imperative. A book, even a very long book, has to have some limits. If I had to discuss the relation of criticism to the practice of literature, I would have to examine, for instance, all the tragedies of Schiller or inquire whether Wordsworth actually wrote poetry in the common language of men. I would quickly abolish the unity of my subject matter, its continuity and development, and would make the history of criticism dissolve into the history of literature itself. Only by limiting the subject can we hope to master it.

But how can it be mastered? How can one reconcile the elementary fact that we have to do with texts that are present today and still think of them as part of the past, as history? One could argue that there is no history of criticism or even of literature. W. P. Ker has stated that the literary historian is like a guide in a museum who points and comments on the pictures, and Benedetto Croce, in many contexts, proclaimed that works of art are unique, individual, immediately present, and that there is no essential continuity between them. In criticism we can say that the problems discussed by Plato or Aristotle are still with us today. We have to do with what W. B. Gallie has strikingly called "essentially contested concepts."[9] We can take such concepts as "imitation," "tragedy," "form," "catharsis," to mention a few key-terms of the *Poetics*, and discuss them as if they were pronounced yesterday. We can ask: Are they true or not? Do they make sense? How do they apply to today's literature? I agree that there are persistent problems present even today, that Aristotle, Kant, Coleridge, Friedrich Schlegel, T. S. Eliot, and others ask questions that we are meant to answer, and they are often the same questions, though often differently phrased, with a new vocabulary. One of the functions of a history of criticism seems to me to show the reader that what has been touted as a new discovery has been said many times over before. Modern criticism can be described as a constant process of rediscovery of old questions. But this whole idea of persistent questions has been challenged by the new historicism. It is said that Aristotle's concepts are not timeless but time-bound, that "tragedy" means for him something very different from what it means for us, because he knew only the Greek plays. Every critic writes in his own time, encapsuled in his own time. I think we must recognize the danger of assuming timeless concepts too readily. We must be aware of the shifts of meaning and not be fooled by the occurrence of the same words or phrases. But this seems to me rather a challenge for the historian than an insurmountable obstacle. I cannot believe in the inscrutable past, in the closed cycles of time-spirits assumed in Hegelianism and such derivatives as O. Spengler or much of German *Geistesgeschichte* with its medieval mind or baroque man.

I myself have written several papers on historical semantics, somewhat on the model of Leo Spitzer's studies on such words as *Stimmung* and *milieu*, papers on the concept of criticism, literature, period, evolution, and five period terms: baroque, classicism, romanticism, realism, and symbolism. But I have rejected the idea of organizing my *History* around the tracing of single concepts or "unit ideas" as recommended in Arthur O. Lovejoy's special method of the "history of ideas." It would break up the systems, admittedly often loosely put together and contradictory, of individual critics; it would make an understanding of their individuality and personality (which must not of course be thought of in biographical terms) impossible. Let us beware of the "trap of spurious persistence," as Peter Gay has called it, but still insist that we can understand the concepts and problems of even remote times and authors. False dilemmas have been pressed by modern hermeneutics. Man can understand someone with a perspective very different from his own. Wilhelm Dilthey has elaborated the view that men share a common potential to be other than they are.

We cannot, however, be content with the idea of the timelessness of criticism if we want to write history even though or because we recognize that concepts persist throughout history. If we dealt with concepts purely as present, we would write not a history of criticism but an introduction to critical problems on the occasion of Aristotle, Dryden, Lessing, Matthew Arnold, Hippolyte Taine, and others. There are books that proceed in this manner. For instance, I. A. Richards's *Coleridge on Imagination* (1934) takes Coleridge out of history and debates the concept of imagination, the coalescence of subject and object and myth in direct argument with Coleridge's pronouncements. *Literary Criticism: A Short History* by William K. Wimsatt and

Cleanth Brooks[10] calls itself frankly "polemic" or "argumentative," though this is a far from sufficient description of a book
full of historical insights.

   The history of criticism, as I conceive it, cannot be simply a
discussion of timeless texts and must not be reduced to a branch
of general or cultural history. We have to find a way of thinking
of an internal history of criticism. Hegel assumes this for the
history of philosophy, and so does Croce in the historical part
of his *Aesthetics*. All philosophy and aesthetics are presumed
to move toward the one divine event: the philosophy of Hegel
or the aesthetics of Croce. These histories could be called "retrospective": they assume that philosophy and aesthetics have found
their final resting point. I have been suspected of sharing this
view and accused of "looking down at the history of criticism as a
series of failures, as doomed attempts to scramble to the heights
of our present-day glories," presumably represented by *Theory of
Literature*. But this is a misunderstanding of *Theory of Literature*,
which is a tolerant and open-minded rehearsal of many theories,
and this misunderstanding is refuted by the text of my *History*. I
have a point of view. I have to make selections of texts and
authors. The idea of a completely neutral, purely expository history seems to me a chimera. There cannot be any history without
a sense of direction, some feeling for the future, some ideal,
some standard, and hence some hindsight. But holding a point
of view and even a specific creed cannot mean that other approaches or perspectives would remain invisible. The function
of a book like mine is to expound the great diversity of views
without, however, giving up one's own perspective. I should like
to think of my *History*, to use the classification that John Passmore[11] proposed for histories of philosophy, as "elucidatory," as
not "argumentative" or "polemical" in the sense of refuting a
critic, but still not shirking from placing him; and not as cultural
history, which would display doctrines only as representatives of
a period or trend. Much in my books must be inevitably "doxo-
graphical," expository, for the books are supposed to be of use to
others and to aim at the exposition of critical ideas from a first-
hand study of the texts. Much is inevitably "retrospective"; I
cannot help selecting and judging from my own vantage point.
Some is cultural history. I must suggest the way critics fit into

their time. But I was always aware of the danger that critics would be treated as mere symptoms of their time and thus would remain without ties to the past of their arguments. The relationship between critics would cease to matter. I know the problem of novelty—the addition or emergence of new problems, the question of originality, the filiation of ideas. I do not think, for instance, that it is unimportant to point to the mainly German sources of Coleridge's theories. It locates him in intellectual history and prevents the kind of judgment pronounced, for instance, by I. A. Richards, when he makes him "the Galileo" of criticism, the forerunner of the presumed Newton: I. A. Richards.[12]

If we allow the possibility of different viewpoints, we are in danger of historicism and even complete relativism. But we need not grant such a conclusion. We can still adjudicate the merits of different ideas, see the relative justification of this or that formula or answer. We need not reconcile deep-seated contradictions and conflicts and claim a "synthesis" to overcome eclecticism. It seems to me that the conception of a greater or lesser understanding of the nature of literature or poetry is objectively determinable. Truth has no history, says Passmore echoing Hegel, but adds, "The discussion of problems has a history."[13]

How can such a continuity be conceived? In my early years I hoped that it would be possible to arrive at an evolutionary history of literature and criticism. On the model of the Russian formalists, one could think of literary history largely as a wearing out, of "automatization" of conventions, followed by an "actualization" of new conventions using radically new devices or concepts. One could think in terms of convention and revolt. Novelty would be the one criterion of change. But I have come to recognize that this scheme is far too simple, that it does not answer the basic question of the direction of change, and that the scheme implies a time-concept that is refuted by modern psychology. Today we recognize a potential simultaneity in a man's mental development. It constitutes a structure that is virtual at any moment. There is an interpenetration of the causal order in experience and memory. A work of criticism is not simply a member of a series, a link in a chain. It may stand in relation to anything in the past. The critic may reach into the remotest history. An evolutionary history of criticism must fail. I have come to this resigned conclusion.

Nor can I accept the model proposed for the history of science in Thomas Kuhn's *Structure of Scientific Revolutions*. Kuhn argues that the canons of scientific theory and practice vary from period to period radically, that there are what he calls "paradigms," or "disciplinary matrices" due to single scientific geniuses such as Copernicus, Newton, Lavoisier, and Einstein. They provide modes, belief systems, texts that Kuhn calls "exemplars." These paradigms are incommensurable, as there is no accretion or accumulation of scientific knowledge except within a single paradigm. Even the words they use have different meanings. "How can they even hope to talk together, much less to be persuasive," says Kuhn.[14] It may be tempting to apply this scheme to the history of criticism. One could argue that there was a model provided by Aristotle and that this model was completely replaced by the romantic view, which presumably originated in Kant and Herder. In the twentieth century one could speak, at least in the English and American world, of a model provided by T. S. Eliot. It might be tempting to speak of completely irreconcilable points of view, to accept a pluralism of methods and thus to account for the present heightened difficulties of communication, for the Tower of Babel, the confusion of tongues.

An attempt has been made to apply Kuhn's scheme to the history of linguistics in a collective volume, *Studies in the History of Linguistics*, edited by the anthropologist Dell Hymes (1974). I was not convinced that linguistics has gone through such complete revolutions. There is a continuity in the history of linguistics, as even some papers in the book prove convincingly. Linguistics is a cumulative science in spite of shifts of emphasis and changing interests. I agree with Keith Percival's recent article in *Language* that accepting Kuhn's view would give rise to an "unhealthy situation": linguists would look upon "all theoretical disagreements as conflicts between rival paradigms, i.e., incommensurable viewpoints and use this as an excuse not to observe the ground rules of rational discussion."[15] The very same arguments hold true of criticism. There are no such complete revolutions in the history of criticism as Kuhn stipulates for the history of science. Nor are there periods completely dominated by one figure and one sacred text. While there are many different points of view, they can and must be discussed rationally. Criticism is an ongoing concern, with a future. I do not believe that things have been settled for good (as Hegel and Croce believed), nor can I believe that my views and those of my contemporaries will be replaced by completely different assumptions. There has been a continued clarification of problems throughout history, a growing core of agreement on many issues despite the ostensible conflicts. My own convictions, I hope, are never imposed or obtruded as a fixed, preconceived pattern.

In practice, I have been content with grouping my critics by countries. National traditions are still very strong, even though there are international currents such as psychoanalysis and Marxism in this century. Still, the gulf between English and American criticism and the developments on the Continent is wide (in spite of some crosscurrents in the last decades) while English and American criticism cannot be treated separately. Three Americans, Henry James, Ezra Pound, and T. S. Eliot, moved to England, and I. A. Richards, a Cambridge don, spent decades in the other Cambridge in Massachusetts. The grouping by critics follows from my conviction that individual initiative rather than collective trends matters in criticism. Critics must never be considered merely as "cases." Both portraiture of critics, intellectual profiles, and a sense of trends and changing conditions make a history. But the order cannot be dialectical or strictly evolutionary. The more I study the situation of a specific time, the more I eschew easy labels and generalities. I trust that in mapping out the field I can indicate its scope and breadth like a surveyor by triangulation. I do not have to measure every foot of the ground. Some ultimate decision will have to remain with the historian. Whether I always made the right choices is a matter I cannot judge myself. As any author, I have to wait for the verdict of readers and critics.

Prospect and Retrospect

A N old friend of mine who occasionally visits Yale wrote to me that he had the shock of his life in seeing books of mine exhibited in the Sterling Library. He thought I might have died—and with no obituary, on account of the newspaper strike. He was reassured when he looked closer. I myself want to think of my seventy-fifth birthday as a stimulus to finishing my big project, *A History of Modern Criticism*. Two more volumes are to come: the fifth, devoted entirely to English and American criticism in the first half of this century; the sixth and last, to the continent of Europe. The fifth is far advanced. Articles on individual critics scattered over several periodicals will be used in an updated and revised form: on A. C. Bradley, on Virginia Woolf, on Ezra Pound, on T. S. Eliot, on I. A. Richards, on F. R. Leavis, to list those devoted to English critics, and on Irving Babbitt, Paul Elmer More, Edmund Wilson, John Crowe Ransom, Cleanth Brooks, Kenneth Burke, R. P. Blackmur, and William K. Wimsatt, to which I shall add a speech reflecting and defending the methods of my *History* and a general essay entitled "The New Criticism: Pro and Contra" recently published in *Critical Inquiry*. An essay on Allen Tate written three years ago has been lying about with a German publisher of a two-volume collection of papers on all the main figures of English and American literary theory from Sir Philip Sidney to Northrop Frye.

The sixth volume is far less advanced, but I have written articles on Benedetto Croce, on the classical tradition in France, on Charles Dubos, on Albert Thibaudet, on Friedrich Gundolf and his erstwhile pupil Max Kommerell, on the three great Romance scholars who wrote in German—Ernst Robert Curtius, Leo Spitzer, and Erich Auerbach—on Emil Staiger, on the Russian for-

An address delivered on 28 September 1978 at the Sterling Memorial Library of Yale University.

malists, on modern Czech criticism, and on the so-called Prague School. Many gaps have to be filled. I have, for instance, nothing written yet on Spanish criticism. Thus my study and writing are planned for several years ahead. I also have other commitments and plans. For years I have promised to bring out a new revised edition of my first book, *Immanuel Kant in England*, which was published by the Princeton University Press in 1931 but was printed in Prague. It contains many misprints as it was set by printers ignorant of English. My own English was then still deficient and there are errors in the transcripts from manuscripts I had trouble in deciphering. Since then I have also turned up a fair amount of new information that I hope to incorporate. I am also less confident of the strongly Hegelian interpretation of Kant to which I was then committed. Most of the book I have retyped in a revised version, but I am still stymied by the chapter on Coleridge. The new edition of Coleridge from the Princeton University Press, both of the *Notebooks* and of the collected writings, is far from complete. I will not see its completion in my lifetime, I fear. Without the full text of the *Notebooks* and without access to the so-called *Magnum Opus*, still unprinted, a completely satisfactory account of Coleridge's relation to Kant cannot be given. I cannot be confident that I shall accomplish everything I plan. There is always the proviso: God willing.

When I look back on my work I see today how clearly it reflects the changes in literary scholarship and criticism which occurred during the fifty-four years of my writing life. When in 1922 I came to the Czech University in Prague to study Germanic philology, I was confronted with the type of philological and historical scholarship prevalent at the time, mainly inherited from the German tradition with its roots in romanticism, implying a glorification of the dim Teutonic and Slavic past and of the Middle Ages. The professor of Germanic philology, Josef Janko (1869–1947), lectured on Gothic vocalism in the first semester and on Gothic consonantism in the second. I came from a *gymnasium* where I had learned to parse and translate Latin and some Greek but had not the foggiest idea about phonetics. I could not distinguish a dental from a labial. The professor of German literature, Arnošt Kraus (1859–1943), gave a seminar on the *Minnesänger*, patiently going through every poet in the

Manesse Manuscript, giving the biography of every poet, the stanzaic form and the analogues of every poem. Reading the *Nibelungenlied* in Middle High German, he was much concerned with the exact route the company took down the Danube to their doom at Etzel's court. In another seminar Professor Kraus distributed letters he had collected from castles and archives in Bohemia, written by more or less well-known German and Austrian writers, and had us edit them. We had to transcribe them from the original, which he entrusted to us freely, ascertain the addressee, the date, explain allusions, and so on. I got a fine letter of Christoph Martin Wieland, the eighteenth-century rococo poet, and one by August von Platen, the early nineteenth-century classicist. It was a good exercise: it let you loose in the library.

For a time I also attended the seminar of Professor August Sauer, then the great light of the German University. I remember having to write a report on a proclamation supposedly written by Napoleon from Elba, which had been concocted by the German pamphleteer and romantic Josef Görres, and being commended that my paper was so thorough and exhaustive that "no grass can grow after Wellek." It was an ambiguous compliment, and even then my attitude toward this kind of scholarship was ambiguous, as it has remained all my life.

I found rather what I wanted in a younger professor of German literature, Otokar Fischer (1883–1938), who had written books on Heinrich von Kleist and Nietzsche. He was a brilliant lecturer, mainly concerned with the psychology of his favorite figures in German literature; his book on Heine, unfortunately buried in the Czech language, grew out of a seminar I attended. In 1908 he had been one of the first (or possibly the very first) literary scholars who had used psychoanalysis for the interpretation of a literary work: the dreams in Gottfried Keller's novel *Der grüne Heinrich*.

In 1924 Fischer founded the new review *Kritika* together with F. X. Šalda (1867–1937), and there I published my very first article, severely criticizing the Czech translation of *Romeo and Juliet*: a bold move for a young man, as the translator, J. V. Sládek, was a revered poet and his translations from Shakespeare considered masterpieces. Šalda had been the dominant figure in Czech literary criticism since the 1890s; he had fought the battles for symbolism and all forms of modernism and had preserved the allegiance of even the youngest avant-garde poets by his sympathy for everything new and revolutionary. During World War I he had been appointed professor of western literatures at the university (though a free-lance journalist), and he still lectured on French literature, reluctantly, casually, even grumpily, obviously considering his duties at the university distractions from his writing. Though I admired his early writings I was disappointed by his performance in the lecture room and soon gave up visiting him in his apartment as he was surrounded by a coterie of young men and pontificated in an overbearing manner I found repellent.

Then there was Václav Tille (1867–1937), professor of comparative literature, a subject then flourishing in the Slavic countries which was conceived largely as comparative folklore, thematology, *Stoffgeschichte*. Tille had written successful fairy tales himself and considered all oral literature to be descended from upper-class literature. He had an amazing memory for themes and plots and was also a dreaded theater critic who would retell the story of a play to make it sound utterly ridiculous and absurd. He was a witty man, basically nihilistic in his views of scholarship and criticism. Still, I sympathized with his elaborate refutation of the determinism of Hippolyte Taine and his general skepticism about causal explanation in literary studies.

Finally there was Vilém Mathesius (1882–1945), the professor of English who later became the founder and president of the Prague Linguistic Circle. He had been an early proponent of descriptive linguistics, of which I knew nothing at that time. But I knew his solid handbooks on Anglo-Saxon and Middle English literature and attended his lectures and seminars, in which he expounded the history of older English literature soberly, descriptively. His literary taste was determined by his admiration for Shaw and H. G. Wells; the tradition of the realistic English novel coincided with his general empirical outlook; he was concerned with the cultural and ethical values of the British Protestant tradition he thought would be good for his nation.

When I look back on these teachers of mine I consider myself lucky to have come to the University of Prague in a time of its flowering, when the old scholarship was changing under the impact of new tastes and the new criticism. The University of Prague, situated in the capital, allowed the collaboration of scholarship and criticism which I still feel to be the ideal solution. But I must confess that I withheld full allegiance from every one of my teachers. I was quite willing to do historical and philological research but felt its limitations strongly. I admired Otokar Fischer immensely but drew back from his psychological and psychoanalytical concerns. I could not become a follower of F. X. Šalda as I did not share his, what seemed to me uncritical, search for novelty. I was quite uninterested in Tille's concern for oral literature. I could not share the view of English literature propounded or implied by Mathesius. I cared then only for Shakespeare, the romantic and Victorian poets, and, after my first visit to England in 1924, for Donne and the metaphysicals. In St. Paul's Cathedral I saw the tomb of John Donne wrapped in his shroud and picked up an anthology of seventeenth-century English poetry compiled by J. H. Massingham which impressed me deeply. I was prepared by what was then the newly revived interest in German and Czech baroque poetry.

I had made one attempt to break away from Prague. In 1923 I had visited Heidelberg, heard a lecture of Friedrich Gundolf, and called on him. I had read *Shakespeare und der deutsche Geist* and his book on Goethe and thought that here literary scholarship was freed from pedantry and allowed bold judgments and generalizations. I shared the new enthusiasm for Hölderlin, on whom Gundolf had written perceptively. But in Heidelberg I was repelled by the atmosphere of awestruck adoration surrounding him; I realized that the unspoken demand for total allegiance and even abject subservience to the ethos and views of the George circle was foreign to my nature. I returned to Prague and shifted from German literature to English. I became the assistant to Mathesius and wrote a thesis under his direction entitled "Carlyle and Romanticism," which mainly concerned Carlyle's German contacts, a topic chosen defiantly to run counter to Mathesius's own predilections. I received a D. Phil. in June 1926 and then spent several months in England preparing a monograph on my new project, Andrew Marvell, whom I wanted to interpret in relation to baroque French and Latin poetry. At that time there was little written on Marvell aside from the splendid essay by T. S. Eliot and a thin biography by Augustin Birrell. It was a great blow when I found out, at Oxford, that a new critical edition was coming out and that a large book, in French, by Pierre Legouis was in preparation.

I had to postpone my plan—indefinitely, as it turned out. I thus welcomed a fellowship to the United States, to Princeton University. I set foot on the soil of this country for the first time in September 1927. At Princeton I attended four seminars as if I were a graduate student (though I held a postdoctoral fellowship). For the first time in my life I had instruction in English literary history, had to write regular papers and do prescribed reading. I was suddenly thrown back into the type of scholarship I wanted to break away from in Prague. At Princeton at that time there was no instruction in modern literature or American literature. I was severely discouraged from taking work with G. M. Harper, the biographer of Wordsworth. Of the five teachers I had, Thomas Marc Parrott taught a seminar on *Hamlet* where we did nothing but make a line-by-line comparison of the two quartos with the folio. Charles Grosvenor Osgood taught a seminar on Spenser which was mainly concerned with sources and background. My first assignment was "Spenser's Irish Rivers," which required looking into old maps of Ireland. Robert Kilburn Root had us read Alexander Pope, and, with his ironic and sarcastic wit, managed to convey something of his ethos, and J. E. Brown, a younger man who died very early, expounded the ideas of Dr. Johnson with sympathy. A fellow student praised a fourth seminar so I added it to the usual load of three. Morris W. Croll propagated Croce's aesthetics and interpreted English lyrical poetry. He was then writing a paper on English baroque prose. A reprint says that I persuaded him to call it baroque (he had called it "Attic" before). But Croll had read Wölfflin and did not need me to know about baroque. From Root and Brown I learned something about eighteenth-century criticism. From reading around I imbibed something of the critical atmosphere of the time. I read H. L. Mencken and the early Van Wyck Brooks criticizing the American business civilization. I read the American New Humanists, then much in the limelight. Later I met Paul Elmer More, who lived in Princeton; he lent me copies of the Cambridge Platonists. I heard Irving Babbitt lecture at Harvard before I returned to Czechoslovakia in June 1930. At Princeton I was impressed by eighteenth-century neoclassicism and the new anti-romantic polemics of the New Humanists, but again I cannot say that I was converted. I realize now that I was lucky, in returning, to escape the depression years, and I thus remained unaffected by the prevailing Marxism of that time. I had read some Marxist criticism in Prague but remained indifferent, possibly because in Czechoslovakia it was identified with the Communist party, rightly considered a tool of Stalin.

When I returned to Prague I had the manuscript of my book *Immanuel Kant in England* more or less in shape. In my two and a half years at Princeton, at Smith, and then again at Princeton, I had developed an increasing interest in philosophy: mainly the standard British authors and the Germans—Kant, Fichte, Schelling, and Hegel. In Prague in my student years I had avoided the professors of philosophy, who seemed to me uninteresting expounders of positivism. As an instructor in Princeton (1929–30), I attended a seminar on Hegel's *Logic* taught by a young Dutchman, Veltman, and Professor Ledger Wood. My thesis on Carlyle had led me to Coleridge, and Coleridge led to Kant and Schelling. In the Widener Library in the summer of 1928, I discovered many totally neglected books, articles, and references to Kant in the 1790s and the early decades of the nineteenth century. Stopping over in London on my way back to Prague I read the manuscript of Coleridge's *Logic* in the British Museum and discovered, to my dismay, that it was nothing but a compilation of passages from the *Critique of Pure Reason*, interspersed with passages from Moses Mendelssohn and pious reflections by Coleridge himself. My chapter on Coleridge made me the exponent of a view of Coleridge's borrowings and his position in a history of philosophy which was and perhaps is still resented.

Back in Prague I submitted *Immanuel Kant in England* as a second thesis (*Habilitation*), which was necessary to be admitted as docent to lecture at the University on English literature. My topic was completely alien to Mathesius, but it testifies to his open-mindedness that he accepted it, though he required me in addition to write a paper on a medieval topic. It was then that I composed a little treatise on *The Pearl* (1933), my only excursion into medieval studies, which confronted me with problems of symbolism, of theological and autobiographical interpretation that I dismissed or solved in a way that, I am told, is still convincing.

When I arrived in Prague after my absence, I learned that the Linguistic Circle had been founded. I joined it immediately and took part in its sessions. I attended a conference on phonology in December 1930 with Roman Jakobson, Jan Mukařovský, and the other members of that splendid group. As the new docent I had to give an inaugural lecture: it was on "Empiricism and Idealism in English Literature," strongly siding with the idealist and Platonic tradition in English poetry. In the Prague years I came more and more under the influence of my older colleagues at the circle and of their models, the Russian formalists. But again I withheld full allegiance. In a review of the Czech translation of Shklovsky's *Theory of Prose* in 1934 I voiced many misgivings about the extremes of his mechanistic formalism, and in a paper on Jakobson's and Mukařovský's history of Czech versification I questioned their views of literary evolution. I argued for modifications of their formalism in the direction of a judgmental criticism and an interest in philosophical implications. I had read Roman Ingarden's *Das literarische Kunstwerk* (1931) and had met Ingarden at the International Congress of Philosophy in Prague in 1934.

In 1935 I was again uprooted. As prospects for a professorship at Prague were distant, I accepted an offer to become lecturer in Czech language and literature at the School of Slavonic Studies of London University, a lectureship paid for by the Czechoslovak Ministry of Education. Still, I kept my foothold at the University of Prague as the presumptive successor to Mathesius. In London I formulated my theoretical conceptions in a paper entitled "The Theory of Literary History," published in English in the sixth volume of *Travaux du Cercle Linguistique de Prague* in 1936. I mention this because the paper was reproduced with little change in the volume *Literary Scholarship*, edited by Norman Foerster, in 1941, and again as the last chapter of

Theory of Literature. I had held these views and formulated them before I returned to the United States and before I knew anything about the American New Criticism.

In England I soon learned something about I. A. Richards, whose behavioristic psychology could not appeal to me, coming as I did from the Prague school and the phenomenology of Ingarden, a student of Husserl. In Cambridge in the summer of 1936, I met F. R. Leavis and some of his friends, Lionel Knights and Henri Fluchère. I sympathized with Leavis's anti-academic attitude and soon began to contribute to *Scrutiny*. I wrote also a long critical account of I. A. Richards, William Empson, and F. R. Leavis for the Czech periodical of the Prague circle (*Slovo a slovesnost*). In a long letter I tried, incautiously, to persuade Leavis that in his newly published book *Revaluation* he had misinterpreted the philosophy of Blake, Wordsworth, and Shelley. He printed the letter in *Scrutiny* and wrote an answer, "Philosophy and Criticism" (1937), in which he took me to task as a philosopher who did not understand that criticism is not concerned with abstract ideas but with concrete sensitive readings. This piece has pursued me all my life: it is reprinted, without my original letter, in Leavis's *Common Pursuit* and is widely quoted. I became a straw man to knock down, though actually I agree with Leavis's general distinction between philosophy and criticism, even though I continue to object to the anti-theoretical bias of much English criticism and of Leavis's in particular.

In addition to my duties as lecturer in Czech, which induced me to study the Czech national revival, English travelers in Bohemia, and the influence of Byron on the Czech romantic poet K. H. Mácha, I pursued a scheme that had emerged naturally from my preoccupation with the theory of literary history. I worked for several years in the British Museum on a history of literary historiography in England. When, after the invasion of Prague by Hitler on 15 March 1939, I had to give up any thought of returning to Prague, I decided to immigrate to the United States. I secured a position in the English department of the University of Iowa through the good offices of Professor Thomas Marc Parrott. I took with me the manuscript of a book, *The Rise of English Literary History*, eventually published in 1941.

Before going out to Iowa I spent six weeks in the Sterling Library at Yale in the summer of 1939 trying to finish my book. Here I met the late James Marshall Osborn and through him Maynard Mack and Louis L. Martz.

I knew only one person at Iowa and nothing of the university. I even had to look up its exact location on a map in the British Museum. But I was grateful to get a foothold in this country, which was the only one that offered a refuge from the approaching war. At Iowa I was immediately plunged into the conflict between historical scholarship and criticism. As I was appointed by Norman Foerster, the director of the School of Letters, a staunch New Humanist, I was lined up on the side of criticism against historical scholarship. I still remember an encounter with one of the literary historians, who reacted furiously to a suggestion that he had also written some criticism. "This is the worst insult anybody ever paid me," he said, flushing deeply. Foerster that very year had brought Austin Warren from Boston University. With a few younger men we made up the "critical faction," and we composed a collective volume, *Literary Scholarship: Its Aims and Methods* (1941), to which Austin Warren contributed the chapter on criticism and I the chapter on literary history. The forties brought about the establishment of criticism as an academic subject in American universities. The textbook *Understanding Poetry* by Cleanth Brooks and Robert Penn Warren (1938) was the main pedagogical breakthrough. R. P. Warren taught twice at Iowa as a visiting professor. At the newly founded English Institute, meeting at Columbia University, I met Cleanth Brooks, Allen Tate, and W. K. Wimsatt in 1940 and 1941. I was deeply impressed by the New Criticism, but again I remained an outsider who had come with different preconceptions. Austin Warren and I felt that we had sailed under false colors when we contributed to a book edited by Norman Foerster. We formed the project of writing a book, *Theory of Literature*, which would combine the new critical outlook of Austin Warren with my knowledge of continental developments. *Theory of Literature* came out after many delays partly due to my involvement with war work (I taught an Army Area and Language Program in Czech) and to Mrs. Warren's illness and death. The date of publication, January 1949, is deceptive: most of the book was written in the years 1945–47 and much dated back to earlier printed work. I mentioned the Prague article "The Theory of Literary History"; the chapter on "The Mode of Existence of a Literary Work of Art" reprinted an article published in the last number of the old *Southern Review* in 1942. The book was not thought of as a textbook, but it made its way in the American graduate schools, and in other countries, to judge from the translations into twenty-two languages. The newest is into Russian, of which I have not yet seen a copy.

At Iowa, as a European with a knowledge of languages, I taught a course in the European novel, and I gave a seminar in German-English literary and intellectual relations. I had long been convinced that no single literature can be studied without going constantly beyond its confines. I embraced the cause of comparative literature as a worthy subject alongside the old national literatures. An ideal of a super-national study of literature seemed to me called for also by the bright hopes of the aftermath of the war.

When I was called to Yale in 1946 as professor of Slavic and comparative literature, I came in something of a missionary spirit. Yale had no chair, no program, and no department, and had never had one. At Harvard and Columbia old departments lay dormant. At Harvard, Harry Levin, in the very same year, was entrusted with resuscitating the subject and brought an Italian Slavicist, Renato Poggioli, to revitalize the program. A quarterly, *Comparative Literature*, began publication in 1949. The first number contains my essay "The Concept of Romanticism in Literary History," in which I tried to refute A. O. Lovejoy's famous argument against its very existence.

At first the Yale program was very small; I was the only person on a full-time appointment. Much later Lowry Nelson, Jr., one of the first Ph.D.'s of the program, was brought in, and joint appointments with other departments were arranged. The program became an independent, full-fledged department as late as 1960. It has flowered also since my retirement in 1972 and has produced a splendid array of students. I myself directed some fifty dissertations. I trust that the company who have come from the department have, whatever the variety of convictions they hold and interests they pursue, at least two things in common: devotion to scholarship and complete freedom to follow their own bent.

After *Theory of Literature* I devoted what energy I had after teaching and administration to writing a large-scale international *History of Modern Criticism*. It seemed inevitable to look for support, justification, and possibly rectification of the theory of literature in history. Theory emerges from history just as history itself can only be understood with questions and answers in mind. History and theory explain and implicate each other. There is a profound unity of fact and idea, past and present.

The volumes that have accompanied the *History, Concepts of Criticism* (1963), *Confrontations* (1965), *Discriminations* (1970), and the new scattered articles that I hope to collect under the title of a key essay, "The Attack on Literature," are conceived in the same spirit and try to come to terms with new developments in America and Europe.

Looking back on my work I am struck with my detachment from all the phases I went through: historical scholarship, symbolist criticism in the wake of Šalda or Gundolf, the American New Humanism, the Prague School shaped by Russian formalism, the Leavis group, the American New Criticism. I may be a Laodicean, but I hope that I have preserved my own integrity and a core of convictions: that the aesthetic experience differs from other experiences and sets off the realm of art, of fictionality, of *Schein*, from life; that the literary work of art, while a linguistic construct, at the same time refers to the world outside; that it cannot therefore be described only by linguistic means but has a meaning telling of man, society, and nature; that all arguments for relativism meet a final barrier; that we are confronted, as students of literature, with an object, the work of art, out there (whatever may be its ultimate ontological status) which challenges us to understand and interpret it; that there is thus no complete liberty of interpretation. Analysis, interpretation, evaluation are interconnected stages of a single procedure. Evaluation grows out of understanding. We as critics learn to distinguish between art and nonart and should have the courage of our convictions. The lawyer knows or thinks he knows what is right and what is wrong; the scientist knows what is true and what is false; the physician knows what is health and what is disease; only the poor humanist is floundering, uncertain of himself and his calling instead of proudly asserting the life of the mind which is the life of reason.

Notes

The Attack on Literature

1. Jacques Ehrmann, "The Death of Literature," *New Literary History* 3 (1971): 43. Also in *Textes suivi de la Mort de la littérature* (Paris, 1971).

2. *New York Times*, 27 October 1968, quoted in Ihab Hassan, *The Dismemberment of Orpheus* (New York, 1971), p. 253.

3. *Essais critiques* (Paris, 1964), p. 254.

4. Quoted by Heinrich Vormweg in "Eine andere Lesart," *Merkur* 25 (1971): 1046. "Das Alphabet kommt von der Obrigkeit."

5. "The Humanist Tradition in Eighteenth Century England," *New Literary History* 3 (1971): 167.

6. "Notes Toward a Radical Culture," *The New Left*, ed. Priscilla Long (Boston, 1969), pp. 422, 424, 426, 431.

7. "The Trouble with Literature," *Change in Higher Education* 2 (1970): 28–30.

8. As in note 6.

9. As in note 6.

10. *Complete Works*, ed. P. P. Howe (London, 1930), 5:347–48.

11. *A Treatise Concerning the Principles of Human Knowledge* (1710) in *Works*, ed. A. C. Fraser (London, 1875), 1:154.

12. *Beiträge zu einer Kritik der Sprache*, 3rd ed., 3 vols. (Leipzig, 1923).

13. *Language, Thought and Reality* (Cambridge, Mass., 1956).

14. *Prosa II*, ed. Herbert Steiner (Frankfurt, 1959), p. 17, "mit dem Herzen zu denken."

15. *Poets of Reality* (Cambridge, Mass., 1965), pp. 38, 36.

16. *Essais critiques*, p. 265.

17. *Les Mots et les Choses* (Paris, 1966), pp. 220, 253.

18. *Styles of Radical Will* (New York, 1969), p. 17.

19. *Textes pour rien* (Paris, 1955). Quoted from George Steiner, *Extraterritorial* (New York, 1971), p. 15.

20. *Le Livre à Venir* (Paris, 1959), pp. 265–67.

21. *Raise High the Roof Beam, Carpenters* (Boston, Mass., 1963), p. 86.

22. *Understanding Media* (New York, 1964), p. 313.

23. "Bücher: Aspekte einer Strukturkrise," *Merkur* 25 (1971): 1087.

24. Ed. Hans Robert Jauss (Munich, 1968).

25. In *Liberations*, ed. Ihab Hassan (Middletown, Conn., 1971), pp. 162, 175.

26. "Art without Artists," *Liberations*, pp. 70ff.

27. *The Presence of the Word* (New Haven, 1967), p. 20.

28. Barthes, *Essais critiques*, p. 125: "Depuis que la 'Littérature' existe (c'est-à-dire, si l'on en juge d'après la date du mot, depuis fort peu de temps), on peut dire c'est la fonction de l'écrivain que de la combattre." Blanchot, *Le Livre à Venir*, p. 242. "Littérature—mot tardif, mot sans honneur."

29. *Institutiones*, bk. 2, chap. 1, sec. 4.

30. Cicero, *Orationes Phillipicae*, 45. De C. Caesare.

31. Eduard Wölfflin, "Litteratur," *Zeitschrift für lateinische Lexikographie und Grammatik* 5 (1885): 49ff. Tertullian, *De Spectaculis* XVII, 6, opposes Christian revelation to pagan civilization, e.g., dramatic performances.

32. Cicero, *Pro Archia Poeta*, 9; Aulus Gellius, *Noctes Atticae*, XIII, 17. Cf. I. Heinemann, "Humanitas," in Pauly-Wissowa, *Reallexikon der classischen Altertumswissenschaft*, supplement 5 (Stuttgart, 1931), pp. 282–310, and Werner Jäger, *Humanistische Reden und Vorträge* (Berlin, 1960), p. 307.

33. *Dictionnaire philosophique*, in *Œuvres*, ed. L. Moland (Paris, 1877–83), 19:590–92.

34. *Eléments de littérature*, 1787 (Paris, 1856, reprint), 2:335.

35. *Life of Samuel Johnson*, ed. G. B. Hill, reviewed by L. F. Powell, (Oxford, 1934), Vol. 1:302.

36. *Experiments in Education* (Ithaca, New York, 1942), p. 75.

37. Quoted from Claude Crispin, *Aux Origines de l'historie littérraire* (Grenoble, 1974), p. 40.

38. Ed. by René Groos, 2 vols. (Paris, 1947), 2:145.

39. *Critical Reflexions on the Old English Dramatick Writers* . . . (London, 1761).

40. Letter to the Rev. Dr. Horne, 30 April 1774, in *Catalogue of the Johnsonian Collection of R. B. Adams* (Buffalo, 1921).

41. Paris, 1743, p. 189.

42. Turin, 1760, p. 6; Paris, 1776; Glasgow, 1771, 1784.

43. Compare Robert Escarpit, "La Définition du terme 'Littérature,' " in *Actes du IIIe Congrès de l'Association Internationale de Littérature Comparée* (The Hague, 1962), pp. 77–89.

Literature, Fiction, and Literariness

1. *The Phenomenon of Literature* (The Hague, 1975), p. 142.

2. "A Program for the Definition of Literature," in *Style in Language*, ed. Thomas A. Sebeok (Cambridge, Mass., 1960), p. 94.

3. "Literature and Its Cognates," in *Dictionary of the History of Ideas*, ed. Philip P. Wiener (New York, 1973), 3:81–89; "What Is Literature?" in *What Is Literature?* ed. Paul Hernadi (Bloomington, 1978), pp. 16–23.

4. See, e.g., Wolfgang Leppmann, *The German Image of Goethe* (Oxford, 1961); Augustus Ralli, *A History of Shakespearean Criticism*, 2 vols. (Oxford, 1932), is a mere compilation, often second hand; Friedrich Gundolf, *Shakespeare und der deutsche Geist* (Berlin, 1911), is the finest book of its kind though limited to the reception of Shakespeare in Germany.

5. *Premières Lundis* (Paris, 1885), 2:299–300.

6. "What Isn't Literature?" in *What Is Literature?* ed. Paul Hernadi (Bloomington, 1978), p. 34.

7. Louis Maigron, *Le Romantisme et les mœurs* (Paris, 1910), collects instances from Paris police records. On Werther, see Klaus Rüdiger Scherpe, *Werther und Wertherwirkung* (Bad Homburg, 1970).

8. *The Dunciad*, ed. James Sutherland, vol. 5 of *The Poems of Alexander Pope* (London, 1943).

9. See Marina Warner, *Joan of Arc: The Image of Female Heroism* (New York,

1981). *Die heilige Johanna: Schiller, Shaw, Brecht, Claudel, Mell, Anouilh*, ed. Joachim Schöndorff (Munich, 1964), contains introduction by Peter Demetz.

10. R. F. Christian, *Tolstoy's "War and Peace": A Study* (Oxford, 1962), esp. p. 82. B. Eichenbaum, in *Lev Tolstoy: kniga vtoraya, 60–e gody* (Moscow and Leningrad, 1931), p. 229 and 414, found the source of the scene with the Tsar on the balcony in the *Reminiscences of an Eyewitness* (1862) by A. Ryázaitsev. The Tsar distributed fruit, not cookies.

11. *Cousine Bette*, chapter 38.

12. Gottlob Frege, *Schriften zur Logik und Sprachphilosophie*, ed. G. Gabriel (Hamburg, 1971); Roman Ingarden, *Das literarische Kunstwerk* (Halle, 1931; English translation, Evanston, Ill., 1973); Monroe Beardsley, *Aesthetics: Problems in the Philosophy of Criticism* (New York, 1958); J. R. Searle, *Speech Acts: An Essay in the Philosophy of Language* (Cambridge, 1969); Gottfried Gabriel, *Fiktion und Wahrheit* (Stuttgart-Bad Cannstatt, 1975); Käte Hamburger, *Wahrheit und aesthetische Wahrheit* (Stuttgart, 1979).

13. *Rage for Order* (Chicago, 1948), p. 50.

14. Benedetto Croce, "Estetica del settecento" in *Ultimi Saggi*, 2nd edition (Bari, 1948), p. 109.

15. Elisabeth Plessen, *Fakten und Erfindungen: Zeitgenössische Epik im Grenzgebiet von fiction und nonfiction* (Munich, 1971), makes great claims for this new hybrid form.

16. "An Apology for Poetry" in *Elizabethan Critical Essays*, ed. G. Gregory Smith (Oxford, 1904), 1:182.

17. "Genre Theory, the Lyric, and 'Erlebnis,'" in *Festschrift für Richard Alewyn*, ed. Herbert Singer and Benno von Wiese (Cologne, 1967), pp. 392–412, reprinted in René Wellek, *Discriminations* (New Haven, 1970), pp. 225–52.

18. Roman Jakobson has argued against the metaphoricalness of all poetry establishing metonymy as the alternative. See "The Metaphoric and Metonymic Poles" in *Fundamentals of Language* (The Hague, 1956). Jakobson cites Pushkin's poem "Ja vas lyubil." One might add Wordsworth's "We are seven" and Robert Bridges's "I love all beauteous things, I seek and adore them."

19. I. A. Richards, *Principles of Literary Criticism* (London, 1924); Thomas C. Pollock, *The Nature of Literature* (Princeton, 1942).

20. In *Qu'est-ce que le structuralisme?* eds. Oswald Ducrot, Tzvetan Todorov, Dan Sperber, Moustafa Safouan, François Wahl (Paris, 1968), p. 108. "La litteralité c'est la capacité pour le signe d'être saisi en lui-même, et non comme renvoi à autre chose."

21. See Fredric Jameson, *The Prison-House of Language* (Princeton, 1972). The title is based on a loose translation of a passage in Nietzsche's *Werke*, ed. Karl Schlechta (Munich 1956), 3:362. Nietzsche speaks only of "sprachlicher Zwang" (the constraint of language). Mr. Jameson does not, of course, approve of the "prison-house."

22. Guy Sircello, *A New Theory of Beauty* (Princeton, 1975), p. 43.

23. *Noten zur Literatur II* (Frankfurt, 1961), p. 164, and *Aesthetische Theorie* (Frankfurt, 1970).

Poetics, Interpretation, and Criticism

1. (Harmondsworth, Middlesex, 1962), pp. 10–11.

2. 3 vols. (Edinburgh, 1762), 2:369, 371, 373. The last sentence is changed in later editions to "in the emotions and feelings of different races of men" (9th ed., 2 vols. [Edinburgh, 1817], 2:450).

3. 2nd ed., 3 vols. (London, 1785), 3:203.

4. A review dating from 1774 of Sulzer's *Allgemeine Theorie der schönen Künste*, in *Sämmtliche Werke*, ed. B. Suphan, 33 vols. (Berlin, 1877–1913), 5:280.

5. "On Poesy or Art" (1818), in *Biographia Literaria*, ed. J. Shawcross, 2 vols. (Oxford, 1907), 2:253.

6. *Shakespearean Criticism*, ed. T. M. Raysor, 2 vols. (London, 1930), 1:224; cf. *Vorlesungen über dramatische Kunst und Literatur*, 3 vols. (Heidelberg, 1817), 3:8.

7. *Poetics* (London, 1852), p. 91.

8. *Practical Criticism* (London, 1929), pp. 248, 349.

9. (Princeton, 1957), pp. 122, 124.

10. *Théorie de la littérature: Textes des formalistes russes* (Paris, 1965).

11. "Présentation," *Poétique* 1 (1970).

12. *Littérature et signification* (Paris, 1967), see p. 9.

13. *Essais critiques* (Paris, 1964), "Écrivains et écrivants" (p. 149), and "La Littérature aujourd'hui" (p. 164).

14. *Qu'est-ce que le structuralisme?* (Paris, 1968), pp. 163–64.

15. See "Stylistics, Poetics, and Criticism," in *Discriminations* (New Haven, 1970), p. 126.

16. Quoted from Fredric Jameson. *The Prison-House of Language* (Princeton, 1973), p. 126.

17. See Richard E. Palmer, *Hermeneutics* (Evanston, Ill., 1969), p. 34, and Wilhelm Dilthey, "Die Entstehung der Hermeneutik" (1900), in *Gesammelte Schriften*, 12 vols. (Leipzig, 1924), 5:317–31.

18. "Das Verstehen (eine Problemgeschichte als Begriffsgeschichte)," *Archiv für Begriffsgeschichte* 1 (1955): 142–99.

19. See H. G. Gadamer, *Wahrheit und Methode*, 2nd ed. (Tübingen, 1965), p. 1 n.

20. (Zürich, 1955), p. 13.

21. "Die Kunst in der Fremde der Gegenwart," in *Geist und Zeitgeist* (Zürich, 1964), pp. 31–59.

22. *La Conscience critique* (Paris, 1971), pp. 299, 311.

23. Letter, in French, dated 6 October 1956.

24. "A propos de la *Vie de Marianne*," in *Romanische Literaturstudien* (Tübingen, 1959), pp. 248–76.

25. *La Distance intérieure* (Paris, 1952), p. 32.

26. *La Conscience critique*, pp. 77, 80; cf. *Journal* (Paris, 1946), 1:65, 399.

27. See Wellek, "Poulet, Du Bos, and Identification," *Comparative Literature Studies* 10 (1973): 173–93.

28. (London, 1930), pp. 2, 12, 17.

29. *Theory of Literature* (New York, 1949), p. 217.

30. *The Wheel of Fire* (London, 1930), p. xix.

31. "The Function of Criticism," *Selected Essays* (London, 1934), p. 32.

32. "Allegory," in *Encyclopedia of Poetry and Poetics*, ed. A. Preminger (Princeton, 1965), p. 12.

33. See "Symbolism in Medieval Literature," *Modern Philology* 56 (1958): 73–81.

34. "Understanding Milton," in *Essays on English and American Literature* (Princeton, 1962), p. 116; "Les Études de style et les différents pays," in *Langue et littérature: Actes du VIIIe Congrès de la Fédération Internationale des Langues et Littératures Modernes* (Paris, 1961), p. 23.

35. (New York, 1967), p. 23.

36. 28 September 1967. Also in *Introduction to Structuralism*, ed. Michael Lane (New York, 1970), pp. 410–16.

37. Reprinted in *The Importance of Scrutiny*, ed. Eric Bentley (New York, 1948), pp. 34, 31; there with my original letter. Also in F. R. Leavis, *The Common Pursuit* (London, 1952), pp. 215, 212.

38. *The Literary Critics* (Harmondsworth, Middlesex, 1962), pp. 11, 13ff.

39. *Anatomy of Criticism*, p. 9.

40. *Figures III* (Paris, 1972), pp. 68–69.

41. "The Concrete Universal," in *The Verbal Icon* (Lexington, Kentucky, 1954), pp. 69–83; Royce, *The Spirit of Modern Philosophy* (Boston, 1892), esp. pp. 222–27, 492–506.

42. *The Verbal Icon: Studies in the Meaning of Poetry* (Lexington, Ky., 1967), pp. 250–51.

43. *Practical Criticism: A Study of Literary Judgment* (New York, 1956), pp. 11.

Criticism as Evaluation

1. (Princeton, 1957), p. 25.

2. *Forme et signification* (Paris, 1962), p. xiv.

3. See E. D. Hirsch, Jr., "Literary Evaluation as Knowledge" in *Criticism: Speculative and Analytical Essays*, ed. L. S. Dembo (Madison, Wisconsin, 1968), pp. 46–57. Reprinted in E. D. Hirsch, Jr., *The Aims of Interpretation* (Chicago, 1976), pp. 95–109.

4. Letter to William Mason, 25 June 1782, in *Correspondence*, ed. W. S. Lewis (New Haven, 1955), 29:256.

5. See *A Short View of Tragedy* (1692) in *Critical Works*, ed. Curt A. Zimansky (New Haven, 1956), p. 164.

6. "Appel à toutes les nations de l'Europe" (1761) in *Œuvres*, ed. L. Moland (Paris, 1877–83), 24:193–203, and letter to D'Argental, 19 July 1776, ibid., 50:58. See René Wellek, *History of Modern Criticism* (New Haven, 1955), 1:33–37.

7. See Hans Robert Jauss, *Literaturgeschichte als Provokation* (Frankfurt, 1970).

8. (Ithaca, N.Y., 1941), new ed. 1947.

9. *Romanische Forschungen* 67 (1955): 287–97, reprinted in *Gesammelte Aufsätze zur romanischen Philologie* (Bern, 1967), pp. 354–63. Used without explicit reference to my work, in introduction to *Literatursprache und Publikum in der lateinischen Spätantike und im Mittelalter* (Bern, 1958). An English version, here quoted, in "Vico's Contribution to Literary Criticism" in *Studia philologica et litteraria in honorem L. Spitzer*, ed. A. G. Hatcher and K. L. Selig (Bern, 1958), pp. 31–37.

10. "The Esthetic Judgment," *Journal of Philosophy* 33 (1936):58.

11. Cf. Herbert Spiegelberg, *Antirelativismus* (Zürich, 1935).

12. In *Das literarische Kunstwerk* (Halle, 1931).

13. *New Shelburne Essays* (Princeton, 1928–36), 3:70, 78, 92.

14. "The Cleft Eliot," *Saturday Review*, November 12, 1932. Reprinted in *Design for Reading*, ed. H. S. Canby (New York, 1934), pp. 333–38.

15. "Modern Currents in American Literature," *New Shelburne Essays*, 1:53–76.

16. *In Defence of Reason* (Denver, 1947), p. 505.

17. *The Function of Criticism: Problems and Exercises*, (Denver, 1957), p. 17.

18. Ibid., pp. 159, 163. The title of the essay on Frost.

19. *The Use of Poetry and the Use of Criticism* (London, 1936), p. 96.

20. *D. H. Lawrence: Novelist* (New York, 1956), p. 120.

21. *Der Dichter als Führer in der deutschen Klassik*, 2nd ed. (Frankfurt, 1942), p. 470.

22. See review of Dámaso Alonso's *Poesía española* in *Romanische Forschungen* 64 (1952): 215.

23. See René Wellek, "New Czech Books on Literary History and Theory," *Slavic Review* 26 (1967): 295–301.

24. "Billets à Angèle" (1921) in *Œuvres complètes* (Paris, 1932 ff.), 2:39.

25. *Variété* (Paris, 1948), 1:70, or in *Œuvres*, Bibliothèque de la Pléiade, ed. Jean Hytier (Paris, 1957), 1:480.

26. In *Criterion* 4 (1926): 5.

27. *On Poets and Poetry* (New York, 1957), p. 147.

28. "What is a Classic?" (London, 1945), p. 31. Also in *On Poets and Poetry*, p. 60.

29. *Grundbegriffe der Poetik* (Zürich, 1946), p. 245. Comment on Horace in 5th ed. (Zürich, 1961), p. 246.

30. E.g., L. I. Timofeyev, *Teoriya literatury*, 3rd ed. (Moscow, 1948), p. 283.

31. See my review in *Kenyon Review* 16 (1954): 299–307.

32. In *Language and Silence* (New York, 1967), p. 149. "A Kind of Survivor."

33. Cf. *The Literature of Silence: Henry Miller and Samuel Beckett* (New York, 1967).

34. *Principles of Literary Criticism* (London, 1924), pp. 16, 110.

35. *Practical Criticism* (London, 1929), p. 204.

36. Roman Ingarden, "Das aesthetische Erlebnis" in *Erlebnis, Kunstwerk und Wert* (Tübingen, 1969), p. 6: "Die Konstituierung des strukturierten, selbstgenügsamen, qualitativen Ganzen bildet das letzte Ziel der schöpferischen Phasen des ästhetischen Erlebnisses."

37. *Prismen* (Munich, 1963), pp. 23–24. English translation *Prisms*, tr. Samuel and Shierry Weber, p. 32.

The Fall of Literary History

1. (Chapel Hill, 1941). New edition, with new Preface (New York, 1966).

2. "Literaturgeschichte als Provokation der Literaturwissenschaft," in *Literaturgeschichte als Provokation* (Frankfurt am Main, 1970), p. 144: "Literaturgeschichte ist in unserer Zeit mehr und mehr, aber keineswegs unverdient in Verruf gekommen. Die Geschichte dieser ehrwürdigen Disziplin beschreibt in den letzten 150 Jahren unverkennbar den Weg eines stetigen Niedergangs."

3. (London, 1969), p. 66.

4. In *The Cambridge Quarterly* 4 (1969–70): 400–402.

5. "The Scandal of Literary Scholarship," in *The Dissenting Academy*, ed. T. Roszak (New York, 1966), p. 43.

6. (Baltimore, 1931).

7. *Noveyshaya russkaya poeziya* (Prague, 1921), p. 11. My translation.

8. In *Časopis pro moderní filologii* 12 (1926): 78–81.

9. In *Western Review* 12 (1947): 52–54.

10. Baugh's "Literary History of England," in *Modern Philology* 47 (1949): 39–45. Robert E. Spiller, W. Thorp, T. H. Johnson, eds., "Literary History of the United States," in *Kenyon Review* 11 (1949): 500–506.

11. "Reflections on the Final Volume of *The Oxford History of English Literature*," in *Refractions: Essays in Comparative Literature* (New York, 1966), pp. 151–70.

12. "Philosophy of Art," in *Essays in Philosophical Criticism* (1883). Reprinted in *Collected Essays* (London, 1925), 2:231–68.

13. On Thomas Warton (1910), also in *Collected Essays*, 1:100.

14. *On Modern Literature*, eds. T. Spencer and J. Sutherland (Oxford, 1955), p. 265.

15. Quoted from G. Watson, *The Study of Literature* (London, 1969), p. 401.

16. *La Riforma della storia artistica e letteraria*, in *Nuovi Saggi di estetica* (Bari, 1926), pp. 157–80.

17. Dated 5 June 1952. "Si dirá che la critica cosí diventa una serie di monografiette o di saggi critici, che bisogna pure mettere in qualche ordine. E per far ciò non occorre il permesso di nessuno. Ciascuno può metterle in quell' ordine che più gli piace."

18. *Estetica*, 8th ed. (Bari, 1945), p. 57. "L'opera d'arte . . . è sempre *interna*; e quella che si chiama *esterna* non è più opera d'arte."

19. "Miss Emily and the Bibliographer," in *Reason in Madness: Critical Essays* (New York, 1941), pp. 107, 116.

20. *Education and the University* (London, 1943), p. 68.

21. (Zürich, 1939), pp. 13, 18.

22. See my *History of Modern Criticism* (New Haven, 1965), 4:27–57.

23. (New York, 1963), esp. pp. 16–23.

24. "For a Literary Historiography Based on Pareto's Sociology," in *The Spirit of the Letter* (Cambridge, Mass., 1965), pp. 291–322. First published in Italian in 1949.

25. *Teoria dell'arte d'avanguardia* (Bologna, 1962). English translation by G. Fitzgerald (Cambridge, Mass., 1968). See comments by R. Shattuck in *The New York Review of Books*, March 12, 1970, p. 43.

26. See my review in "Recent Czech Literary History and Criticism" (1962), in *Essays on Czech Literature* (The Hague, 1963), pp. 194–205.

27. See, e.g., *Skizze einer Geschichte der neueren deutschen Literatur* (Neuwied, 1965), pp. 12, 13. Written in 1952.

28. *The Hidden God*, English translation by P. Tody (New York, 1964), p. 96. "Matérialisme dialectique et histoire de la littérature," in *Recherches dialectiques* (Paris, 1959), p. 62. "Mais *l'analyse sociologique* n'épuise pas l'œuvre d'art et parfois n'arrive même pas à la toucher."

29. *Weltgeschichtliche Betrachtungen*, ed. Rudolf Marx (Leipzig, n.d.), p. 6. "Immerhin ist man dem Kentauren den höchsten Dank schuldig und begrüsst ihn gerne hier und da an einem Waldesrand der geschichtlichen Studien."

30. (Princeton, 1970), pp. 69–70.

31. (New Haven, 1962). Kubler is much concerned with artifacts from pre-Columbian America. He must rely on purely archeological and stylistic evidence unrelated or hardly related to any definable historical events.

32. First in *Journal of Philosophy* 39 (1942); reprinted in *Readings in Philosophical Analysis*, eds. H. Feigl and W. Sellars (New York, 1949), pp. 459–71.

33. A. C. Danto, *Analytical Philosophy of History* (Cambridge, 1968); W. Dray, *Laws and Explanation in History* (Oxford, 1957); W. B. Gallie, *Philosophy and Historical Understanding* (New York, 1968); P. Gardiner, *The Nature of Historical Explanation* (Oxford, 1952); W. H. Walsh, *Philosophy of History: An Introduction* (New York, 1960); M. White, *Foundations of Historical Knowledge* (New York, 1965).

34. *The Idea of History* (Oxford, 1946), p. 214. Written in 1936.

35. *Experience and Its Modes* (Cambridge, 1933), esp. p. 131.

36. Coleridge's account, first printed in 1816, differs from an earlier shorter version first printed by A. Snyder in the *Times Literary Supplement*, August 2, 1934, p. 541, which does not mention the interruption nor the "person from Porlock."

37. M. White, *Foundations of Historical Knowledge* (New York, 1965), pp. 200–201.

38. In *History and Theory* 6 (1967): 77.

39. *The Meaning of Human History* (La Salle, Ill., 1947), p. 102.

40. "Formermüdung" in *Zur Aesthetik der Architektur* (Stuttgart, 1887).

41. "Critical and Historical Principles of Literary History," in *The Idea of the Humanities and Other Essays Critical and Historical* (Chicago, 1967), 2:45–156. Quotations from p. 151.

42. In *Politiques et moralistes du dix-neuvième siècle*, 3ème série (Paris, 1900), pp. 237–314.

43. (New York, 1948), pp. 60, 63.

44. In *Polákova Vznešenost přírody* (Prague, 1934), p. 9; reprinted in *Kapitoly z české poetiky* (Prague, 1948), 2:100–101. My translation.

45. "Dějiny českého verše a metody literární historie," *Listy pro umění a kritiku* 2 (1934): 437–45; "The Theory of Literary History," *Travaux du Cercle Linguistique de Prague* 6 (1936): 173–91.

46. *Journal of the History of Ideas* 30 (1969): 127–33, and my answer, ibid. 30 (1969): 281–82.

47. *The Idea of the Humanities*, 2:174.

48. Jan Huizinga, "The Idea of History," in *The Varieties of History*, ed. F. Stern (New York, 1956), p. 293.

49. E. H. Carr in *What is History?* (Harmondsworth, Middlesex, 1964), pp. 123–24.

50. *The American Scholar* (Chapel Hill, 1929), p. 36.

51. Brooks's sketch in *Modern Poetry and the Tradition* (Chapel Hill, 1939), pp. 219–44.

52. In *For Roman Jakobson* (The Hague, 1956), pp. 653–61; reprinted in *Concepts of Criticism* (New Haven, 1963), pp. 37–53.

53. In *Daedalus* (Spring 1970): 355–83.

54. *The Burden of the Past and the English Poet* (Cambridge, Mass., 1970), p. 130.

55. Cf. "Literaturgeschichte als Provokation der Literaturwissenschaft," in *Literaturgeschichte als Provokation* (Frankfurt am Main, 1970), pp. 144–207.

56. In *The Disciplines of Criticism*, eds. P. Demetz, T. M. Greene, and Lowry Nelson, Jr. (New Haven, 1968), pp. 173–92.

57. Cf. W. B. Gallie, *Philosophy and Historical Understanding* (New York, 1968), pp. 153 ff.

58. *Die Welt als Wille und Vorstellung*, 3rd book, paragraph 36, in *Sämtliche Werke*, ed. A Hübscher (Leipzig, 1938), 2:218: "So ist dagegen die Kunst überall am Ziel."

Science, Pseudoscience, and Intuition in Recent Criticism

1. "The Study of Literature in Graduate School: Diagnosis and Prescription," *Sewanee Review* 55 (1947): 610–26.

2. See *In Search of Literary Theory* (Ithaca, 1972), pp. 73–90.

3. Quoted by Roman Ingarden in "The Physicalistic Theory of Language and the Work of Literature" in *Problems of Literary Evaluation*, ed. J. Strelka (University Park, Penn., 1969), p. 82.

4. *A Statistical Method of Determining Authorship: The Junius Letters 1769–1772* (Göteborg, 1969).

5. *A Quantitative Approach to the Style of Jonathan Swift* (The Hague, 1967).

6. *Eras and Modes in English Poetry* (Berkeley, 1964); *The Continuity of Poetic Language* (New York, 1965).

7. (New York, 1969).

8. Ed. Rul Gunzenhäuser and Helmut Kreuzer (Munich, 1965).

9. *Mathematik und Dichtung*, ed. Gunzenhäuser and Kreuzer (Munich, 1965), pp. 89–94, 191–92, 212, 230.

10. *Nach allen Regeln der Kunst* (Stuttgart, 1968), p. 126: "Eine fundamentale Schwierigkeit mit der Sprache besteht darin, dass, wenn immer man spricht, schreibt, liest, oder hört, gleichzeitig ganze Schwärme von Assoziationen und Emotionen das Lesen, Schreiben und Hören begleiten."

11. *Some Aspects of Text Grammars* (The Hague, 1972), pp. 291–92.

12. E.g., *Littérature et signification* (Paris, 1967); *Introduction à la littérature fantastique* (Paris, 1970); *Poétique de la prose* (Paris, 1971).

13. In *Figures III* (Paris, 1972), pp. 65–282.

14. See "Stylistics, Poetics, and Criticism" in *Discriminations* (New Haven, 1970), pp. 327–43.

15. *Über Literatur* (Olten, 1966), pp. 213–14: "[Das Subjekt] reduziert sich . . . zu einem Bündel Redegewohnheiten. . . . Das seiner selbst bewusste Ich erweist sich als fiktiv und löst sich auf in ein Feld von Bezugpunkten."

16. See *Critique et vérité* (Paris, 1966).

17. *The Critical Moment* (London, 1964), pp. 127–28. Also in *Essais critiques* (Paris, 1964), p. 256: ". . . non à *découvrir* l'œuvre interrogée, mais au contraire à la *couvrir* le plus complètement possible par son propre langage."

18. *Die Zeit als Einbildungskraft des Dichters* (Zurich, 1939).

19. *Geist und Buchstabe der Dichtung* (Frankfurt, 1940), Vorbemerkung: "Ein Zurückgehen auf das Einfachste, wenn auch nicht Leichteste . . . auf das unbefangene Befragen des Gegenstandes."

20. *Holzwege* (Frankfurt, 1950), p. 197: "Eine rechte Erläuterung versteht jedoch den Text nie besser als dessen Verfasser ihn verstand, wohl aber anders."

21. *Goethe* (Zürich, 1959), 3:474, 476, 478–79. Staiger draws on Gustav Becking, *Der musikalische Rhythmus als Erkenntnisquelle* (Augsburg, 1928).

22. *La Conscience critique* (Paris, 1971), p. 311: "Un même *J E* devait opérer chez l'auteur et chez le critique."

23. "Le Categorie rettoriche e il prof. Gröber" (1900) in *Problemi di Estetica*, 4th ed. (Bari, 1949), p. 155: "Quando io penetro l'intimo significato di un canto di Dante, *io sono Dante*."

24. "Alcune massime critiche e il loro intendimento" (1913) in *Nuovi Saggi di estetica*, 3rd ed. (Bari, 1948), p. 222.

25. *La Conscience critique*, p. 104: "Ce qui resemble le plus à un traité de dévotion du XVe ou du XVIIe siècle, c'est un essai critique écrit au XXe."

26. *Holzwege* (Frankfurt, 1950), p. 25, repeated p. 28.

27. *Méditations cartésiennes* (Paris, 1931), pp. 38–39.

28. "Zur Morphologie" (1822) in *Sämtliche Werke*, Jubiläums-Ausgabe, ed. E. von der Hellen (Stuttgart, 1901–3), 39:60: "Die Wissenschaft wird dadurch sehr zurückgehalten, dass man sich abgibt mit dem, was nicht wissenswert, und mit dem, was nicht wissbar ist."

The New Criticism: Pro and Contra

1. *Critics and Criticism*, ed. R. S. Crane (Chicago, 1952), p. 45.

2. In Thomas Daniel Young, *Gentleman in Dustcoat* (Baton Rouge, La., 1976), p. 152.

3. *Essays of Four Decades* (Chicago, 1968), p. 153.

4. *New Republic* 41 (1927): 330.

5. *The Function of Criticism* (Denver, 1957), pp. 24, 17.

6. *The Lion and the Honeycomb* (New York, 1955), p. 181.

7. *Kenyon Review* 2 (1940): 349–50.

8. *English Institute Annual, 1946*, pp. 155, 134.

9. *Nation* 122 (1926): 532.

10. *The Literary Correspondence of Donald Davidson and Allen Tate*, ed. John Tyree Fain and Thomas Daniel Young (Athens, Ga., 1974), p. 189.

11. *Essays of Four Decades*, p. 406.

12. *The Well Wrought Urn* (New York, 1947), p. 194.

13. *Literary Criticism* (New York, 1957), pp. 737–38.

14. *Poems and Essays* (New York, 1955), p. 171.

15. *The Function of Criticism*, pp. 79ff.

16. *The Well Wrought Urn*, p. 191.

17. *Kenyon Review* 7 (1945): 294.

18. *In Defense of Reason* (Denver, 1947), p. 11.

19. *This Quarter* 5 (1932): 292.

20. *The World's Body* (New York, 1938), p. 198n.

21. *Essays of Four Decades*, pp. 202, 105.

22. Jonathan Culler, in *Comparative Literature* 28 (1976): 250.

23. (Evanston, Ill., 1969), p. 7.

24. In "What Was New Criticism? Literary Interpretation and Scientific Objectivity," *Salmagundi* 27 (1974): 72–93.

25. (New Haven, 1970), pp. 56, 57; the essay dates from 1966.

26. *Critics and Criticism*, pp. 95, 105.

27. "History versus Criticism in the Study of Literature" (1935), repr. in *The Idea of the Humanities*, 2 vols. (Chicago, 1967), 2:3–24.

28. *Essays of Four Decades*, p. 619.

29. "Goethe's *Faust I*," in *Language as Symbolic Action* (Berkeley, 1966), pp. 139–62. See René Wellek, "Kenneth Burke and Literary Criticism," *Sewanee Review* 79 (1971): 183–84.

American Criticism of the Sixties

1. In *Kenyon Review* 28 (1966): 326.

2. *New York Times*, special supplement, 30 December 1969, p. 21.

3. *Fools of Time* (Toronto, 1967), p. 6.

4. Ibid., p. 51.

5. Ibid., pp. 51–52.

6. *Anatomy of Criticism* (Princeton, 1957), p. 136.

7. *Fables of Identity* (New York, 1963), p. 35.

8. *Anatomy of Criticism*, p. 367.

9. *Whitman*, ed. R. H. Pearce (Englewood Cliffs, N.J., 1962), p. 40.

10. *A Natural Perspective* (New York, 1965), p. 70.

11. René Wellek and Austin Warren, *Theory of Literature* (New York, 1949), p. 217.

12. *The Tragic Vision* (New York, 1960), p. 24.

13. *Styles of Radical Will* (New York, 1969), p. 17.

14. *Against Interpretation* (New York, 1966), p. 7.

15. Ibid., p. 14.

16. *Styles of Radical Will*, p. 58.

17. J. Hillis Miller, *Poets of Reality* (Cambridge, Mass., 1965), p. 327.

18. *William Carlos Williams*, ed. J. Hillis Miller (Englewood Cliffs, N.J., 1966), p. 12.

19. In *Modern Language Notes* (1966), reprinted in *Beyond Formalism* (New Haven, 1970), pp. 42–57.

20. In *Review of Metaphysics* (1969), reprinted in *Beyond Formalism*, pp. 337–55.

21. James Dickey, *Babel to Byzantium* (New York, 1968), p. 101.

22. Howard Nemerov, *Poetry and Fiction* (New Brunswick, N.J., 1963), p. 12.

23. Norman Podhoretz, *Making It* (New York, 1967), p. 118.

Russian Formalism

1. *Oeuvres complètes*, ed. Y. G. Le Dantec (Paris, 1961), pp. 296–97. A good history of the concept of modernity is in Matei Calinescu, *Faces of Modernity* (Bloomington, 1977).

2. *De la mission de l'art et du rôle des artistes* (Paris, 1845), p. 4. Calinescu has found earlier uses of avant-garde in Etienne Pasquier (1529–1615) and in Saint-Simon (1825). See *Faces of Modernity* pp. 97–98, 103.

3. Full text of manifesto in Vladimir Markov, *Russian Futurism* (London, 1969), p. 46.

4. *O teorii prozy* (Moscow, 1929), p. 192. All translations are my own.

5. *Khod Konia* (Berlin, 1923), p. 39.

6. *O teorii prozy*, p. 226.

7. *Noveyshaya russkaya poeziya* (Prague, 1921), p. 11. Reprinted in Roman Jakobson, *Selected Writings* (The Hague, 1979), 5:310.

8. *O teorii prozy*, p. 35.

9. *Selected Writings*, 5:305.

10. This definition of poetry occurs in A. W. Schlegel and the forgotten K. F. E. Trahndorff before Belinsky, in "The Idea of Art" (1841, first printed in 1862), popularized it in Russia. Cf. René Wellek, *History of Modern Criticism* (New Haven, 1965), 3:252, 363.

11. *O teorii prozy*, pp. 13, 24.

12. As in note 7.

13. "T. n. Formal'nyj metod," in *LEF*, no. 1 (1923): 213–15, quoted in Victor Erlich, *Russian Formalism* (The Hague, 1955), p. 221.

14. "Kak delat stikhi?" (1926) in *Sobranie sochinenii v osmi tomakh* (Moscow, 1968), 5:466. Cf. *How are Verses Made?* translated by G. M. Hyde (London, 1970), p. 11.

Reflections on my *History of Modern Criticism*

1. George Saintsbury, *History of Criticism* (Edinburgh, 1908), 1:36.

2. R. S. Crane, "J. W. Atkins's *English Literary Criticism: 17th & 18th Century*," *University of Toronto Quarterly* 22 (1953): 376–91. Reprinted in *The Idea of the Humanities and Other Essays Critical and Historical* (Chicago, 1967), 2:157–75.

3. G. W. F. Hegel, *Vorlesungen über die Geschichte der Philosophie*, in *Werke* (Frankfurt, 1971), 18:16, 37, 55, 56, 57, 24.

4. Erich Auerbach, "Wellek's *History of Modern Criticism*," *Romanische Forschungen* 67 (1955): 87–97. Reprinted in *Gesammelte Aufsätze zur romanischen Philologie* (Bern, 1967), pp. 354–63.

5. Bernard Smith, *Forces in American Criticism: A Study in the History of American Literary Thought* (New York, 1939), p. vii.

6. Ernst Gombrich, *In Search of Cultural History* (London, 1969), p. 31.

7. "The Fall of Literary History," 1973, above, pp. 64–77.

8. Morris R. Cohen, *The Meaning of Human History* (La Salle, 1947), p. 102.

9. W. B. Gallic, *Philosophy and Historical Understanding* (New York, 1958), pp. 153ff.

10. William K. Wimsatt and Cleanth Brooks, *Literary Criticism: A Short History* (New York, 1957), p. vii.

11. John Passmore, "The Idea of a History of Philosophy," *History and Theory: Studies in Philosophy of History* 5 (1965): 1–31.

12. I. A. Richards, *Coleridge on Imagination* (London, 1934), p. 232.

13. Passmore, "Idea of a History," p. 31.

14. Thomas Kuhn, *Structure of Scientific Revolutions* (Chicago, 1970), p. 200.

15. Kenneth Percival, "The Applicability of Kuhn's Paradigms to the History of Linguistics," *Language* 52 (1976): 285–94.

Bibliography of the Writings of René Wellek

from 1 January 1970 to 1 January 1982
(Supplementing the Lists in *Concepts of Criticism* and *Discriminations*)

A. Books

3t. *Teoria da literatura*. Portuguese translation by José Palla a Carmo. Lisboa: Publicagões Europa-América, n.d.

3u. *Litteraturteori*. Norwegian translation by Haakon Hofgaard Halvorsan. Oslo: Gyldendal Norsk Forlag, 1970.

3v. *Teoria literatury*. Polish translation by Macej Zurowski. Warszawa: Pań stwowe Wydawnictwo Naukowe, 1970; 2nd ed., 1975.

3w. *La Théorie littéraire*. French translation by Jean-Pierre Audigier and Jean Gattégno. Paris: Éditions du Seuil, 1971.

3x. *Az irodalom elmélete*. Hungarian translation by József Szili. Budapest: Gondolat Kiadó, 1972.

3y. *Theorie der literatuur*. Dutch translation by Tom Etty, T. Anbeek, and J. Fontijn. Amsterdam: Athenaeum–Polak and Van Genep, 1974.

3z. *Nazariatu al-adab*. Arabic translation by Yahya ad-Dm̃ Subhi. Damascus, Syria: The High Council for the Custody of the Arts, Literature, and the Social Sciences of the Ministry of Culture, 1976.

3aa. *Sahitya-Siddhant*. Hindi translation by B. S. Palival. Ilahabad, India: Lokbharati Prakashan, n.d.

3bb. *Teoriya literatury*. Russian translation by A. Zvereva, V. Kharitonova, I. Il'ija, Introduction by A. A. Anikst, Commentary by B. A. Gilenson. Moscow: Progress, 1978.

3cc. *Wen-hsüe-li-lun*. Chinese translation by Liang Po-chieh. Taipei, Taiwan: Ta-lin, n.d.

3dd. *Wen-hsüeh lun Wen-hsüeh yen chiu fang- fa lun*. Another Chinese translation by Wang Meng-ou and Hsü Kuo-heng. Taipei, Taiwan: Chih-wen, 1976 (a third printing, 1979).

4e. *Istoria criticii literare moderne*, vol. I. Rumanian translation by Rodica Tiniş, Preface by Romul Muneanu. Bucarest: Editura Univers, 1974.

5e. *Istoria criticii literare moderne*, Vol. II. Rumanian translation by Rodica Tiniş. Bucarest: Editura Univers, 1974.

4f and 5f. Reprint of 4a and 5a in one volume. Berlin: Walter de Gruyter, 1978.

7c. *Conceptos de Crítica Literaria*. Spanish translation by Edgar Rodríguez-Leal. Caracas: Ediciones de la Biblioteca Universidad Central de Venezuela, 1968 (actually 1969).

7d. *Conceptele critici*. Rumanian translation by Rodica Tiniş, Introduction by Sorin Alexandrescu. Bucarest: Editura Univers, 1970.

7e. *Concetti di Critica*. Italian translation by several hands: Maria Alvernia, Marcella Morelli, M.B., Stefania Casemurata, Augusto Simonini. Bologna: Massimiliano Boni Editore, 1972.

172   Bibliography

7f. *Conceitos de crítica.* Portuguese translation by Oscar Mendes. São Paulo, Brazil: Editora Cultrix, 1979.
7g. *Pojęcia i problemy nauki o literaturze.* Wybrał i przedmowa popredził Henryk Markiewicz. Translated by Andrzej Jaraczewski, Maria Kaniowa, Ignacy Sieradzki. Warszawa: Państwowy Instytut Wydawniczy, 1979. Combines translation of *Concepts of Criticism* with selections from *Discriminations, Confrontations,* and essays on T. S. Eliot and F. R. Leavis.
9b. *Historia da crítica moderna,* Vol. III. Portuguese translation by Hildegard Feist. São Paulo: A Transição, Herder, 1971.
9c. *Historia da crítica moderna (1750–1950): Los Años de Transición.* Spanish translation by J. C. Cayol de Bethencourt. Madrid: Editorial Gredos, 1972.
9d. *Geschichte der Literaturkritik 1750–1950,* Vol. 2, *Das Zeitalter des Übergangs.* German translation by Cornelie and Gert Ueding. Berlin: Walter de Gruyter, 1977. (corresp. to Vol. 3)
10b. *Geschichte der Literaturkritik 1750–1950,* Vol. 3, *Das späte 19. Jahrhundert.* German translation by Lisa Rüdiger. Berlin: Walter de Gruyter, 1977. (corresp. to Vol. 4)
11a. Italian translation in *Critica e storia letteraria: Studi offerti a Mario Fubini* 2 (Padova, 1970): 881–904.
11b. Reprint of original in 12.
12. *Discriminations: Further Concepts of Criticism.* New Haven and London: Yale University Press, 1970.
12a. *Grenzziehungen: Beiträge zur Literaturkritik.* Partial German translation by Marlene Lohner. Stuttgart: W. Kohlhammer, 1972.
12b. Partial translation in 7g.
13. *Four Critics: Croce, Valéry, Lukács, Ingarden.* Seattle: University of Washington Press, 1981.

B. Contributions to Books

7a. Reprinted in W. K. Wimsatt, ed., *Literary Criticism: Idea and Art*, pp. 44–65. Berkeley: University of California Press, 1974.
12–53. 26 articles, with some revisions and updating. Reprinted in *Columbia Dictionary of Modern European Literature*, edited by Jean-Albert Bédé and William B. Edgerton. 2nd ed. New York: Columbia University Press, 1980.
    Bezruč, Petr, p. 86
    Březina, Otokar, p. 118
    Čapek, Josef, p. 139
    Čapek, Karel, p. 140
    Čapek-Chod, Matěj, p. 141
    Čep, Jan, p. 154
    Durych, Jaroslav, p. 217
    Dyk, Viktor, p. 223
    Fischer, Otokar, p. 252
    Holeček, Josef, p. 365

Hora, Josef, p. 369
Langer, František, p. 460
Machar, Jan Svatopluk, p. 495
Masaryk, Tomáš G., p. 530
Neumann, Stanislav K., p. 562
Nezval, Vítězslav, p. 563
Novák, Arne, p. 575
Nováková, Teréza, p. 576
Olbracht, Ivan, p. 579
Šalda, F. X., p. 709
Sova, Antonín, p. 762
Šrámek, Fráňa, p. 771
Svobodová, Růžena, p. 787
Theer, Otokar, p. 805
Vančura, Vladislav, p. 839
Wolker, Jiří, p. 876

57b. "Coleridge's Philosophy and Criticism (to 1956)." Reprinted in *The English Romantic Poets: A Review of Research and Criticism*, edited by Frank Jordan, pp. 209–31. 3rd rev. ed. New York, Modern Language Association, 1972.

64a. Reprinted in A12.

75a. Reprinted in A12.

81. Polish translation in B7g.

84d. Reprinted in A12.

86a. Reprinted in A12.

90a. Reprinted in A12.

91a. Reprinted in A12.

91b. German translation by Renate and Karl R. Hudson. In *Methodenfragen der deutschen Literaturwissenschaft*, edited by R. Grimm and Jost Hermand, pp. 268–94. Darmstadt: Wissenschaftliche Buchgesellschaft, 1973.

92d. Reprinted in A12.

96b. Reprinted in A12.

97b. My German translation. In *Die Tschechoslowakei, 1945–1970*, edited by Nikolaus Lobkowicz and Friedrich Prinz, pp. 227–36. Munich: Oldenbourg, 1978.

98. "Literary Criticism." In *Encyclopedia of World Literature in the Twentieth Century*, edited by W. B. Fleischmann, 2:284–328. New York: Ungar, 1969. English expanded and updated version of B73.

99. "Preface" to Henry Hallam, *Introduction to the Literature of Europe in the Fifteenth, Sixteenth, and Seventeenth Centuries*, pp. v–xvii. New York, Johnson Reprint Corporation, 1970.

100. "American Criticism of the Last Ten Years." In *Yearbook of Comparative and General Literature*, 20:5–14. Bloomington, University of Indiana Press, 1971.

100a. Also in *Amerikanische Literatur im 20. Jahrhundert*, edited by Alfred Weber and Dietmar Haack, pp. 14–28. Göttingen: Vandenhoeck und Ruprecht, 1972.

101. "Stylistics, Poetics, and Criticism." In *Literary Style: A Symposium*, edited by Seymour Chatman, pp. 65–75. London and New York: Oxford University Press, 1971. Also in A12.

102. "Šalda, František Xaver." In *Encyclopedia of World Literature in the Twentieth Century*, edited by W. B. Fleischmann, 3:222–23. New York: Ungar, 1971.
103. "Albert Thibaudet." In *Modern French Criticism from Proust and Valéry to Structuralism*, edited by J. K. Simon, pp. 85–107. Chicago: University of Chicago Press, 1972.
104. "John Crowe Ransom's Theory of Poetry." In *Literary Theory and Structure: Essays in Honor of William K. Wimsatt*, edited by Frank Brady, John Palmer, and Martin Price, pp. 179–98. New Haven: Yale University Press, 1973 (actually 1972).
105. "Coleridge's Philosophy and Criticism (from 1956)." In *The English Romantic Poets: A Review of Research and Criticism*, edited by Frank Jordan, pp. 232–58. 3rd rev. ed. New York: Modern Language Association, 1972.
106. "The Fall of Literary History." In *Geschichte: Ereignis und Erzählung*, edited by Reinhart Kosseleck and Wolf-Dieter Stempel, pp. 427–40. Munich: Wilhelm Fink Verlag, 1973.
106a. Reprinted in *Proceedings of the VIth Congress of the International Comparative Literature Association, Bordeaux, 1970*, pp. 29–36. Stuttgart: Kunst und Wissen, Erich Bieber, 1975.
106b. Reprinted in *New Perspectives in German Literary Criticism*, edited by Richard E. Amacher and Victor Lange, pp. 418–31. Princeton, N.J.: Princeton University Press, 1979.
107. "Introduction" to *Czech Poetry: A Bilingual Anthology*, edited by Alfred French (Michigan Slavic Translations), 1:xv–xix. Ann Arbor: The Czechoslovak Society of Arts and Sciences in America and The Department of Slavic Languages and Literatures of the University of Michigan, 1973.
108. "Walter Benjamin's Literary Criticism in His Marxist Phase." In *The Personality of the Critic*, edited by Joseph P. Strelka (*Yearbook of Comparative Criticism*), 6:168–78. University Park: Pennsylvania State University Press, 1973.
109–
17. "Baroque in Literature," 1:188–95.
"Classicism in Literature," 1:449–56.
"Literary Criticism," 1:596–607.
"Evolution in Literature," 2:169–74.
"Literature and Its Cognates," 3:81–89.
"Periodization in Literary History," 3:481–86.
"Realism in Literature," 4:51–56.
"Romanticism in Literature," 4:187–98.
"Symbol and Symbolism in Literature," 4:337–45.
All in *Dictionary of the History of Ideas*, edited by Philip P. Wiener. New York, Scribner's, 1973.
111a. Reprinted in *What is Criticism?* ed. Paul Hernadi. Bloomington: Indiana University Press, 1981, pp. 291–321.
118. "Littérature comparée." In *Dictionnaire international des termes littéraires*, edited by R. Escarpit, 50:54–58. The Hague: Mouton, 1973.
119. "Introductions" to Flaubert's *Madame Bovary* and to Chekhov's *Cherry Orchard*. In *World Masterpieces*, edited by Maynard Mack, 3rd ed. 2:720–

24, 737. New York: W. W. Norton, 1973. Also in Continental Edition of *World Masterpieces*. New York: W. W. Norton, 1974.

120. "Introduction" to Tomáš G. Masaryk, *The Meaning of Czech History*, translated by Peter Kussi, pp. vii–xxiii. Chapel Hill: University of North Carolina Press, 1974.

120a. Czech translation by Milič Čapek in *Proměny* 16 (1979): 13–26.

121. "Literary Criticism: Recent Developments." In *Encyclopedia of World Literature in the Twentieth Century*, edited by Frederick Ungar and Lina Mainero, 4:223–26. New York: Frederick Ungar, 1975.

122. "Max Kommerell as Critic of Literature." In *Teilnahme und Spiegelung: Festschrift für Horst Rüdiger*, edited by Beda Allemann and Erwin Koppen, pp. 485–98. Berlin: Walter de Gruyter, 1975.

123. "A. C. Bradley, Shakespeare and the Infinite." In *From Chaucer to Gibbon: Essays in Memory of Curt A. Zimansky*, pp. 85–103. Iowa City: University of Iowa Press, 1975.

123a. Also in *Philological Quarterly* 54, no. 1 (Winter 1975): pp. 85–103.

124. "The Price of Progress in Eighteenth-Century Reflections on Literature." In *Transactions of the Fourth International Congress on the Enlightenment*. Studies on Voltaire and the Eighteenth Century, edited by T. Bestermann, 5:2265–84. Oxford: The Voltaire Foundation at the Taylor Institution, 1976.

125. "Critica letteraria." In *Enciclopedia del Novecento (Enciclopedia Treccani)* 1:1123–33. Rome: Instituto della Enciclopedia italiana, 1976.

126. "Vilém Mathesius (1882–1945), Founder of the Prague Linguistic Circle." In *Sound, Sign and Meaning: Quinquagenary of the Prague Linguistic Circle*, edited by Ladislav Matejka, pp. 6–14. Ann Arbor: Michigan Slavic Contributions, Department of Slavic Languages and Literatures, The University of Michigan, 1976.

127. "Collaborating with Austin Warren on *Theory of Literature*." In *Teacher and Critic: Essays by and about Austin Warren*, edited by Myron Simon and Harvey Gross, pp. 68–75. Los Angeles: The Plantin Press, 1976.

128. "Foreword" to Jan Mukařovský, *The Word and Verbal Art: Selected Essays*, translated and edited by John Burbank and Peter Steiner, pp. x–xiii. New Haven: Yale University Press, 1977.

129. "Criticism as Evaluation." In *Herkommen und Erneuerung: Essays für Oskar Seidlin*, edited by Gerald Gillespie and Edgar Lohner, pp. 39–55. Tübingen: Max Niemeyer, 1976. Expanded version of C61.

129a. German translation by Wolf Küster. In *Literaturkritik und literarische Wertung*, edited by Peter Gebhardt, pp. 331–51. Darmstadt: Wissenschaftliche Buchgesellschaft, 1980.

130. "Il Realismo critico di De Sanctis." In *De Sanctis e il realismo*, Introduction by Giuseppe Cuomo, 1:21–44. 2 vols. Napoli: Giannini, 1978.

130a. English version "The critical realism of Francesco De Sanctis." In *Comparative Criticism: A Yearbook*, ed. Elinor Shaffer, pp. 17–36. Cambridge: Cambridge University Press, 1979.

131. "What is Literature?" In *What is Literature?* edited with an Introduction by Paul Hernadi, pp. 16–23. Bloomington, Indiana: Indiana University Press, 1978.

131a. German translation. In *Lili: Zeitschrift für Literaturwissenschaft und Linguistik* 8 (1978): 15–19.

132. Introduction to Henrik Ibsen, *Hedda Gabler*. In *The Norton Anthology of World Masterpieces*, edited by Maynard Mack and others, pp. 727–31. 4th ed. New York: W. W. Norton, 1979.

133. "Allen Tate: Literary Theorist and Critic." In *Englische und amerikanische Literaturtheorie*, edited by Rüdiger Ahrens and Erwin Wolff, 2:557–72. Heidelberg: Carl Winter, 1979.

134. "James Marshall Osborn, 1906–1976." In *Evidence in Literary Scholarship: Essays in Memory of James Marshall Osborn*, edited by René Wellek and Alvaro Ribeiro, pp. v–xv. Oxford: Clarendon Press, 1979.

135. "Science, Pseudoscience, and Intuition in Recent Criticism." In *Actes du VIIe Congrès de l'Association Internationale de Littérature Comparée [Montreal-Ottawa, 1973]* 2:465–69. Stuttgart: Kunst und Wissen, Erich Bieber, 1979.

136. "Introduction." In *Alice Garrigue Masaryk, 1879–1966: Her Life as Recorded in Her Own Words and by Her Friends*, compiled by Ruth Crawford Mitchell, pp. xix–xxiv. Pittsburgh: University Center of International Studies, University of Pittsburgh, 1980.

137b. "Reflections on my *History of Modern Criticism*" in *Proceedings of the VIIIth Congress of the International Comparative Literature Association*, Budapest, 1976, pp. 439–47. Budapest: Akadémia Kiadó, 1981.

138b. "Literature, Fiction, and Literariness." In *Proceedings of the IXth Congress of the International Comparative Literature Association, Innsbruck, 1979*. Vol. 1 of *Classical Models in Literature*, edited by Zoran Konstantinović, pp. 19–25. Innsbruck: AMOE, 1981.

C. Articles in Periodicals

13a. Reprinted in *American Transcendentalism: An Anthology of Criticism*, edited by Brian M. Barbour, pp. 103–23. Notre Dame, Ind.: Notre Dame University Press, 1973.

28b. Polish translation in B7g.

29b. Reprint of Italian translation. In *I Critici per la storia della filologia e della critica moderna in Italia*, edited by Gianni Grana, 1:194–219. Milan: Marzorati, 1969.

29c. Partial reprint from volume 4 of the *History of Modern Criticism* in Italian translation. In *La Letteratura italiana per saggi storicamente disposti: L'Ottocento*, edited by Lanfranco Caretti and Giorgio Luti, pp. 374–79. Milan: Mursia, 1973.

37a. German translation. In *Begriffsbestimmung des literarischen Realismus*, edited by Richard Brinkmann, pp. 400–433. Darmstadt: Wissenschaftliche Buchgesellschaft, 1969.

38a. Reprinted in A12.

45a. Greek translation as pamphlet. *Germanikós kai agglikós romantismós*, Athens, Erasmos, 1976.

45b. Polish translation in B7g.

47a. Reprinted in A12.

52. "Comparative Literature at Yale." *Ventures: Magazine of the Yale Graduate School* 10 (1970): 24–32.

53. "Kenneth Burke and Literary Criticism." *Sewanee Review* 79 (1971): 171–88.
54. "R. P. Blackmur Re-examined." *Southern Review* 7, new ser. (1971): 825–45.
54a. Reprinted in *English Studies Today*, 5th ser., edited by Sencer Tonguç (Istanbul: Matbassi, 1973): 453–76.
55. "Russian Formalism." *Arcadia: Zeitschrift für vergleichende Literaturwissenschaft* 6 (1971), 175–86.
55a. Reprinted in *Russian Modernism: Culture and the Avant-garde, 1900–1930*, edited by George Gibian and H. W. Tjalsma, pp. 31–48. Ithaca, Cornell University Press, 1976.
56. "The Early Literary Criticism of Walter Benjamin." *Rice University Studies: Studies in German in Memory of Robert L. Kahn* 57 (1971): 123–34.
57. "The Attack on Literature." *American Scholar* 42 (December 1972): 27–42.
57a. Also in *Expression, Communication, and Experience in Literature and Language: Proceedings of the Twelfth Congress of the International Federation for Modern Languages and Literatures*, edited by Richard G. Popperwell, pp. 3–16. London, Modern Humanities Research Association, 1973.
58. "Poulet, Du Bos, and Identification." *Comparative Literature Studies* 10 (1973): 173–93.
59. "Cleanth Brooks, Critic of Critics." *Sewanee Review* 10 (1974): 125–52.
59a. Reprinted in *The Possibilities of Order: Cleanth Brooks and His Work*, edited by Lewis P. Simpson, pp. 196–229. Baton Rouge: Louisiana State University Press, 1976.
60. "Poetics, Interpretation, and Criticism." *Modern Language Review* 69 (October, 1974): xxi–xxxi.
61. "Criticism as Evaluation." *Proceedings of the American Philosophical Society* 119, no. 5 (15 October 1975): 397–400.
62. "Yvor Winters Rehearsed and Reconsidered." *Denver Quarterly* 10, no. 3 (Autumn 1975): 1–27.
63. "Ezra Pound's Literary Criticism." *Denver Quarterly* 11 (Spring 1976): 1–20.
64. "The Literary Theory of William K. Wimsatt." *The Yale Review* 66 (1977): 178–92.
65. "Virginia Woolf as Critic." *Southern Review* 13 (Summer 1977): 419–37.
66. "Reflections on my *History of Modern Criticism*." *PTL: A Journal of Descriptive Poetics and Theory of Literature* (Amsterdam) 2, no. 3 (October 1977): 417–27.
66a. Also in B. 137.
67. "The Literary Criticism of Ernst Robert Curtius." *PTL: A Journal for Descriptive Poetics and Theory of Literature* 3 (1978): 25–44.
68. "Edmund Wilson (1895–1972)." *Comparative Literature Studies* 15 (1978): 97–123.
68a. Reprinted in *History as a Tool in Critical Interpretation*, edited by Thomas F. Rugh and Erin R. Silva, pp. 63–95. Provo, Utah: Brigham Young University Press.
69. "The New Criticism: Pro and Contra." *Critical Inquiry* 4 (1978): 611–24.
70. "Propagace české literatury." *Proměny* 15 (1978): 28–33.
71. "The Literary Criticism of Lionel Trilling." *New England Review* 2 (1979): 26–49.

72. "The Literary Theories of F. W. Bateson." *Essays in Criticism* 29 (1979): 112–23.
73. "Auerbach and Vico." *Lettere Italiane* 31 (1979): 457–69.
73a. Reprinted in *Vico: Past and Present*, edited by Giorgio Tagliacozzo, 2: 85–96. Atlantic Heights, N.J.: Humanities Press, 1981.
74. "Prospect and Retrospect." *The Yale Review* 69 (1979): 301–12.
74a. Also in *Journal of Comparative Literature and Aesthetics* 1 (Orissa, India, 1978): 1–12.
75. "Bakhtin's View of Dostoevsky: 'Polyphony' and 'Carnivalesque.'" *Dostoevsky Studies* 1 (1980): 31–39.
76. "The Later Leavis." *Southern Review* 17 (1981): 490–500.
77. "David Herbert Lawrence Critico Letterario." *Belfagor* 36 (1981): 129–43. Translated by Remo Ceserani and Anita Piemonti. The English original will appear in the *Sewanee Review*.

D. Reviews

75. Gian N. G. Orsini, *Coleridge and German Idealism*. In *Comparative Literature* 22 (1970): 279–82.
76. Thomas McFarland, *Coleridge and the Pantheist Tradition*. In *Comparative Literature* 22 (1970): 282–86.
77. Milada Blekastad, *Comenius: Versuch eines Umrisses von Leben, Werk und Schicksal des Jan Amos Komenský*. In *Slavic and East European Journal* 14 (1970): 511–12.
78. Ignazio Ambrosio, *Formalismo e avanguardia in Russia*, and Krystyna Pomorska, *Russian Formalism and Its Poetic Ambiance*. In *Comparative Literature* 23 (1971): 167–73.
79. Claudio Guillén, *Literature as System: Essays toward the Theory of Literary History*. In *Yale Review* 61 (1972): 254–59.
80. Fredric Jameson, *Marxism and Form: Twentieth-Century Dialectical Theories of Literature*. In *Yale Review* 62 (1972): 119–26.
81. James E. Magner, Jr., *John Crowe Ransom: Critical Principles and Preoccupations*. In *Revue Belge de Philologie et d'Histoire* 1 (1973): 101–2.
82. Robert Scholes, *Structuralism in Literature: An Introduction*. In *Journal of English and German Philology* 73 (1974): 459–62.
83. Ellis Sandoz, *Political Apocalypse: A Study of Dostoevsky's Grand Inquisitor*. In *Slavic and East European Journal* 19 (1975): 445–46.
84. Václav Černý, *Dostoevsky and his Devils*. In *Slavic Review* 35 (1976): 384–85.
85. G. N. Giordano Orsini, *Organic Unity in Ancient and Later Poetics: The Philosophical Foundation of Literary Criticism*. In *English Language Notes* 14 (1976): 74–76.
86. *Semiotics of Art: Prague School Contributions*, ed. L. Matejka and I. R. Titunik. In *Dispositio* (Michigan) 3 (1976): pp. 361–63.
87. Sigrun Bielfeldt, *Die čechische Moderne im Frühwerk Šaldas*. In *Slavic Review* 37 (1978): 542.
88. S. S. Prawer, *Karl Marx and World Literature*, and Terry Eagleton, *Marxism and Literary Criticism*. In *Slavic Review* 36 (1977): 530–31.
89. John Fekete, *The Critical Twilight: Explorations in the Ideology of Anglo-*

American Literary Theory from Eliot to McLuhan. In *Modern Language Review*
74 (1979): 440–41.
90. Walter A. Davis, *The Act of Interpretation: A Critique of Literary Reason*. In
Modern Language Review 74 (1979): 897–98.
91. George Bistray, *Marxist Models of Literary Realism*. In *Slavic Review* 38
(1979): 711–12.
92. Christopher Norris, *William Empson and the Philosophy of Literary Criticism*.
In *Modern Language Review* 75 (1980): 182–85.
93. Grant Webster, *The Republic of Letters: A History of Postwar American Literary
Criticism*. In *The Georgia Review* 34 (1980): 182–88.
94. Robert Boyers, *F. R. Leavis: Judgment and Discipline of Thought*; R. P. Bilan,
The Literary Criticism of F. R. Leavis; and Francis Mulhern, *The Moment of
"Scrutiny."* In *Modern Language Review* 76 (1981): 175–80.

E. Miscellaneous

11a. German translation. In *Begriffsbestimmung des literarischen Realismus*, ed.
Richard Brinkmann, pp. 448–52. Darmstadt, Wissenschaftliche Buchgesellschaft, 1969.
20. Summary in German of "The Term and Concept of Classicism." In *Archiv
für das Studium der Begriffsgeschichte* 13 (1961): 112–13.
21. "Mr. Wellek replies to Margaret Sharon Feary's comment on 'The Attack
on Literature.'" In *American Scholar* 42 (1973): 365–66.
22. Comment on Robert Gorham Davis, "The Professors Lie." In *The
Columbia Forum* 2 (Winter 1973): 43–44.
23. "Zur methodischen Aporie einer Rezeptionsgeschichte." In *Geschichte:
Ereignis und Erzählung*, ed. R. Kosseleck and Wolf-Dietrich Stempel, pp.
515–17. Munich: Wilhelm Fink Verlag, 1973.
24. "Editor's Notes" to *British Philosophers and Theologians of the 17th and 18th
Centuries in 101 Volumes*, ed. René Wellek, pp. 1–3. New York: Garland
Publishing Company, Inc., 1975.
25. "The Comparative Method, Sociology and the Study of Literature,"
comments on Leo Lowenthal's contribution. In *Yearbook of Comparative and
General Literature* 23 (1974): pp. 18–20.
26. "Editor's Note" (on the *Lucia di Lammermoor* episode in *Madame Bovary*). In
World Masterpieces, ed. Maynard Mack, 2:750–51. 3rd ed. New York: W. W.
Norton, 1973.
27. "Critical Response: Notes and Exchanges" (with Wayne Booth). In *Critical
Inquiry* 4 no. 1 (Autumn 1977): 203–6.
28. German preface to A9d and A10b.
29. "Literary history and literary criticism." In *History as a Critical Tool*, ed.
Thomas F. Rugh and Erin R. Silva, pp. 43–48, 51–61. Provo, Utah:
Brigham Young University Press, 1978.
30. "Notes and Exchanges," between René Wellek and Wayne C. Booth. In
Critical Inquiry 4 (1977): 203–6.
31. "A Rejoinder to Gerald Graff." In *Critical Inquiry* 5 (1979): 576–79.
32. An obituary of *Karel Krejčí (1904–79)*. In *Revue de littérature comparée* 54
(1980): 122–23.

33. "Concluding Remarks" (to a discussion of the periodization of twentieth-century literature). In *Proceedings of the VIIth Congress of the International Comparative Literature Association*, edited by Milan V. Dimić and Eva Kushner, 2:201–2. Stuttgart: Kunst und Wissen, Erich Bieber, 1979.
34. "An Answer to Roman Ingarden." In *Komparatistik. Festschrift für Zoran Konstantinović*, ed. Fridrun Rinner and Klaus Zerinschek, pp. 21–26. Heidelberg Carl Winter: Universitätsverlag, 1981.

Index of Names

Index of Topics and Themes